W9-AJR-707

OTHER BOOKS BY THE AUTHOR

POETRY
Music from Home: Selected Poems
Winters Without Snow
Lie and Say You Love Me
Queen of the Ebony Isles
Bone Flames
What Madness Brought Me Here: New and Selected Poems

SHORT FICTION
Jesus and Fat Tuesday
Driving Under the Cardboard Pines

NONFICTION
Speech and Language of the Preschool Child
Over the Lip of the World: Among the Storytellers of Madagascar

CHAPBOOKS
The Mules Done Long Since Gone
Looking for a Country Under its Original Name
Talk Story

A LONG WAY FROM
St. Louie

TRAVEL MEMOIRS :: COLLEEN J. MCELROY

I remember well just where
I used to be
But now I'm on the road
To where I meant to be
    "Sarah"—B. Ighner

COFFEE HOUSE PRESS :: MINNEAPOLIS

Copyright © 1997 by Colleen J. McElroy. Cover art by Jody Kim. Cover design by Kelly Kofron. Back cover photograph by Eleanor M. Hamilton.

Some of these pieces appeared in slightly different versions in the following publications, "Why My Camera Fails When the Picture Is in View," *Calapooya Collage II;* "Going Home," *Homeground* (Blue Heron Press, 1996); "Journey to Ulcinj," *Western Humanities Review,* Winter 1991; "Moon and Malaysia," *Kenyon Review,* Winter 1992; "The Butcher's Ear," *Left Bank 3: Sex, Family, and Tribe;* Winter 1992; "To Market To Market," *The Writer's Solution Sourcebook* (Prentice-Hall, 1997). Excerpt from "Route 66" by Bobby Troup © 1974 Capitol Londontown Music, Inc. Excerpt from *For Colored Girls who have Considered Suicide / When the Rainbow is Enuf* by Ntozake Shange reprinted with the permission of Simon & Schuster; copyright © 1975, 1976, 1977 by Ntozake Shange.

Coffee House Press is supported in part by a grant provided by the Minnesota State Arts Board, through an appropriation by the Minnesota State Legislature, and by a grant from the National Endowment for the Arts, a federal agency. Additional support has been provided by the Lila Wallace-Reader's Digest Fund; The McKnight Foundation; Lannan Foundation; Jerome Foundation; Target Stores, Dayton's, and Mervyn's by the Dayton Hudson Foundation; General Mills Foundation; Butler Family Foundation; St. Paul Companies; Honeywell Foundation; Star Tribune/Cowles Media Company; The James R. Thorpe Foundation; Dain Bosworth Foundation; The Beverly J. and John A. Rollwagen Fund of The Minneapolis Foundation; and The Andrew W. Mellon Foundation.

Coffee House Press books are available to the trade through our primary distributor, Consortium Book Sales & Distribution, 1045 Westgate Drive, Saint Paul, MN 55114. For personal orders, catalogs, or other information, write to: Coffee House Press, 27 North Fourth Street, Suite 400, Minneapolis, MN 55401.

LIBRARY OF CONGRESS CIP INFORMATION
McElroy, Colleen J.
A long way from St. Louie / Colleen J. McElroy.
    p.m.
ISBN 1-56689-059-4 (alk.paper)
1. Afro-American women—Poetry. 2. Afro-American women
poets—Journeys. 3. McElroy, Colleen J.—Journeys.
1. Title.
PS3563.A2925L66 1997
811'.54—dc21   96-53099   CIP

10   9   8   7   6   5   4   3   2   1

CONTENTS

For my aunt, Jennie Mae Ritchie, who told me
to wander through this big old world

I wish to thank Denise Levertov for urging me to write about my travels. A very special note of thanks to Janie Smith, who was my reader and confidante as I mapped this book; to Professor T. Subramanuium Saraswathi, who insisted that I put the same demands for the music of language in prose as I had placed on poetry; to Jodie Kim, who gave me my dreams of the blue woman; and to Stephen Rush of Crossroads Travel, for his years of patient assistance in the many complications of routing my journeys, both near and distant. I also appreciate the assistance of Edna Daigre, who has kept me dancing through the years, Rob Weller, who taught me to speak in bytes, Mira Shimabukuro, who helped me sharpen my memory of lost names, and Laura McKee, who sees form the way sculptors see shapes in stone.

The author expresses her appreciation to the Fulbright Foundation, the DuPont Distinguished Scholars Program, the Rockefeller Foundation, Arts America, the Council for International Exchange of Scholars, and the Bellagio Study and Conference Center in Como, Italy, for their generous support and for providing the time and space to complete this work.

Introduction

This is a book about my travels, but it is not a travel book, not a description or tour guide, but rather impressions of journeys, memories held in fragments: like footprints on a sandy beach, the familiar scent of perfume, or the special spice in a dish prepared by a favorite cook. These impressions are interwoven, one linked to and dependent upon another. One memory distinct, the other blurred. This book, like my travels, was not planned—I had no great scheme to plot my trek from one country to the next, nor did I have a master plan directing the retelling of these journeys. For years, I beleaguered my friends with anecodotes, half-finished stories of one trip or another: how I thought I'd seen someone who could have been a cousin's twin peering through a window of a house in the Andes, how in Naples a young Ethiopian woman had mistaken me for someone she knew, speaking first in Amharic, then Italian, then English. How I'd felt trapped in English even when I'd attempted to answer in Italian. Or how mountain ridges in other parts of the world reminded me of the Northwest, how certain smells in another country brought me back to my mother's house in St. Louis or to farm houses in Georgia, how when you travel, time is relative, shifting across invisible borders according to the needs of the day. Even now, the many clocks in my house are not synchronized.

"You have to write down these stories," my friends said. For years, I resisted. After all, the accounts were only one part entertainment but three parts revelation, what I had learned about the world and how the experience had caused me to see myself in another way. When finally I relented—I would write a book—I had no idea where to begin. I have been traveling for almost as long as I can remember. Because my father was in the army, I've always felt I belonged nearly everywhere and was on my way to someplace else. But in the seventies, long after my father had retired, I became determined to see as much of the world as I could on my own. For a book of memoirs, both starting points seemed too logical, too self-consciously chosen. That was never my style. My traveling was always built on the desire to go someplace distant and soon.

Partly, I travel to discover more about myself. My journeys have taught me that a definition of who I am cannot be mapped on the simple black-and-white limits of state lines and borders. The identification of myself and my country has not been an easy task. In this country, I fall into that big, simple, overwhelmingly inaccurate category: black (negro, colored, African American). Outside of this country, I am expected to explain what that means in terms of my history. But there are few literal markers of my history. Instead of heroes like Harriet Tubman, Nat Love, Charles Drew, and Bessie Coleman, I have read about vaudeville stereotypes, have seen Rastas hawking Cream of Wheat, and the Gold Dust twins locked in stereotypes on labels crowding grocery store shelves. I've toured the slave castles on the island of Gorée; the monuments to freedom fighters in the Père Lachaise in Paris and the Kragujevac memorial in Yugoslavia; Auschwitz and Hiroshima; and a dozen churches where the Inquisition claimed the lives of Indians; but I've found no national museums for the holocaust of American slavery; no Ellis Island markers to place the entry of Africans on slave ships; no statues for those lynched by night riders or for the victims of race riots in cities we call democratic. The historical reminders for African Americans are verbal—stories passed from one generation to the next: slave narratives, the adventures of Anansi and Br'er Rabbit, conjure tales, and grandmother stories.

When I was young, eight or so—I'll guess eight since that year seems to have become fixed as the magic age when my memory takes on its own momentum—I would plague my grandmother for stories of faraway places. My grandmother, Anna Belle Long, had never traveled farther north than our neighborhood in St. Louis or farther south than our relatives' houses in Texas. But in the forties, while my father was in the army and my mother worked long hours in the defense plant, my grandmother was the source of all stories, so I assumed she knew the mysteries of distant places. I'd pull my grandfather's atlas from the bookshelf, a 1930s rendition of the world with foldout maps, some of them detailing countries that no longer exist at this end of the century, and I'd choose an unlikely destination, one where I knew no one and where no one in my neighborhood had ever ventured. My grandmother was patient, watching me point to this place and that. I'd spread out the maps, letting my fingers roam the globe. "Mama, there's Mali and Chad," I'd say. "Do they have black people in Mali?" I'd ask. "That's Africa," she'd say. "We come from there a long time ago. My mother's mother . . ." she'd tell me, and launch into a story about my ancestors. I'd ask questions, taking mental note of who was from where, but when she came too close to home, lingering on tales of endless lines of cousins and who was married to whom, I'd move on. "And what about Greenland?" I'd ask. "They got black people in Greenland? And Russia and China? And the Himalayas," I'd say, remembering a book I'd read. "What about there?" I'd ask. Exhausted by my endless questions, she'd laugh. "Chile, they got some of us everywhere," she'd say. "Wearing all manner of clothes and speaking in every kind of tongue." And thus began my wanderlust.

Half of any trip is the excitement of getting there, which explains my romance with airplanes. In those early morning hours when I'm half asleep, when I hear the drone of a jet as it pierces the cloud cover, gaining altitude before heading west over the Pacific, I wistfully think of my next trip, the yearning so strong, I keep myself awake long enough to confirm that indeed, I will be going somewhere in three months, six months, soon. "It's an addiction," my friends tell me when I identify airlines by the insignias on a plane's tailfin. "Look, there's United," I tell them. "Alaska, TWA, and British Air." To me, those names are like magic, keys to doorways full of secrets. I am in love with the act of traveling, and yes, I must confess, I also hold a strange, rather perverse, love for all the missed connections and canceled flights. After all, I have read Nancy Drew mysteries and know that adventures should not be easy, which brings me to that uneasy fondness I have for my fellow travelers, even the ones who seem to bring aboard furniture disguised as carry-ons. On every flight, cabin attendants intone: "All items must fit under your seat or in the overhead compartment." But I have watched a family of six attempting to shove their entire household possessions into 20 x 12-inch spaces. Yet the moment those doors close and the captain announces preparation for takeoff, we are equals, all of us, from the first-class passengers with luxurious leg room to the cattle car arrangement of coach class. We are all at the mercy of cabin pressure, radar, and weather. We are all bound for a place far from home where, often, we will find no one of our acquaintance and language will elude us.

I know not everyone has the itch to travel. I know army brats who say their traveling days ended when their fathers mustered out of the service. "I had enough of always moving and never belonging anywhere," they tell me. And certainly I wasn't raised with images of black explorers. In history books, my past was connected to the vast diaspora of slavery, race riots, and a few expatriate artists who fled this country. Accounts of great travels never included black people, so I had no role models. In fact, until I escape the airport red tape of each new destination, my traveling companions more than likely will be white: the lone Englishwoman making do with emergency rations of tea and a medical kit for inevitable accidents; ruddy-faced Germans in sturdy shoes and hand-tooled backpacks; groups of healthy young Americans in snappy sportswear and hiking gear—all of them with cameras of multitudinous lenses. I have found no stalwart African American ladies, fresh from climbing the Himalayas or surviving the swelter of tropical heat, romanticism intact. I have only my own wanderlust—and my grandmother's belief that there are black folks everywhere on this earth.

I doubt if Anna Belle Long ever expected her grandchild to become addicted to travel any more than my mother did. My mother, who never quite expects me to be home to receive her phone calls, who still expects that I will wind up lost in some place that she cannot find on any map. "I'm just going on a trip," I tell her. "I'm not leaving the planet." Even over the phone, I know my mother is frowning. My mother, who grew up in a segregated world where women, especially black women, were not expected to venture too far away from home. "But why do you have to go to all those places?" she asks. "Because they're there," I tell her. And I hear her sigh. My mother, worried that her only daughter will come to no good end, out there traveling where no one she knows has ever been.

"You stay on the road too much," my mother tells me. "When I get you on the phone, I don't know whether you're coming or going. You best stay where your family can see for you." It is one of those endless mother-daughter conversations. I know why my mother worries, but I want to see for myself, to traverse the globe in random flight paths to places full of both surprise and disappointment, to give myself the vision of what it is like to be black and female on an unknown landscape, where my adjustment to leaving home has often been easier than my readjustment upon return. These are the memoirs of those travels, some poetic and some anecdotal. These are the journeys on which I have sometimes been displaced, losing time or leaving a footprint, gaining a scrap of memory, a bit of this, a bit of that, learning to speak without words and translate into languages I did not know.

I am fortunate to have a life that has fueled my passion for travel—first with my father during his years in the military, and later, with my own work as a writer and folklorist. Although over fifty years have passed since I first nagged my grandmother for stories of places she'd never imagined visiting, my passion for marking destinations on a map has hardly subsided. Sometimes I choose a place for no more reason than the sound of the name fits the corners of my mouth and the very act of speaking it fills me with anticipation of the visit: Malaysia, Fiji, Majorca, Venezuela. Sometimes the choice is made because my work takes me there: a fellowship to research folk stories and oral histories or an invitation to attend an international convention of writers and scholars. I have cultivated ways of funding my travels, and when I am lucky, those methods are successful. When I am lucky, I find the less traveled path, where tour buses will not appear in convoys like invading armies. This is not to say I try to become one of the people—none of this New Age business of stepping out of my Westernized self in order to wear the spiritual cloak of another culture, or even worse, of cruising through a country as if browsing the shelves of a convenience store. I refuse to see the rest of the world as a place where I can escape myself, becoming, as my writer-friend, Robert Anderson, put it, "a lookey loo" intent on viewing what is strange and exotic. Living poor without indoor plumbing does not help you gain spirituality any more than abundant wealth harbors intelligent civilization. We are the keepers of our past. Like all of us, I carry my past with me. I know that my percep-tions are shaped by that past, the bags and baggage of America—from my grandmother's kitchen and public schools to modern appli-ances and network television news. I am the great-granddaughter of a slave, a member of the sixth generation of African descendents who have survived diaspora on American soil with a little bit of this, a lit-tle bit of that. I am a Western woman, and I must always, always be aware of how that life has affected my vision, my ability to see myself as akin to and different from the people I meet. In short, I must fol-low the Malagasy proverb: *Enjoy yourself to the fullest but remain the perfect stranger.*

WHY MY CAMERA FAILS WHEN THE PICTURE IS IN VIEW

The woman in Peru had a rough twenty-odd years.
　　Her skin shows the wear—brown face webbed
　　in the wonder of an unlucky past; present
　　too close at hand and trapped in the wrong
　　angle and lens. Her child waits for handouts—
　　head bent like a comma into stunted body,
　　but patient. Behind them the Museo del Oro
　　holds national treasure. There is all the time
　　in the world. Or none at all.

It is fall and the fire dancers of Fiji are suddenly
　　sixteen and gawking like street kids too
　　hip to be anything else. With their ashes
　　removed, they blink with normal fear into
　　lens or fire. For eight minutes, they demanded
　　its attention, playing flames to foot or hand
　　like kittens. Now they're boys again—almost
　　men—flicking their eyes over a woman's
　　skin, hot.

Five men pissing on a wall in Venezuela are not
　　lined up for a local execution. They are
　　commuters, business suits pressed precisely
　　as an accountant's. They lean at wide angles
　　against the lines of the wall, the tallest
　　to the left, and above their heads, fading
　　lines of graffiti from someone taller still,
　　while their common urinal glows yellower
　　with rage.

The fortune teller in Ikebukuro worked that corner
       before the war. Life to him is a knotted
       string, creases in the palms, the absence
       of planes overhead and soldiers underfoot.
       Customers or not, he works his roots daily
       and saves his one gaijin speech for my
       appearance. Glancing at muddied lines
       in my hands, he clips English vowels and
       whispers, "No pictures here."

The old men in Palma call me African and cockstrut
       for the occasion. Umbrellas held high against
       hot Mediterranean sun, they pull their pants
       crotch tight like uncles in Georgia or Nigeria.
       But this is Spain and life is simply more than
       my camera still locked in its leather case.
       One move toward the shutter and they will slump
       against the bench, playing dead, one bleary
       eye opened to watch me pass.

I am waiting in another town for the chance geography
       of what will not make us foreign and different.
       I am home and full of calendars and postcards of
       rough paper. I have no photos of any acquaintance.
       My passport is stamped with triangles of countries
       as complicated as talk-stories. I turn the camera
       toward me, waiting for the right angle of sun,
       the climate that will get the picture right.

—Colleen J. McElroy
Seattle, Washington

Going Home

*I know the old saying that it is not
the voyage but the voyager that matters.*
—An African in Greenland

My travels began in St. Louis, Missouri, not going to it, but coming from it. There I learned how to see myself as both separate from and a part of several lives. This has happened repeatedly over the years: going away seems to bring me back to whom I have become. Wherever I go, I take pieces with me. That is how my story begins and continues: with pieces, bits of things remembered, details of home moving on a fuzzy landscape. Smells, sounds, textures clearer even than names and dates. My mind recording changes. My life growing out of events that occurred away from home. The world giving me a sense of home. So that is how I will tell it, a story where I move away from and back to whom I have been and what I have become. This is my chronometry of travels, the bits and pieces, my goings and comings.

Each trip reorders my map, until like some ancient sailor's, the known world is dead center. The rest spirals out. Spokes and arcs, light and water, an aside where it all belongs.

To get out of town, you had to pass the fountain in front of Union Station. The Wedding of Rivers. The pull of the mighty Mississippi. Then on to Creve Coeur (kids said Grieve Car in Missouri French). After that, it was a clear shot. Of course, you avoided the old men on benches and the old women in their kitchens and the snaggletoothed children and the rococo statues at the fountain shooting rusty water that keeps going nowhere.

I'm still out here on that road. Occasionally getting caught in cul-de-sacs, a thousand and one shops. Avoiding the final exit.

Chile, why do you go to all them places? I never heard of such. Nobody in our family ever did all that going. Why you always got to be going?

Because they're there, those places. Everything we know is in constant motion. Earth, air, water. This room, this piece of paper, these words. All traveling along some map, through systems in motion. Rising, falling, willingly or forced, we are brought together at some point. We move apart, move closer, move away. It is natural to move. As natural as breathing or dying or loving or freedom. All that movement didn't stop with the Emancipation.

What are you? he said. Serious, I answered: Negro. *No,* he said. *Not what are you called, but what do you claim?* America? I answered. And he said: *I am German. Verstehen? This place is the place of my people. What place holds your people to this earth?* It was the first time I was asked that question. And never asked at home.

> *One two three O'Leary*
> *Four five six McCleary*
> *Allen Adams Grunewald Carey*
> *Ten O'Leary Dandy*

What you remember: jump rope songs, ol' man Farrow's store, the all-white playground at the end of the street, races down Ash Hill, the eight block walk to school—no bus. Getting out.

They have torn down every house you've ever lived in. The house on Kennerly gone. Aunt Jennie's house on St. Ferdinand gone. The flat over Mrs. Scales's bar gone. The house on McMillan gone. And all the others mushed in a new riddle of one-way streets leading to vacant lots. Not one damn map familiar and comfortable.

Tonight, another ubiquitous immigrant salutes the good ol' days. *I remember,* says the fat man, *when this land was free—we come here with nothing more than what my daddy could put on a half-load wagon. Weren't nothing here but some scraggly trees, a few Indians, and lots of rattlesnakes. Carved everything we own outta this dirt.* Funny, I think, no black cowboys. No Bill Picketts or Isom Darts or Nat Loves? No black folks heading West for Oklahoma and the territories, stopping off in St. Louis for one last home-cooked meal?

Pick a color: black, white, black and white, white and black.

Eighth grade. We graduated eighth grade in those days. No one expected us to do better. Cote Brilliante School. The system was George Washington Carver. Our bootstraps hooked to a libretto.

All year we practiced. *The Caravan,* an operetta. With Bedouins, Arabs, and slaves. I could sing every role, but Mr. Billups found me no matter where I hid. "Off-key!" he'd shout. "Off-key!"

What twisted mind let thirty-two black kids sing about caravans and slaves on a hot day in June 1947 in the middle of St. Louis?

A woman whose lip peels back to gum and nasal ridge brags of her descent from English stock. She loves all that is Old World except its dysentery, scarlet fever, plague, and syphilis. When the round of questions on heritage ends on your plate, she asks: *Where do you live, dear?*

You nod, your safest bet. Everyone is polite. They speak in confidential tones of conquests. Give each other gentled names. Nothing is as it seems. Adventure means plunder. They are pirates turned captains of industry.

3

Just in case you'll never get it right, he clarifies: *We were giving it away, from Indian Hills clear to Cherokee.* The names slip off his tongue: Potawatomee, Unondoga, Shawnee . . . *Good little towns,* he says, *my brother was the sheriff round about the time the Crees migrated here. Don't 'member too many of the colored—'cept that one town had 'em all. Jebediah.*

The thieves are counting their jewels. They give each coin a name of exclusion. Their women are bent under the weight.

And you wonder how migrations fared under the guns of cavalry and manacles and backbreaking marches with no time to stop for babies or sore feet.

> *Cherries, cherries in my basket*
> *Heel toe stamp and over*
> *Gold and silver in my basket*
> *Front and over heel toe*

You still remember eighth grade, don't you? In those days your folks graduated eighth grade. Nobody thought they could do more. "The Caravan" and the whole class was a choir. Most could sing. Not you. The boys sang all the slave parts: *We are old with labor/bended low/and our steps are weary/weary and slow.* The girls sang answers: *Heed not the slaves melancholy song/Heed not their moaning along.* Everyone laughed when you sang: *The guards are forming a-head.*

Your problem has always been mouth. Most folks expect you to prove the truth, yet they accept the other stuff. Well, here's the truth: you were on your way to a planet of three moons and some-how got sidetracked here. Once you landed, there was no turning back. But in your world, the dead are white and walk backwards. The rest just are. Same problem as here.

Now the statistics: In the black, 12–16%—depending on the calcu-lator. In the service, 25%. In the pen, 55%. On the pity of welfare, 65%. On the move, 35%. Abroad, 03%. Two of them male.

Girl, what you doing out there by yourself? Best be careful among those foreigners.

What are you? he said. Serious, I answered: Negro. *Not where, but who? American?* He says: *I am German. Verstehen? This place is the place of my people. What place holds your people to this earth?* Silence. It is the first time I have been asked that question. And never at home. Silence. *How can you understand someone else's history if you don't know your own? Do not come back until you can answer the question.* I don't.

Watusi. Xhosa. Eritrean. Seminole. Chinese. Saxon. Which names matter? Herr Doktor Professur what I remember is eighth grade. Cote Brilliante School. An operetta I couldn't sing.

James's boy wants to marry a Eurasian girl, Mama says. Don't know what's happening to this family. First you go off and stay for Lord knows how long with all them foreigners, then your brother gets himself a wife from one of them places in the Pacific and brought her here to St. Louis. Colored people got enough trouble without all that mess. And James, he's fit to be tied now. 'Course, the girl looks like your cousin Mae.

What else is there left to say? Your aging cousins show you their fur coats. They have traded them for men. Mink as mean as their eyes. Your aunt, their mother, greets you as always with hostile indifference. She thinks you've passed over. Not dead but just as well could be in a sea of pink faces.

What travelers invent for themselves is a journey of unimaginable lengths.

I am standing in the middle of a dusty square. The sun is boiling and tropical. A woman comes up to me. She wears something Punjabi. Speaks Haitian. Eats European, fork in left hand always. She is thirsty. I hand her a map. She sticks it full of pins and falls asleep. When she dreams, she smiles. When the bus arrives, she demands a ticket. Home.

In the right light, my mother looks a bit like her mother, but she really favors her father, my grandfather, Papa. Papa, who worked for Anheuser. Papa, who gave me my long legs and slender fingers. Papa, who died before I began all this traveling stuff. Now I do it with his memory in my head. Odd, since it was my mother's mother, Mama, who always greeted us when we came home.

My mother and I have similiar feet, long and narrow. Made for walking, my grandmother would say. Grandma had feet with ankles that ended right on the ground, and a roll of flesh around the heels like a small inner tube. She had feet that grew corns like an annual crop. Her feet could dig into the earth, walk a mile, and dance as if they had wings. I knew those feet didn't like shoes, but when we came home from one of my father's tours of duty, my grandmother's feet virtually flew down the stairs of that house on Kennerly and didn't even touch the ground. She wouldn't know which of us to hug first. She sort of scooped us all against her, and we fell into one of those clumsy hugs that involved too many people squished together at strange angles, bits of them left out in the open like extra body parts. She'd grab me around my ears and neck, leaving my left shoulder wedged between her chest and my mother's armpit. My left side picked up the heat from those women. My right side stuck out unattached and cold in the nippy St. Louis air. Ready to go again.

Come September and Mama sent me home for school: in St. Louis, where I'd get a good education in a colored school, the family said. And my cousins, Irma Jean and Cora Jean squealing like birds whose nest had been mangled: *Colleena Mobeena Stick Stack Steena.* And everyone moving in sort of a circle of laughing and ooh-ing and ahh-ing and *Lord Jesus, so long a time* . . .

The first problem of adjustment upon returning anyplace is that everything seems smaller than you remember. I remembered the house on Kennerly as bigger than any place we'd lived in in the army. I remembered rows of coffee-colored flats with whitewashed stoops.

Or my Aunt Jennie's house, set in a block of houses with long summer porches. Jennie, who always took you back when you came
home. What I saw when I returned was a line of squat houses made
of fake brick with postage-stamp front porches of faded yellow and
blue paint, and all that curlicue wrought iron. Houses where one
neighbor knew exactly what the other neighbor was doing. Houses
stacked together wall-to-wall, like those houses of cards Daddy built
to show me how strong a deck could be.

> Heel toe kiss O'Malley
> Pull him way back in the alley
> Soap and water gums and belly
> End to end O'Malley

What are the telltale signs of the inveterate traveler? She loves the
act of traveling: the motion, the confusion of tickets and luggage,
strangeness waiting like presents about to be opened.

What is home if the road that draws you away from it is more familiar, more comforting? Home is what you find when you get there.
Home is anyplace on this planet. And no silver arch over the "Mighty
Miss" to pin you there. They got some of us everywhere, Grandma
said. In Ecuador, in 1977, on the seventh day of the seventh month, I
stood at the equator: latitude 0'00. In Istanbul, I stood with one foot
in Asia and the other in Europe.

The only sunrise I ever want to see is over the wingtip of a 747 at
35,000 feet. Otherwise, don't wake me before noon.

Overseas, I am always the sight to see. Some turn, smile, say: Buon
giorno or Buenos dias or Comment allez-vous or G'day t'ya. Some
just grin: Coffee? Tea? Their treat. In the market on Fiji, the vendors
were pretty and black and when they learned my name, they called
me Col-lee-een, and I started tripping 'cause I heard my mama calling me home when I had to run swimming among fireflies and all
those bad boys trying to get me in trouble.

Out in the world, I think of Josephine, La Bakaire. Me and Josephine, a long way from St. Louie.

On the Isle of Marjorca, near the home of Junipero Serra who wrestled the Indians of the Californias into Christianity, three boys and an old man stand outside my car for an hour and a half while I rest my swollen feet. In the end, they consent to one photo—none of them smiling. In Belgrade, everyone stared, jeered, flapped behind me like geese. My trick: Find the dullest storefront display (old keys, sockets and wrenches, shoelaces and heelcaps). When a crowd gathered, (and it would), straining to see what it was I saw—this strange black woman in Western clothing—I slip away and leave them there. It always worked.

You always remember men who smiled shyly, their eyes soft as a caress: Stëin and Chaupè . . . Stephanovic and Nikki . . . Lau and Georgio and Anton . . . They taught you languages you'll never forget. Some nights you still dream of them.

Perhaps everything you love should be put on wheels.

Outside, the sun is making its daily comeback. And the sea is dancing its one damn dance again. But yours is a water sign, and that's what this is all about. This moving. You are making love. The sheets are hot, the air is hot, your skin is hot, your lover. Lips, arms, skin. Where are you traveling now? You've always liked lovers with strong thighs. After all, someone has to carry all those damn bags. And you always overpack.

When the plane bound for New Jersey left the Azores, the last landmark we saw was the castle, Torre-de-Belem. Our pilot tipped the wings so we'd catch that final glimpse of land. It was a noticeable lurch, the kind taken by pilots who still dreamed of the old days and wars, when they skimmed the clouds to avoid ground fire. Beneath us, the sunset turned leaves gold and red, then we winged out over the endless ocean, going home.

My greatest hassles with customs agents have always been stateside.

How did you pay for this ticket? they ask. *Where were you born? Why did you go to these places? Do you know anyone there? Is there anyone at home who can vouch for you?*

Is there anyone home?

> *Heel toe cross and over*
> *Heel toe back and over*
> *Put O'Leary in the clover*
> *Cross and over heel toe*

When we stepped into the terminal in New Jersey, I discovered culture shock in reverse. I'd landed in a sea of black faces. Away from home for a few months, and I find myself swimming in a sea of black faces. Hundreds of black folks everywhere and of every shade. Not just some scattered here and there, as in the cities of Europe or Asia. Black folks swirled around me, words echoing with the sounds of Texas, Georgia, Missouri, New York—and all in color. Out of the country, I was the stranger, stared at because I was the curiosity, the exotic, the myth they'd told stories about. Out of the country, white Americans thought they knew me better than I knew myself. But stateside was another matter. Straight color, like so much White and so much Black, I couldn't breathe without pushing against it. All answers depended on color. Three hundred years of racism, a history of slavery, and headlines about Supreme Court decisions became eyeball-to-eyeball looks. Folks looked knives, looked buzz saws and grenades. "They look like damn-it-I'll-bite-you," Mama said. Somewhere overseas, I'd lost the knack of that look. Somewhere, I'd dropped my mask and stood up: "Black and the hell with you, I'm here." Now I was home, and color was straight out and head on. Color was the prison where, like any concentration camp, both the guards and the inmates were bound by the rage.

He says, *It says here you've traveled quite a bit.* Yes, I say. *Visa stamps on almost every page.* An old passport, I tell him. He picks up the entry stamp. Turns the pages again. Triangles, squares, blue ink, green ink—half the world turned into symbols. He brings the stamp down slowly. *Don't you ever stay home?* he asks. I am home, I say.

She was Japanese, short and muscular. I didn't give a damn. It was the last luggage cart in customs and three other inbound planes had landed. I didn't care if she was a sumo wrestler. She squatted, stared, yanked the cart, said something that sounded like sand hitting the side of a bowl. I held fast. Yanked back. Turned street. It's always surprising how "fuck you" translates instantly in all languages.

Somewhere in the late afternoon of that first day home, when my body clock was collapsing under the change in time zones, I listened to the rhythms of the house.

Listen to the music of geography: Paradox, Colorado; Hellville, Madagascar; Darwin, Australia; Chantilly, France; and Peera Peera Poolanna.

Home alone, with the children gone now and the rest of the family in the Midwest. If I'm quiet, I can still hear the familiar sounds of home. Perhaps I hear Aunt Jennie saying: Chile, you are so brave. Go out there and see this world. Wish I could go with you. Or my grandmother pulling out old photographs to match the ones I'm showing her of places she'll never see. That's your Uncle Roman, she says, just so I won't lose track of the family. And that's you, she says. A silhouette done at the carnival when you was just about five years old. But you so big now. I member when you was no bigger than this. Then she pops her fingers and hardly a sound comes out and we both laugh because Grandma could never make her fingers pop. And my father will cook a meal of a thousand starches highlighted with greens and beans and beets. And my mother will shake her head and say: I just don't understand. Full grown and always on the go. And I'll look at the tapestry hanging over my grandmother's sofa. The one with the desert scene, a hand at the tent flap, one eye peeking out.

One two three O'Leary
Give the basket to McCleary
Pinch her if she hollers dearie
That's O'Leary Dandy

The plane was filled with orphans, babies belted in airline cradles all the way from Korea. Chicago was the last leg of their trip. Two nuns accompanied them, but no one else could touch them, not even hold them when they cried. Against regulations. Finally, an hour outside of Chicago, they fell asleep. Then we went into a holding pattern over O'Hare. It was too quiet. All the babies woke up. The plane nosed through the heavy cloud cover and rocketed past the lights of the city with forty orphans wailing.

Thirty-two of us singing *The Caravan*. Four will be dead before they're twenty. Eight more before they're thirty. One will be an opera singer, the toast of Europe, naturally. Two will head corporations, one of which will go bankrupt during someone else's savings and loan scandal. One will dance on Broadway. One will form his own singing group. He'll be famous. One day, on tour, I'll stop by his hotel. The concierge will not admit me to his room.

There's a name somewhere on the tip of your tongue. Like an island in a sea of words. Nadi. Majorca. Krk. Ischia. Langkawi. Why does it always taste so good to say names in foreign languages? Like loving someone you can hardly bear to touch? Smells like flowers—sweet plumeria, raw rafflesia. The texture of washed silk. A crisp ticket for a new port. The body adjusts, sighs. Beautiful, you think, beautiful. You move.

Even now, you can recite entire verses of *The Caravan*.

Home. I turned to the window. The air lanes were dotted with planes, some like the American carrier I had traveled on, others with foreign designations. I've traveled them as well. The airfield held a strange kind of symmetry, planes lined up wingtip to wingtip, underbellies dragging or pointed noses painted like beaks. When the airport limo turned onto the highway, I watched cars zip past. Too many colors, too many different faces, too many billboards for "buy this" and roadside stores selling a little bit of that. A fast-talking disc jockey handed out bad news on the hour, every hour. And we eased past the strangeness of airports, heading where? Home ain't but a place, I tell myself.

Why you got to go to all those places? Mama asks. Because they are there, I say. All that going and coming, she says. Always going home, I think.

Route 66

If I had to name two things that have turned me toward writing and traveling, I would choose my grandmother's dressing room mirror and Route 66.Odd as it may seem, they are connected. As a child, my grandmother's mirror gave me my place of imagination, and Route 66 provided me with my first observation of worlds outside of St. Louis.

> *Take the highway, take the byway that's the best*
> *Get your kicks on Route 66.*

The truth is: I have spent my life traveling from somewhere to the next place, either physically or in the stories I have created and retold. My romance with language began in my grandmother's attic with her full-length mirror and wind-up Victrola, feather boas and wide-brimmed hats, and stacks and stacks of thick 78 rpm records—recordings of everything imaginable from opera and vaudeville to march tunes and early blues, all of them essential accoutrements for a lonely child to play out stories. I took on the roles of both speaker and listener—and when words failed, I mimicked adult conversations with body language and intonation. It was there I learned the 1920s and '30s songs of Ethel Waters, Valaida

Snow, and Florence Mills, women I chose as my heroes, the stars of my dressing room mirror stories and later, my poems, because they dared to defy someone's notion of what they were supposed to be. If the St. Louis of my youth had been a more reasonable world, I might have become an actress, but I was born into a St. Louis of segregated schools, occasional race riots, and a world on its way to a war in which my father would wear the uniform of a segregated army, a world where I saw clearly that the only acting parts offered black folks were limited to the serving and singing roles of Stephin Fetchit, Hattie MacDaniels, Bojangles Robinson, or Josephine Baker sporting a bunch of bananas at the Folies Bergère. So before I had a chance to try Route 66 or any other highway, I tried make-believe conversations in worlds I dreamed would be there when I finally arrived.

I grew up as a storyteller: first in a family full of women who reveled in storytelling, women who, in fact, held their families together with stories when husbands and sons were called into the military or when racism pushed the men into jobs in other cities. And later, when I changed schools, which I did once my mother began to follow my father on his tours of duty with the military, I used storytelling as a way of making friends. With twelve years separating me and my younger brother, I was virtually an only child in a family of adults. I had to learn to amuse myself. I fell in love with the sounds of language—the music of words and the images they create. I had a passion for reading. I read everything from Shakespeare and *Tales of the Decameron* to Aesop's fables and Marvel Comics, and in all of them, I looked for images of myself. I gravitated to dark-haired women in lieu of women of color. The Dragon Lady in *Terry and the Pirates* and Scheherazade from *Tales of the Arabian Nights* joined Florence Mills and Josephine Baker on my list of "women who took no stuff"—remembered, as Milton Caniff said of the Dragon Lady, "because they poisoned empires." My female heroes showed me how to search out places other than where I was as surely as I believed Route 66 was the dream road to those other worlds. Still, I was more entranced with the beauty of language than I was with the particular beauties of any given writer or star of a stage act. The stories in those books carried me into worlds of language where the music and texture of sounds brushing the tongue flickered on the page as clear as those fireflies I saw floating in midwestern heat, or the crystals of ice frozen on a window pane, cool water tumbling from the fountain in front of the train station, or the spray from a neighborhood fire hydrant opened on a summer's day. Later, when I became a speech pathologist, I posted a quotation on my office wall: *The limits of my language mean the limits of my world.*

When I was a child, Route 66 represented for me something waiting, something pulling me along to who knows where. Travel was, and is, the second source of my writing. Richard Hugo, a wonderful poet and writer, once tried to explain to me how the landscape of the writer determined the language of what was to be written: "In the city, the rush of living speeds up the writing," he said. "It is only by looking back that we learn to focus on what has triggered the work." I have had the time, finally, to look back on Route 66, and I hold in my memory an event that is as clearly connected to my need to travel as it is to my need to write.

> *Now you go through St. Louie, Joplin, Missouri,*
> *Oklahoma City is mighty pretty*
> *You see Amarillo—Gallup, New Mexico . . .*

The year was 1943, or thereabouts, and my mother, one of her sisters, her brother, and I were heading for California. It was the year the Allies fought in Bataan and Corregidor, the British attacked the Vichy in Madagascar, enemy submarines shelled Vancouver Island and the Aleutians, and the military claimed all the grown men in my neighborhood, including my father, my uncle, and my cousins. In fact, it was the last summer my uncle, my mother's only brother, would be a civilian. One of his last duties before entering the army was to be the driver on our trip to California. There is a part of me that wants to say I remember absolutely every detail about my first time on that highway, but what I remember most is the sense of freedom, the changing smells from St. Louis to the open road, and what the rest of the family warned us would be "way-out-West and no telling what can happen." I remember it as the first time I really pulled clear of what locked me into the half-mile radius of streets bordered by Taylor, St. Ferdinand, Cottage, and Kennerly avenues: the whites-only playground at Cote Brilliante School, the pickle jars full of penny candy at Ol' Man Farrow's store, the rumors of white folks rising out of their graves in the segregated cemetary next to Ash Hill, the sugar-soaked ice cream at the Velvet Freeze, and White Castle's ten-cent hamburgers. It was to be the first summer I would not spend long afternoons clinging to the shady side of the gangway between our brownstone and Farrow's store.

Even while I was packing, I knew I'd miss those sweet purple-black grapes hanging in heavy clumps in the bee-infested backyard arbor. After years of travel, after journeying halfway around the world in either direction from Missouri, that was to be the last summer I would taste any grapes quite like those: so sweet and fat, as deeply purple on the inside as on the outside, with a sugary pulp that left me deliciously drunk after I'd stuffed myself sick during tea parties with Valaida and Josephine under the arbor's dappled shade. Out on that road, everything gained perspective, and no sense of knowing was ever as clear to me as what I saw down Route 66. After I had grown up, after the war was over and my father finally retired from the military, after the army camps from Missouri to Germany had blended together in my memory, my travels would take me to back to Europe and on to Africa, South America, Japan, Fiji, and the Pacific, but the initial sense of the world I place in my poems and stories is connected always to that first trip down Route 66.

It was late June, and the St. Louis humidity was swelling against the hinges of my uncle's Dodge sedan. I had put away my broken crayons, skate keys, and jacks in favor of a foldout map of the forty-eight states, a fresh load of Nancy Drew mysteries, my grandmother's trusty *Farmer's Almanac* of places to see and weather reports, and the best book of all—a brand-new diary with a lock and key for all those private thoughts I was sure I would have. In those days, before my baby brother was born, I had the backseat to myself, and while the adults contemplated the safest route through unknown territory, I wrote letters to my diary, then marked the map as we hummed along the asphalt past Joplin, Oklahoma City, Amarillo, Gallup, and Flagstaff.

Nowadays, Route 66 has dwindled to a mere whisper along certain sections of Interstate 40, or, in some places, a narrow slip of a road winding away from the roar of cross-country travel as desolute as a farmer's horse-drawn cart. But back then, when I was just beginning to learn how the body picks up the rhythms of a vehicle and shifts the flow of blood to match the pulse of wheels and motors, Route 66 was the road that connected the main street of one town to the main drag of another. It was a lineup of red Coca-Cola signs with grinning white faces placed cheek-to-glass against bottles of Coke built like busty women. It was Aunt Jemima grinning silly over pancakes, the Phillip Morris bellhop and Johnnie Walker's whiskey jockey marching across landscapes as if they were rushing to wait for me in the next town. At that age, I was easily impressed. Not so my family; my family knew that any stretch of road with signs announcing FOR WHITES ONLY signaled danger for black folks. In those days, some towns along Route 66 displayed those signs, and folks back home told jokes about traveling Negroes falling through the door on tired feet, greasy bags of fried chicken clutched in their hands, except it was no joke. That was the reality of what to do when you had no Howard Johnsons, Holiday Inns, or Motel 6. It was how to survive while changing jobs or avoiding sheriffs if rednecked anger reached its peak. So with enough gas ration stamps to make it to California, we pushed the limits of that Dodge, stopping only when we had directions to a distant relative's house or the address for a friend of a friend.

We left St. Louis with a network of places to spend the night. Aside from being delayed by the occasional line of transport trucks carrying supplies and soldiers, the only real traffic seemed to be farmers creeping out of country lanes in slow-moving cars or barreling head-on around blind curves as if they had only driven tractors across open fields until the very day we encountered them on the road. I amused myself by connecting towns on the map, counting the number of Hudsons and DeSotos against the Packards and Fords, and writing down all the dumb Burma-Shave signs we passed:

If your mind is a muddle. And your life is a puddle.
Take a tip from the sun. Smile upon everyone.
Burma-Shave.

I remember how my mother and her sister amused themselves by recalling all the gossip ever uttered about a family member, one by one, from birth on, and my uncle drove and ignored orders from the women when they told him to "stop here" or "turn there." But by the time we reached Gallup, New Mexico, and the nephew-of-somebody's-first-wife, my uncle's enthusiasm for the open road had dwindled, and we had run out of safe houses. That meant we saw fewer black faces, and without the name of a friend-of-a-friend, it was either "making those white folks give us a room" or driving straight through to California.

After we left Gallup, carrying a box packed to the brim by the nephew-of-somebody's-first-wife with "a little bit of traveling food"—meaning enough food for a couple of five-course meals—an argument started about what we should do come nightfall. I buried my head in Nancy Drew's *Mystery of the Gila Monster Gang,* surfacing only to stare at the crystallized trees in the Petrified Forest, frozen in the act of dying, and the pink, blue, yellow, and red clay of the Painted Desert, brillant as a dish of multicolored crayons left to melt in the sun. As we started to skirt the rim of the Navajo Reservation, I occasionally left the outlaws of my mystery book long enough to wave at the unsmiling faces of Indians staring at us as we passed them on the roadside, Indians my mother swore had not forgotten what the soldiers did to them when the cavalry had swept through the territory. But my uncle was more concerned about the notice of his impending duty with the modern army, and as we sped across the mesa toward Flagstaff, he decided he wanted to see the Grand Canyon before Uncle Sam pointed a finger his way.

No one should tell women, already nervous about the prospect of driving through desert country, that they are about to detour from the main road into canyons full of hidden cliffs and ridges, but that was what my uncle did. "We'll just sleep out in the open," he said. While my mother and her sister chewed on reasons for going straight to Flagstaff, Uncle headed for the south rim of the canyon, and I followed the posse tracking the Gila Monster Gang back to their hideout in the foothills. The scenes in my book and what I saw through that Dodge's back windows were similiar: Nancy Drew couldn't convince anyone she knew how to enter the secret cave, and my uncle refused to listen to the women complain about sleeping in the car all night. The sun made the trail twice as difficult for the posse. The heat in our car rose with every chorus of complaints. Lizards skittered through descriptions of Nancy's trail. Any view from the window offered me the sight of a strange bird circling overhead or the tail of some small creature scurrying away from the road. Exhausted from the chase, I fell asleep long before we parked for the night.

But I was the first to awaken at dawn. What I saw outside the window became my first remembered attempt at the language of poetry.

I had been dreaming of gila monsters—of that, I am certain, because I woke up itchy and rubbing the chill off my arms. Half awake, I thought for a moment that my uncle had parked the car in the mouth of the Gila Gang's cave. Although the silvery rays of early morning sun filled the side windows, no light seeped through the windshield. I slipped on my glasses and squinted over the front seat. Now the darkness covering the window had detail—short little spikes like scrub brush or hair. And it was breathing.

I counted the rise and fall of inhales and exhales before I eased toward the front seat and gently tapped my uncle's shoulder. He was a slow riser, and by the time he had blinked the sleep from his eyes, the windshield's fur coat was stretching itself awake to greet the day. Now it had a mouth, four legs, a tail, and was unmistakably catlike. It slipped away from the glass, took one lazy yawn, and turned toward us. Uncle whispered something that sounded like "Oh Lordy Jesus," and the cat shook the sound from its ears. Even that small movement rocked the car, but the women did not awaken, just as none of us had awakened when the cat had climbed onto the warm hood the night before. I held my breath and reached toward my mother, then thought better of it. Uncle was making little sounds deep in his throat. The cat lifted its head and sniffed the air. Morning light tinted its eyes gold, almost the same color as its fur. My uncle, who was usually clumsy, had slipped noiselessly into position behind the steering wheel. The cat stared at us, winking, and my uncle, who has beige cat's eyes himself, stared back. I wondered how long it would take the cat to drag us to its cave, one by one, or eat us right there in the car. The front window offered me no solace. When the cat's breath coated the windshield, it lazily licked the mist from the glass until it was distracted by a movement in the bushes. Slowly it rose, turned, and slid to the ground as if it were leaving an easy chair. The hood held a clear imprint of its body. Without missing a beat, my uncle popped the clutch and started backing down the mountain. Before the women were fully awake, he was doing thirty in reverse, and while they asked what happened, I wrote my first big observation in my diary:

> We saw a mountain lion. It covered the whole
> front of the car and it looked like a big rug
> and had golden eyes and winked at me. When it
> yawned, I could count all its teeth. Uncle
> Brother was so scared he backed the car all
> the way down the mountain like he was driving
> the rollercoaster ride at Grandview carnival.

There is quite a gap between that first bit of diary writing and the time when I formally began writing poems, but if my grandmother's mirror were available to me now, I would baffle it with my sprin-klings of dimly remembered foreign tongues and conversations overheard in more airports than I'd care to count. My notions of the open road have taken wing, and I have lost the details of billboards; my roads border countries instead of towns, and in the wash of fast travel, the lines of black and white blur with language changes: strangers become neighbors, cities blend into maps of ruins, and taxi drivers remain surly in every language.

I was lucky to have had both my grandmother's mirror and Route 66, for all of its shortcomings. Eventually, that road, and hundreds like it, took me from St. Louis to halfway around the world. Part of me wants to say I remember everything about trips I have taken, even those I took as a child, but what memories I have of early trips blur into fuzzy lines of army camps from Missouri to Wyoming, and trips to California that seem to fade somewhere around Arizona. What I remember are impressions of moving, the absolute sense of freedom, the changing smells from St. Louis to the open road.

There was that time when I could map my travels from St. Louis to Joplin, Oklahoma City, Amarillo, Gallup, Flagstaff, and San Bernadino. Now, Route 66 is a will-o'-the-wisp of a road that bor-ders sections of Interstate 40, but when I was learning how the world was complicated by traveling, my view was country stores with ice chests full of cold soda pop and gas stations where the tops of the pumps were transparent, like blenders or Pyrex tumblers, quarts of petrol that turned gold in the sunlight. It was the grandest road I knew, except for Kingshighway Boulevard in St. Louis. It was the first road where I learned how to push against the black/white limits of anyone's map.

> *Farewell old verse along the road*
> *How sad to know you're out of mode*
> *Burma-shave*

Swinging and Swaying with Arthur Murray in a Hurry

My mother used to tell me I was built like a boy, all arms and legs—
no hips, no bust, just everything hanging loose and ready to move.
"High pockets," they called me. And my grandmother would say,
"Chile, what did you do when the Lord was giving out body parts?
Stand in line twice to get them long legs?" But on my private stage in
the attic, I was Josephine Baker at the Moulin Rouge, and Florence
Mills dancing her way through *Bye-Bye, Blackbird* on Broadway.
Having hips might have depended on my imagination, but I let my
imagination run wild, swaying my body like Katherine Dunham and
Carmen Miranda combined, even to the point of wrapping a towel
around my head and filling it with oranges and grapes. If I got
through a whole dance of shaking my shoulders and moving my hips
without dropping the fruit on the floor, I'd reward myself with a
snack. Some days, all I ate was bruised fruit. But I could create a
world of my own making: spinning, spinning, and dizzy with the
movement, with the sheer joy of making the world go loopy. I
twirled and shimmied my ten-year-old version of the jitterbug, the
hucklebuck, and the camel walk. I lip-synched tunes, twisting my
bony hips this way and that, and as soon as I'd memorized the steps

until I could do any dance forward, backward, and sideways, I was ready to show every kid on the block what I knew. "Look at this," I'd say. "Look at this." And I'd sing: *If your feet get tired and you don't want to walk . . . Put a hump in your back and do the camel walk.* Then I'd fall into some syncopation that I was sure Bojangles would have noticed if only Bojangles had known I was waiting for him in St. Louis. Little did I know that it was Arthur Murray who was waiting for me.

Twilight. When I was growing up, that was the very best time of the day. That was when the light turned pearl blue and the sky seemed to hold both day and night, when the sounds of the neighborhood wound down and we could really hear the Hodiman streetcar *ding-ding* its bell as it crossed the intersection a block away. The air was sweet with flowers closing for the night, and fireflies blinked under an early evening sky already shadowed by the moon. Swirls of gnats drifted off breezes blowing across vacant lots filled with chickweeds and dandelions. And after dinner, the kids gathered for one more round of stoopball or one last ring game. I always made sure I got picked at least once before darkness erased the street.

Looking back, I guess that was when I was dancing without even knowing that's what I was doing. Sometimes the boys watched the girls, but rarely did they join us. We knew they were watching, and we set our moves to get their attention, the girls singing: *Little Sally Walker sitting in her saucer . . . Rise Sally Rise . . .* And when it was my turn, I'd rise in one move, my body set to strut and prance and my eye on some boy playing stickball or jackknife. I was no more than seven or eight, acting like I was going on twenty-eight, and the girls were clapping and yelling, *Put your hands on your hips and let your backbone shift. Ohh, shake it to the east . . . Ohh, shake it to the west . . . Ohh shake it to the one you love the best . . .* I'd march to the center of the circle, my head in the air and my butt sticking out like Ms. Nellie Simmons, who lived at the end of the block and wore tight flowered dresses. I'd switch my hips and move my feet like I was walking on sand and had an itch somewhere down in the small of my back. Or I'd fling out my arms and let my body go loose like the women at the sanctified church who could shake all over when they got the holiness. The girls would giggle, and the boys would pretend they didn't know who I loved the best.

The summer of my fourteenth year, I ran away from my mother's house and went across town to live with Aunt Jennie. The two Jeans—my cousins, Irma Jean and Cora Jean—were there when I arrived. Irma Jean was a year older and Cora Jean a year younger than me, and like me, they also had run away from their mothers to come live with Jennie, the childless aunt in the family. They weren't sisters, but that didn't seem to matter, because they were forever connected by their middle names. And by Aunt Jennie. I still can't decide if my aunt was crazy or sainted, but even then, I knew she was special. She wore silk dresses and high heels, and she wouldn't serve dinner until everyone was sitting down at the table. Mama tried, but dinner at our house was always haphazard, everybody operating on a different schedule. My father was in the army, which meant that until he came home for furlough, Mama and I were left at home with my grandmother and Mama's younger brother. I got along fine with everyone but Uncle Brother, and it was trying to live with him that made me take refuge at Aunt Jennie's.

Jennie took me in without blinking her eyes. The rules were simple. Break one and you go straight back to your mother's house. The two Jeans and I worked hard at keeping Jennie happy. In return, she taught us manners. We learned how to dress, which fork to use, and what books to read. But her real gift was in letting three teenage girls see the world for what it was, not with a flood of warnings as our mothers did, but with practical stuff, like nail polish and mascara, cut flowers and cloth napkins, sweet perfume, silk scarves, and yes, dancing. Jennie had a Motorola phonograph, the deluxe style in a wooden cabinet with a turntable that could hold ten records. I think the two Jeans and I wore out more needles in six months than Jennie had used in a whole year.

On Saturdays, after we'd finished our chores, we commanded that Motorola. We'd throw back the rug and do the Stroll or Bugaloo, trucking along with Ray Charles or Ruth Brown, the Cadillacs, the Moonglows, or the Clovers, the two Jeans and I working each line and sometimes adding a little routine of our own, like *slide-step-double fist-turn, and . . . doohwahdoohwah . . .* I taught the two Jeans how to do the quickstep and the Camel Walk. They taught me how to stand with my knees slightly bent and flirt with one shoulder, the way girl groups like the Chantels did. And when Irma watched Cora jerking her hips as if the lower part of her body were a washing machine, Irma decided to teach us how to move smooth and easy, until we could write our names on the wall with our butts, the whole name in cursive: first, middle, and last. I was glad my name was all loops, with no i's to dot or t's to cross.

"Com'on," Irma would tease us. "You got a boody. Shake it." But best of all, Irma Jean showed me how to follow someone else's lead. I was still dancing as if Grandma's Victrola had been cranked up just for me. "Girl, what you doing?" Irma said. "You wear out some boy moving your feet like that." Boys? I thought and mentally closed the lid on that Victrola.

"This is slow dancing," Irma said. "Hang loose and act like you kinda sleeping. Let *him* do all the work." Then we'd put on records by Billy Eckstine or Ivory Joe Hunter. Cora and I learned how boys would hold us close and move their hips against us until our bones grew warm and ready to dissolve. I didn't believe it would work, all that dancing with body against body until you couldn't tell where yours ended and the other began. I stumbled and Cora giggled, and Irma almost gave up on both of us. But one day, it clicked. One day, I told my body to wait, and it did. I felt myself go loose, not with Cora Jean's sad slump that left her hanging around Irma's neck like an old towel, but with a looseness that hummed with the music and held back just long enough to be carried on the next note. It was as if I'd stepped across an invisible line where, for the first time, dancing meant moving along with someone else's rhythm. When Irma

Jean turned, my feet fell into place where hers had been. When she leaned, I leaned with her. I let her pull me against her and off center until one hip was brought up to meet her oncoming hip. And I learned to glide and sway as if I were trying to use the hem of my skirt to polish a glass. Bring on the boys, I thought.

I have this picture in my head of my Aunt Jennie kicking up her heels in the dining room of her house on St. Ferdinand Avenue. I'm standing in the doorway with the two Jeans, the three of us trying desperately to be older than fifteen. We've been assigned to wash the dinner dishes, but we're watching what the grown folks are doing instead. As clear as I can remember, it is summer, one of those hot St. Louis days that makes the Mississippi look like an inviting place to swim. The humidity has exceeded the temperature, and although three or four fans are blowing humid air from doorway to doorway, ice cubes still crackle and melt as soon as my mother pours fruit punch into a glass. My father, on leave for a week, is nursing his whiskey straight, and my cousin, Anna, whom we called Sweet, is complaining about how hard it is to teach the project kids in her third grade summer school class. Across the room, my Uncle Phillip is sorting through records to add to the stack of LPs spindled on the phonograph. "Cupid's Boogie" falls under the needle and when Little Esther starts to sing, Aunt Jennie lets go, twirling and spinning and rocking right along with the record.

No one is surprised when Jennie cuts loose. She's the redhead in the family and given to fancy dresses and high living, as my grandmother would say. But halfway through the song, the throw rug slips on the floor that the two Jeans and I have waxed that morning, and before Uncle Phillip can reach forward to save her, Jennie goes spilling into the living room as if she's been ejected off the tip of Little Esther's high note. She sits there, splat-legged the way people do when they don't expect the ground to come up so suddenly underneath them. For a second, the only sounds are the ice melting in the drinks and Little Esther moaning about the pain of love. Then Mama says, "Um-um- um," and Jennie says, "I guess I'm out of practice." And the two Jeans and I have to hold each other up to keep from falling over laughing.

Practice? How old was I when I started? Eight? Nine? Was it when I danced through all those sidewalk games or was it in Grandma's attic when I moved like the wind, like the flowers, like the leaves on the red oak tree in Aunt Jennie's backyard? When I got older, Mama warned me, "You best make something of yourself. White folks think all we can do is sing and dance." Of course, I remembered her slow dancing with my father, but that was different, she said. "You'll be ruint behind all that stuff," she told me. "Look at how they talk about Josephine Baker. No telling what's happened to her behind all that singing and dancing. And she was born right here in St. Louis." And I thought about Josephine and Paris and my feet just itched to move. "Don't be acting like those fast tail gals out there in the street," Mama said. I nodded OK, but it was too late.

I was at a sock hop at the downtown Y when I stumbled upon George Darlington Love, a sweet brown-skinned boy who, I swear, could have been pulled from one of those stories I read in *True Romance* or *Teen Magazine*. Most of the boys I knew had three-part names like Warren Hope Davis and Harry Blackinston, Jr., but not even in my wish book had I dreamed of *George-Darlington-Love*. Later, the two Jeans would taunt me with his name, but that first night when he stepped away from the milky shadows of the YWCA dance floor, I didn't question his name or where he came from. I only thanked whatever guardian angel or fairy godmother had thrown him in my path.

He was cruising the floor and I was groping my way back from the little girls' room, my nearsightedness made more acute by my refusal to wear my glasses in the presence of prospective boyfriends. This meant I saw the room in a sort of dreamy blur, accentuated by the dappled light streaming off a silver ball that hung like the moon over the dance floor. The DJ was playing one of those belly-rubbing songs, you know, some tune where the baritone croons "I Need You So"; "For You My Love I'd Do Anything"; or "Cross My Heart, I Love You."

The swish-swish of sock-clad feet sounded like a dozen brushes stroking the drum. That's when George Darlington Love, in full air force uniform, stepped out of the shadows and gathered me in his arms. It was a deadly combination: that blue uniform, the chandelier light sprinkled across the floor, and all those bodies floating from note to note. He was thin and wiry, a rail of a boy with cat-gray eyes, hair plastered down with brilliantine hair creme, and a smile that made me swallow surprise. I was almost afraid to breathe as I nestled my head against his shoulder. He smelled of Old Spice and skin turned hot from the sweat of muscles. He held me close—one hand in the small of my back, the other low down at my side to shove me in gear. Not that we were going anywhere. We moved cool and slow, brush-brush-slide and hip to hip, my body fitting against his like a hand fits a glove. And just as Irma Jean had told me: we never paid any attention to our feet. We danced, George Darlington Love and I, as if we were the only ones under that glittering light, just me and a slightly built boy with an improbable name, my first beau. No dance would ever be the same.

And then there were times when I dreamed about being Conchita, Rosita, Flame of Old Mejeeco . . .

I was two years away from Arthur Murray when I fell victim to demon rum. The two Jeans and I were at a kitchen table club, a jook joint, Aunt Jennie would've called it if we'd ever had the misfortune to explain to her where we were. But our luck held. Rumor had it that the club was a hangout for boys visiting town from Spanish Harlem, so we were trying to look grown-up. Only Irma Jean was succeeding. None of us knew it, but that was to be the year Irma finally ran away from us for good, lured by a boy with empty pockets and a mouth full of promises. Meanwhile, the three of us tried looking as if we didn't care where we were.

Everyone was fooled except the bartender. He sent over Shirley Temples with two cherries in each glass. As soon as his back was turned, we drank half the soda and Irma poured rum to the lip of the glass. I guess you could say rum was my downfall, either that or the Latin beat that carried me headlong onto the dance floor. Whatever the case, I was on my feet as soon as the band started. The place was filled with boys who had marcelled their hair to a fare-thee-well, and girls shaking their hips as if they could wear out their dresses from the inside. The girls wore off-the-shoulder blouses that seemed to stay up by sheer willpower. They were girls of quick tongues, sharp looks, and satin skirts slit up to the dangerous part of the thigh. And the boys, with no shoulders and biceps as big as Popeye's. Some boy with a hard chest and tight pants covering an ass like a fist. Some boy with bean breath and eyes like liquid. Some boy who slid by and asked for a dance like he was snitching something off a rack while looking the other way, looking cool.

But the music saved us all. The band was drums, timbals, and congas, with enough horns for Prez Perado and Cal Tjader combined. They slammed into a cha-cha or mambo beat, holding it precise and tight until even the floorboards began to shake. And I was in heaven, calling up the memory of Katherine Dunham and Carmen Miranda. How had I done it? The towel wrapped around my head, the fruit staying put, and my hips gyrating into tomorrow. I had forgotten nothing, and when some boy locked me in a dance, my very bones picked up the heat of the drums. I let him lead, my moves flowing into his until our bodies spoke the same language. The problem was that sometimes, at the end of the dance, the same boy who had moved his hips like I was the last uncharted continent he wanted to march into, would turn on his heels and walk away— no word, just a glimpse of him trucking toward some other unexplored territory. But the next dance had already started and I would shout, "aRRiba!" trilling my tongue against the roof of my mouth like a wild parrot sounding an alarm, holding onto it for the sheer joy of it, for the rush of sound, for the whistled, whispered, laughing riot of noise.

I'm sure it was rum that threw me into the clutches of the Chico Cha-cha Champs. By the middle of summer, I no longer waited for the two Jeans to go club hopping. I'd find a date or he'd find me, some Henry or Bobby or Clarence. And the drinks arrived already spiked. That's how I fell in with Chico. One sip of rum, and I was ready to mambo on Mars. The Champs had two couples, but Chico needed a partner for the Afro-Cuban finals in Chicago. I wanted to dance forever. It sounded like a good idea at the time, but then at sixteen, any idea sounded good. His name was José Eduardo Something-or-Other. Blessedly, I have forgotten his last name. But I'll never forget his hair. I swear, that man had the greasiest hair in the Western Hemisphere. On the dance floor, his hair cast its own glitter, a wink of waves and one curl languishing on his forehead. He was a dark brown version of Rudolf Valentino, but his glamour had a price. I spent the season try-ing to keep him from smoothing back his pompadour before we went on stage. If I didn't succeed, one spin could send me reeling off the oily end of his fingertips clear to Canada. Still, I'm here to tell you, that man could dance. His speciality: Cuban mambo, step-step, and hip-to-hip. He was Belafonte, Piro, and Cuban Pete, all rolled into one. And I have to give him credit. With him, I learned to dance with my whole body. He taught me how the legs move from the hips, not the knees, and the arms from the shoulders so that your wrist finishes the step your feet had started. I learned to count steps and know how the body was kept clear in the eye: the feet separate from the legs, the legs from the trunk, the shoulders from the arms, each defined so that when he turned, everything seemed to move from the hips. And the hips, how they moved, like serving rum in a teacup. Rum and a Latin beat. That was my downfall. One sip, and all I saw was Chico's laugh-ter, the sweat on his skin winking like black pearls just washed clean from an oyster's shell.

We danced for three months, sometimes winning a competition, sometimes barely placing in the lineup. He told me that was longer than he'd ever spent with any partner. It was easy to see why: Chico demanded attention. On the floor, he'd start a movement that looked like a two-step, then up the tempo: four, six, and eight beats to the bar until, before I knew it, he'd shift from mambo to rhumba and back again. That was all right, except sometimes he'd change his mind in the middle of a breathtaking turn, and I'd find myself hanging onto the end of a cha-cha that never materialized. The effect was magic. One minute I'd catch a glimpse of Chico's hair, a wink, and a gold-toothed smile. The next, I'd pirouette off the tips of his fingers and untangle myself from the twirl of my own skirts to find him halfway across the room. Sans glasses, I couldn't really see him, so I'd have to guess the number of steps to close the distance. In my off-the-shoulder blouses, high, high heels, and gypsy skirts, I was hot, or so I thought. It was all show-biz, which is probably why we never made it past the local circuit. But to this day, I stay away from demon rum. After all, the last time, I wound up dancing with a slick-haired Puerto Rican in Chicago.

I guess Chico's legacy was that he made me believe I could dance with anybody. So when an instructor from Arthur Murray asked me to stop by the studio, I figured the job was a piece of cake. Besides, I was a gate-crasher. "The first black instructor ever," they said. But it was Kansas, 1957, and anything was believable. In the end, my tour of duty with Arthur Murray was about as routine as taking a lab class in zoology. Instead of flowing dresses and big bands, I had tiny studio rooms decorated with those damn diagrams. They were waiting for me everywhere, and each time I followed the path, I became a stenographer of dance, recording what had already been done, counting out the steps—"always in a cheerful voice," I was cautioned: *one-two-three-four . . . turn, turn, slide, stop . . . One more time and left foot first . . .* At least that was partly right. My students were left-footed—soldiers who abandoned all they knew at the front door. After a week of corporals and sergeants walking on my insteps, I laid down the law: no combat boots. And no hands on my butt. I'd turn on the tape, reel-to-reel, an endless loop of Nelson Riddle, Lawrence Welk, and Frank Sinatra. Arthur beamed at me from a wall poster as I put each client through the paces: *One-two-three . . . one-two-three . . . One more time, left foot first* ... For six weeks, I suffered the waltz, stiff-backed and unyielding, before I was promoted to Latin rhythms where the body was real and present, and I could dance hip-to-hip again.

For years, I never told anyone that I had actually taught dance for Arthur Murray. It's sort of like admitting you move your lips when you read, you know what I mean? Besides, I hardly look like the Arthur Murray type. Face it, can you imagine me and Arthur grooving to the Sloop and the Philly Dog, his eyebrows arched in a state of endless surprise? And nowhere in my old neighborhood would you find a floor that was pasted with footprints diagramming dance steps, tracks of high heels and brogans scattered all over the place as if crazed ghost couples had spent the night trying to Fox-trot and Samba their way out of purgatory. "We don't move our hips here," I was told. "It's all in the feet."

I remember looking down at the square-toed patent leather pumps encasing my long skinny feet. *These flat feet?* I thought. I looked up at the posters of Arthur Murray and his partner plastered on the walls. Their spines were so straight, I figured they must have had rods strapped to their backs. "No hips, just feet," Arthur seemed to be warning. So I straightened up and counted: *One-two-three . . . one-two-three . . . One more time, left foot first. . . .* I'm here to tell you, at the height of my Arthur Murray years, there were nights where my dreams were filled with those damn footprints, except they'd take on random designs, detailing some dance no human could follow. On those nights, I'd wake up to the sound of my own voice counting out the rhythm: *one-two-three-four . . . turn, turn, slide, stop . . . One more time and left foot first. . . .* And me, moving my feet like dogs when they dream of chasing cars.

Now fast-forward thirty years. I'm in Ixtapa, Mexico, a little town near Zihuatanejo that's more tourists than town. I'm traveling with a friend. We're on vacation, Johnnella and I, on leave, trying not to be professors of English for at least a few weeks while we nose around Ixtapa. We've walked down the beach to a cantina. It's early evening, and we seem to be the only two black Americans in the room. Sometimes it's hard to focus when you're feeling so very foreign, so we cop an attitude—cool, almost snooty, certainly not paying any attention to anyone who might be staring at us. The band is hot, but then, so is the weather. Tall sangrias start to taste real good in hot weather. By the time we've downed one or two, we can finally bring the room into view. Our timing is perfect. A voice says, "Buenas noches."

His name is Armand. "Armando?" Johnnella asks. "Is Armand short for Armando?"

"No, just Armand," he corrects her. "I am not Spanish. But you are from America?"

"How did you know?" Johnnella answers. It's a polite question that doesn't really require an answer—just a way of opening the conversation. He will take us shopping in Zihuatanejo, he says. He knows the best shops for silver and antiquities. How about air conditioning? I say to myself and try my best not to worry the beads of sweat at the nape of my neck.

"Wonderful. I want to shop for masks," I tell him.

Johnnella frowns at me. It's one thing to chat in a public place but quite another to suggest we'll meet later.

We have come to the cantina, Johnnella and I, thinking that at night, the heat will have abated and we will at least feel the ocean breeze. But the cantina is on the leeward side of the beach hotels along a stretch of stores and shops that seem to have no purpose other than to serve touristas. The band is part mariachi, part disco, but the music is definitely Latino. Everyone is swaying in tune. The memory of Chico and his Cha-Cha Champs may as well have come from another planet, far far away. I hug my chair.

After years of being an academic, I just know I've lost all my moves—or as the musicians say, I've lost my chops. I've only felt this way once, in the sixties, when my new husband took me into a western bar full of Montana cowboys whose speech seemed taken

straight from the twang of guitar strings. They had all called me
ma'am. "Care for a dance, ma'am?" they'd ask. I'd stayed glued to that
seat all night.

"We must have a dance," Armand says, as the band cranks up with
enough brass to put Herb Alpert to shame. I nod to Johnnella. "Go
ahead," I tell her. She won't buy it. "You're the dancer," she says.
Armand escorts me onto the floor.

Make the hips move, I tell myself. Don't count the steps, I tell
myself. "Mambo-one-two-pequeño Mambo—just a little footwork,
hip, slide . . ."

It wasn't like getting back on a horse after you've fallen off, but for
a minute, with Armand reminding me a little too much of Chico, I
was, as the playwright Ntozake Shange says: *twirlin hippin givin much
quik feet & bein a mute cute* . . . did I say, Mexicana?

Paris, 1990. The Métro. We have twenty minutes to get to the
Ministry of Culture, although I've explained that I hate subways.
They're crowded, confusing, and you can't see a damn thing underground. But protocol takes precedence, and I'm with the u.s. repre-
sentatives at a conference on African Americans in Europe. I'm
dressed for a cocktail party, cute little sequined bag slung over my
shoulder. It's zipped tight, I remember. He's French, North African I
think, maybe Algerian. I see him at the turnstile, and later, on the
train. But I don't notice that he's handsome because I'm still in the
mood to complain about subways and undergrounds and why I
won't take them. So I don't notice the first body contact, except his
face, smiling pretty. And then there's the second bump, not quite a
grope, but full body and familiar. Too familiar, I think, and check my
purse. It's open and that flash of burgundy in his left hand looks just
like my wallet. He's behind me and heading for the door. The train
sounds a warning buzzer. I pirouette. We're hip to hip. Handsome or
not, I want my wallet. We two-step, then he's halfway on the platform. I see a flash of purple leather, like a leaf falling from his hand,
then caught, in one move, between his thighs. Amazing style! But I

don't even stop to think about how good he is, not when he's tangoed with my wallet. He holds up his hands as if he's surrendering. My eyes are on the prize. I follow—one foot in the car, the other on the platform. My friend screams: *Don't!* I plié. Perfect form. My dance teacher would be proud. I rake down his butt, extend one hand between his legs, and snatch my wallet. I think I feel a nail break. His arms, still raised, falter a bit, but I'm already into the next step: lift and arch, complete the pirouette, and step inside before the doors click shut. I'm safe, minus one fingernail. My last glimpse: a lone figure on the platform, his expression puzzled as the train zips away from the station. Perhaps his pants were that thin, I muse. A car full of Métro riders applaud. I pocket my wallet and take my bows. Ah, dance—you do serve me well.

Sometimes I can forget about dancing for days, weeks, months even—then something happens and I've got the itch again. Even Seattle cooperates with an installation of Art-in-Public-Places that leaves brass footprints diagramming dance steps on every corner for a six block stretch of Broadway. Samba, Cha-cha, Tango in an impossible combination of steps—it's all there, Arthur Murray style. Anyone for a Mambo on the way to the supermarket? I'll always volunteer. I don't mean I drop everything for a one-two step around a ballroom floor, although I performed a dance for my sixtieth birthday party, but hey, how many times do you get to celebrate turning sixty with two handsome backup dancers at a black-tie affair in the aquarium? I swear, those fish were dancing too. Maybe it was all that champagne. And me, all done up formal in sequins with a hundred or so of my friends cheering me on. I explained that I'd forgotten half the steps. "You even look good when you don't know what you're doing." Not much change from my Chico days, I think.

But whenever I get too smug about dancing, I remember how long it's been since Chico took me for a spin across the floor. At a gypsy wedding in Yugoslavia, I enviously watched young girls slide into the rhythms of the dance, their dons wearing thin mustaches and slicked-back hair. One even had a tan overcoat draped across his shoulders. As I watched him cruise the room in his white suit, black shirt, and white tie, I fantasized for a second that he and Chico had gone to the same tailor. Then I told myself that it was merely the magic of the dance, that familiar walk and stance, the look that said: *Hang on if you dare.*

These days, I tell my creative writing students about the time I finally joined a professional dance troupe. I had survived the two Jeans, the Chico Cha-cha Champs, and Arthur Murray. In the first session, the dance master asked us to walk across the floor. We were thirty or so neophytes, all of us young and cocky. So we walked. One by one and in pairs, from one end of the room to the other. In a patient voice, the dance master said, "Please, walk across the floor again." And again we walked. We pranced, we strutted, we strolled, we paced. By the fourth or fifth time, the dance master was losing his patience. "Ladies and gentlemen, I want you to listen," he said. "One more time: show me how you walk across the floor." *There's a trick to this,* I thought. But I couldn't find the clue. After all, what was there to walking anyway?

By the end of the morning session, after walking-across-the-floor for hours, the dance master held his head. "Tomorrow," he said, "you will walk across the floor again. Tomorrow, you will walk—across — the—floor. Not walk/across/the/floor. But walk —as if you and the floor are one. As if you communicate with the floor and it with you. Your whole body. Not your legs and feet. Not your hands swinging wildly as if you're signaling ships at sea. But walking, ladies and gentlemen. Walking for the joy of moving."

I tell my students that poetry, like dance, is knowing how to walk—across—the floor. That we are all molecules in motion, meeting other molecules in motion. The art of it all is in how we represent what we see: a flower, a baby, lovers, the act of walking, the dance.

"Poetry, like dance, is a metaphor," I say. "It is how we recreate this life we live." I tell them: I am a poet, and that has been my dance, how I learned to walk—across—the floor. Ohh, feet don't fail me now.

The Butcher's Ear

The day I arrived in Germany was neither sunny nor cloudy but filled
with a swell of noise and confusion that rose and fell like the movements of the ocean. The air was blue-gray from the last thrums of the
ship's engines and the diesel fumes of cargo loaders and nearby loco-
motives. Coils of cable, bundled near gangways, fell in a maze of
lines along the dock, and hung from the sides of the ship, hung from
the sky itself. Gulls screamed insults, and the tide reeked with the
bounty of dead fish, oil, and the debris of ancient shipping lanes.
Only the ocean smell of salt saved us from a foulness that would have
been unbearable.

It was the grandest sight I'd ever imagined. I was not yet eighteen,
and my mother had just given me the ultimate reprieve: a ticket to
some place miles away from her house. And not just any place, but
one full of the glitter and sparkle of unfamiliar words, curlicues and
inflections of French, German, Portuguese, Greek, and a symphony
of other languages. That day at the dockside in Bremerhaven, I
plunged into a world of new sounds without any notion of what was
expected of me, a St. Louis colored girl, wide-eyed and trying to
look cool. Aside from the rumors of entertainers who had left the
States, and West Indians who showed up at weddings and family
reunions, I'd had no close contact with black folks who spoke

something other than English. Moreover, I had "the butcher's ear" —*L'oreille du boucher,* or *der Hörerschlächter.*

As far as I know, my grandmother coined the term *butcher's ear.* It was her way of describing the neighborhood butcher's reluctance to follow her instructions regarding which cut of meat she wanted him to prepare. In those days, neighborhoods were segregated, and butchers sent the choicest cuts of meat to the white side of town. My grandmother took me with her if she had to talk to the butcher. But no matter how many ration stamps she had or how precise her descriptions and my reinforcements, the butcher translated our order into a request for the fatty end, the bony cut, the gristle, as if he had suddenly grown deaf. And so for my grandmother, to be deaf, to not hear what you were told to do was to own the butcher's ear. If I forgot an errand or did my chores haphazardly, she accused me of having the butcher's ear. If I continued to play a game of stickball or sweet-rosie-in-the-cornfield instead of coming home as soon as she called me, she would claim my good sense surely had been possessed by the butcher's ear.

"Chile, what's the matter with you?" she'd say. "You act like you can't listen to me no better than that butcher."

I may not have been totally possessed by the butcher's ear in my youth, but I certainly came to acknowledge its presence later when I was older and attempted to speak a foreign language. I have, in the course of some forty years of travels, heard languages with an ear trained on the Mason-Dixon line, the mythical gateway to the West, the border state—Missouri. Not exactly southern but certainly not northern, my speech was as confined to region as those cuts of meat the butcher foisted off on my grandmother—the sounds of language dulled by the limitations of a monolinguistic culture and tempered by dialect, often leading me down dangerous paths where I wander like some luckless tourist, lost in a casbah of extra syllables and wayward sounds.

When I arrived in Germany in 1953, I was bound for the university, equipped with a Missouri accent and a pocketful of textbook phrases. My mother doggedly pulled us through the customs office, where she managed the maze of red tape as long as we were confronted with u.s. personnel, most of whom carried the same drawl of sounds she had been accustomed to hearing in the States. Once we left dockside, she deposited me on a train for Munich.

The last English I would hear for a while was my mother saying, "I want you to take care-ah of y'rself, you hear-ah?"

I waved my mother a cheery good-bye and looked down the length of the train. For a moment, I imagined I had stumbled into one of the movies I'd seen during Saturday matinees at the Antioch Theater near my grandmother's house. That train was a relic out of films in which spies lurked in corridors and spoke the language of espionage, the kind of conversations found in movies starring actors like Claude Rains, Adolf Menjou, Una Merkel, Charles Boyer, or Marlene Dietrich. When we got underway, each whistle's shriek and clatter of wheels brought me back to those matinees at the Antioch.

And that train ride was my first real encounter with another language. Any other contacts had been confined to classroom imitation and rote. Given the opportunity, I could say, without hesitation, in French or in German, "The teacher is at the blackboard," or "The book is on the table." (Although I was a dutiful student and memorized whatever was required of me, to this day I have never had a reason to use either of those phrases in real life.) I settled into my train compartment and tried to look suave—suavé, I whispered, convinced a word so full of worldliness needed an accented ending. As the train sped through the German countryside, moving away from the gray hillsides of mining towns into vineyards and farms linked by thick patches of woods, I opened my map and read aloud the names of places that tracked the route to Munich.

"Düsseldorf," I began. "Kaiserslautern. Tübingen. Ulm," trying to slide past glottal stops without swallowing my tongue.

"Bist du eine Amerikanerin?" a woman seated across from me asked.

"Yeah . . . uh . . . Ja," I said, recovering quickly. "Studenta," I said, aiming for a word that was vaguely German, even if just a bit on the Spanish side of language.

The woman seemed to not notice my efforts. "Willkommen in Deutschland," she smiled.

"Dun-ker shine, mayan Frau-ah," I slowly answered, decorating each word with Missouri vowels.

"Jawohl," she laughed. "Willkommen."

I had begun my first conversation. Sure, it was a poor beginning, but remember: I had the butcher's ear, one trained in a land plowed flat as an altar board, flooded each spring by the mighty Mississippi River, and pocketed with hidden caves. Language was merely another detail on an unforgiving landscape, one to be mastered with an ear that had been trained to hear only certain sounds. Geography marked the speech of both blacks and whites. Vowels were heard as gulps of sound flipping through the air of consonants, and the consonants themselves sometimes falling short of finding their places in words. So I know I'm not too far from home when I hear someone say pen so that it sounds like pin, or celery equals salary, while "Little aw'fun Annie aw'fun goes to the store," and Washington becomes Warshin'ton. I can conjure up memories of St. Louis whether I hear these sounds from a redheaded flight attendant who tries to reassure me when midwestern weather creates death-defying air pockets, or from my mother, who is convinced that my obsession with traveling will be the death of me yet. Whoever the speaker, I know we have been trained with the same ear.

My strange meanderings through foreign languages began with that first trip to Europe where I learned to breathe in the sounds of other languages, all the cacophonies and glides, the hums, clicks, and hisses that unraveled into an abundance of new words holding lives so clearly unlike mine, yet somehow very familiar. In this country, I had not been expected to learn another language, and was in fact suspected of not really knowing English. Stateside education had not prepared me for the likes of Alexandre Dumas, Léopold Senghor, or

Aimé Césaire. I'd only heard about two kinds of black folks—those in Africa and those in America. (Speaking the Spanish of Central America and the Caribbean was not enough to place anyone of color outside of those categories, and African languages were depicted as a gumbo mixture of grunts and gestures straight from Hollywood.)

But although I now can say that my world has expanded beyond the limits of textbook rituals, in truth, I began practicing for other languages when I was living with my grandmother.

An only child, I was stuck in my grandmother's house through snowy St. Louis winters and entertained myself with a windup Victrola. The inside of its lid was embellished with the RCA logo of a black-and-white terrier forever listening to his master's voice. The needle arm was chrome and bulky, like a knob off a Studebaker, but when that needle landed on a 78, I was bathed in the blues of Bessie Smith, the ragtime of Scott Joplin, and the megaphone voice of Rudy Vallee calling out "The Varsity Drag" and "The Bristol Stomp." I mostly listened to the music black dancers used, the songs recorded on Decca and Race Records labels. That Victrola held my orchestras. I learned to step-slide-turn to the wail of Andy Kirk's saxophone recorded at the Savoy ballroom. And when Valaida Snow and her all-girl band sang, "I can't dance, I got ants in my pants," my legs and arms would fly out in all directions, heel-tapping and hand-slapping on the downbeat. In that attic, just out of range of the safety of adults, my companion had been a 1920s boudoir mirror, silver plated and wood framed, crowned with a finial that curled like a lady's hairdo.

In front of that mirror, I plotted my invasion of the world with all the wonderful blues ladies of 78 rpm records. I mimicked adult conversations, not knowing exactly what words to use but aiming for the intonation and nuance of utterances. What I did not hear, I approximated. With my butcher's ear, I could not always distinquish where one word ended and another began, so I relied on the weft and warp of inflection. Valaida Snow and I discussed how she'd come to own a golden trumpet. "Chile, don't you know I got it in the Netherlands?"

she said, shrugging off consonants with a hint of French—or was it Russian?—in her voice. And I answered in my own made-up tongue, shrugging my shoulders and sashaying to the beat of Valaida's all-girl band. When Josephine Baker fell under the command of my grandmother's Victrola needle, I threw an old feather boa around my shoulders and imagined myself in Le Beau-Chêne, resting after a round of supper clubs. I heard only the words that rhymed, but I could trill R's, and *mon, ton, bon*, right along with Josephine.

"Don't you go acting like Josephine Baker," the women in my family would say. "Took herself over to Europe and didn't come back. No telling what went on over there."

So naturally, I paid special attention to Josephine's songs. What better teacher than a black woman who had defied convention, who could set my pulse racing on a tremolo of accented and circumflected sounds? I strained to hear the words and mimicked what she sang. But it would take more than Josephine to help me wrestle with the butcher's ear.

"All you have to do is try," American friends said, although they giggled in amazement at what happened to German under the influence of Southern speech. Still I tried, *dun-ker shining* and *wheater-sayun* my way from phrase to phrase, and surprisingly, I quickly found a circle of friends, German and others, who expected me to speak their language. In fact, in Europe I discovered that language was not color exclusive. For the first time, being black was not a line that separated me from other languages. For the first time, I had as much trouble with being identified as an English-speaking American as I had with someone's reaction to the color of my skin.

My best German lessons began when I met Wilma Hessel. Winter was a slate-gray sky cast over classrooms, gasthauses, side streets, and little parks with twig-bent trees. I had come to the park because it was important to get away from American students. When I was with Americans, all the Germans I met wanted to practice English. Wilma had no such intentions. German or English—it was a trade-off for her. She was a "brown baby," not from World War II, but from between the wars, when her mother, a singer, had met her father, a bistro owner.

"There some of us everywhere," my grandmother had told me. "Don't need to look for 'em. They find you."

Wilma Hessel had found me—or I had found her—by accident one afternoon on the bridge near the Deutsches Museum. I was watching German families strolling past and fat little kids in lederhosen scattering birds trying to eat the few seeds sprinkled on the ground. The leaves were rustling like the sound of nylon stockings brushing together under a woman's skirts, and the sun had bronzed everything.

"Ich bin Deutscher," Wilma had said.

The words did not ring true until I understood how I identified myself as American first, black second. "Ich bin Amerikanerin," I said. "Negro," I added, as if that were necessary.

Wilma placed her hand over mine. Our hands together, one light brown, one dark brown, were not very different. "Amerikanerin," Wilma said. "Und Deutscher." When she looked at me, there was laughter in her eyes. I joined her, and we both laughed, knowing how little we actually had said with those words. It is what happens when words betray you, when they hide what you truly want to say.

Wilma became my anchor, my touchstone with reality in a time that still seems to me unreal. But she was genuine—an in-the-flesh, bona fide motorcycle mama. Her only problem was that there were damned few motorcycles in postwar Germany. So Wilma was stuck with a motor scooter, a Vespa painted jazzy yellow, with a windscreen curved like a VW hood. We zipped past VWs, around 1930s German trucks, putt-putts that seemed to run on sheer willpower alone. Wilma especially liked to take on old cars, revving the Vespa engine when we raced alongside sedans with running boards and high windows that looked as if they'd been pulled off the back lot of a Claude Rains movie. "Third Reichers," Wilma called them.

We sped down streets that had been swept cleaner than in any town I'd ever seen. And not just swept but picked clean, until every dustpanfull of gravel, every brick, door, and windowpane was accounted for as the country went about the business of coming to life after decades of horror. Most streets held the ruins of some building: an archway guarding an upheaval of bricks or the shell of a house hidden behind a scarred wall on which politicians' flyers announcing the rebirth of West Germany had been posted.

Munich, 1953, was no different from Köln, Düsseldorf, Frankfurt, or other cities. Rebuilding went on alongside the obvious traces of Hitler's disaster: the ruined spires of Frauenkirche looming above a ragged skyline, scaffolding hugging the fire-blackened skeleton of the opera house near the Hofgarten, and from the upheaval of cobblestones banked on either side of Marienplatz, the niches of the Glockenspiel, gaunt and empty of the clock's guardians. Two blocks away, a new building stood like a messenger out of the future.

"Nein, nein . . . Go right! Rechts! Rechts! Schnell!," Wilma would yell as I swerved to avoid a vw, a Mercedes, or a lorry. My greatest fear was the trolley cars—old wooden trams with unpredictable brakes and drivers who plowed through traffic with a vengeance. The strassenbahn bell was like a ten-second warning. Those who dared took the outside lanes, where the rush of oncoming traffic and narrow streets was not unlike riding the downhill loop on a roller coaster. Even today, I can swear better in German than in any other foreign language, perhaps because I learned those phrases when death was barreling toward me in the form of a strassenbahn, its seats removed for firewood and a maniac at the wheel.

I kept confusing my right with my left, so whenever I signaled a turn, I looked as if I was waving off the fertilizer smells of some invisible honey wagon. Wilma would yell, "Vamanos! Vamanos!" as if I weren't going fast enough already. Except when Wilma said, Vamanos, it sounded more like "Vomiting! Vomiting!" so I didn't know whether to stop or to pick up speed. I think I may have wanted time to stop, to capture the two of us forever, in our leather bomber jackets, pedal pushers, saddle shoes and sunglasses, scooting down the highway, singing, "Hey bop-o-rebop," as if we were practicing for *Ted Mack's Amateur Hour*.

Some afternoons, Wilma and I would sit with friends in outdoor cafés, drinking beer and smoking contraband cigarettes, the raw burnt leather smell of local tobacco mingling with the smoke from Camels and Viceroys. Our companions were German, French, Italian, Senegalese, Turkish, and a few, I suspected, whose papers were not in order, as Claude Rains invariably would say before the spy movie ended.

Evenings we'd head for the Hofbrauhaus for bockbeer and fat sausages, or to a club in Schwabing to see someone like Jeanne Marcelle, billed as *Der Fisch und Ihrer Angel*. But in that café crowd of artists, poets, students, and drifters at the Tabu or Atelier, no one asked for official papers. In fact, by tacit agreement we had a great disdain for anything official. We argued the merits of life where all rules were broken. And when the talk turned to heritage, confusing color and race, as I had been taught to do back home, did not let me off the hook. I was expected to carry my weight in the conversation and was asked to explain what I meant when I said I was a "Negro" or had African roots. It was the first time I'd been asked those questions, and I began to understand how, in a world that could be turned inside-out and upside-down, color was too simple and American usually meant white, Anglo-Saxon, Protestant.

I began by looking at who we were. We represented a hodgepodge of races, a sort of impromptu version of Josephine Baker's adopted "Rainbow Tribe," but more loose knit. We played at being family the way I remembered playing "let's pretend" games in grade school, when younger kids who had no siblings claimed an older playmate as playsister and playbrother to give them status in the schoolyard. There was Seglinde, who spent far too much time trying to explain how young Germans had been sucked into defending the Vaterland. And Stëin Eric, whose family had fled both the Italian and German armies and whose brother had been killed fighting with the Vichy French. And Lily, who remembered the war as the crackle of a radio constantly attended by her family at their farmhouse in Wales. And Dedes, who saw his first Black American when soldiers landed near his village in Morocco. "They were black, like me, but I could not understand why they did not speak French," he said. And Rosemary Farmer and Claudette Gerard and Mike Tushman and all the others who swore we'd keep in touch forever, even while the world went to hell in a handbasket, as we knew it someday would. We were fatalists, but by the same token, we thought we were invincible. (Perhaps that is the way I can explain challenging fate on a motor scooter.) I only know that when a handsome suitor insisted on drinking a stein of the Hofbrau's finest beer from my slipper, I swear I heard Josephine laughing along with me as I limped home in a soggy shoe.

Despite my bobby socks, angora sweaters, and poodle skirts, Josephine Baker was certainly with me on my first visit to Europe. But where she had found the high life of Paris and Berlin, I mostly saw the ordinary days of Bavaria, days punctuated with the hunger of postwar Germany and the unsettling beauty of Black Forest country.

Unlike Josephine Baker, I could not say, "J'ai deux amours." The only love I developed was a romance of possibilities—the love of travel. My first trip abroad was a journey into a fairy-tale land of gingerbread houses, eiderdown beds, gabled roofs and chimney pots, pretty decorations in a land that had housed concentration camps. But it was a step away from the u.s., a foreign place where I no longer had to rely on my memory of Adolf Menjou and matinees at the Antioch.

My travels have become my own stories of adventure. For six months, three months, three weeks I take my leave of the world I know in order to step, for a moment, into other worlds where playsisters await, bright with stories. I still blunder into languages other than English with the awe I had when I first listened to Josephine Baker on my grandmother's Victrola, but now, more than ever, I try to shed the butcher's ear.

By my second year in Germany, I was living on the economy, working as an au pair girl and going to school part-time. I began to frequent a butcher shop near my flat on Hansa Allee. Unlike the one in St. Louis, this butcher shop presented another kind of trap. No purchase was simple. In exchange for an exorbitant number of Deutschmarks, I had to listen to the butcher's stories about the old days—"When the king was Prussian," he would boast. He had a line-up of pictures on the wall: idyllic settings with castles and the remains of castles scattered throughout Germany, near Nymphen-burg, Grünwald, Friedberg, and a score of other places I can't re-member. Each time I went to the store, I received another story about the castles.

"After the war, not so many," he'd say. "Nicht sehr viele." But no matter how much he talked, he always sliced a choice piece of schnitzel or pork cut according to my request.

"They are beautiful," I'd tell him. "Ja, Schönheit. Sehr gut," I'd say, and watch the butcher turn to me, smiling.

I'd smile too. We had spoken to each other, the butcher and I. So I shifted my singular rucksack of English and midwestern sounds, and made do, as my grandmother would have advised.

Wandering in the Time of Butterflies

It's hot in the Yucatan, a kind of heat that soaks through the skin and doesn't let go, even in sleep. Usually I revel in this kind of heat, have welcomed it in places where incoming planes descend as if they are surfing the almost visible waves of air that gather and break like ribbons of cellophane in the jet stream above the runway. This, for me, is the romance of travel—the plane cutting through that shimmering of ground and sky—the anticipation of shedding heavy shoes and jackets for straw hats and sandals, the freedom of opening my arms to the sun. I almost forget how hot it can be until I arrive in the thick of it, until I step from artificial air into nature's own furnace.

As soon as I step away from the plane, memory closes in on me. The heat intrudes itself into all kinds of private places: behind my knees, in the seams of my hips and thighs, behind my ears. At first I welcome it, wanting to be enveloped in the rush of it, a kind of sweetness that prickles my skin and tells me to breathe deep, even though my face feels flushed and I have trouble catching my breath. After months of the coolness of northern weather, my skin soaks up the warmth. I get the strange feeling that although I'm on the road, I'm finally at home inside a body made for the tropics, "goin' where the weather suits my clothes," as the song goes. Except in the Yucatan, the heat is about the business of undressing me. It welcomes me like a rowdy old lover, fingers clasped against the back of my neck, body rudely pressed into mine in a greeting that makes me question why I ever planned to visit in the first damn place. I begin to sweat. It's too sudden, too close. I want to yell, "Back off!" but all I can do is stagger toward the terminal, wondering how I'll keep my dignity through the rest of the trip. The heat doesn't care. I've arrived, so live with it. Or sweat it out. And sweat I will.

There is nothing subtle about the heat of a Yucatan summer, not like Hawaii's, where the blanched air is softened by trade winds carrying the scent of plumeria and gardenia, all mingled in my first taste of a tall, frosty piña colada. Or Fiji, where the moment I leave the plane, I know I'm heading for some palm-lined beach and already imagine cool ocean waters. Oh yes, I know the beach is out there in the Yucatan, if for no other reason than all those beach towels and flip-flops forever on sale at the airport. But the folklorist in me, that eavesdropper who wants to hear one more story, one more myth of how things have come to be as they are, is intent on turning away from the ocean and heading for the interior. That's when all my romanticizing of heat begins to falter, when I quickly have to learn either to love the heat or hate it. I say I love it, or I try to, but I must admit it is a love affair with many ups and downs.

Always there is beauty in the midst of that heat. In July, butterflies
arrive—literally thousands, swirling dipping pirouetting
flutters that separate and cluster, separate and cluster until
the air is filled with them—a spray, a cloud, a storm of
butterflies, suddenly, between one sunset and the next. Brilliant
Sulfurs, Sleepy Oranges, Dwarf Yellows feeding on milkweed
and bougainvillea. They hover two or three feet above mud puddles or flutter
among cabbage plants and morning glories. Bright flashes
of pale brown or white, and a few, Monarchs perhaps, copper
with false eye markings of red or bright blue. They swirl
like colored air, in abandoned fields and muddy patches

near the road. They flicker among the trees, dance in
reedy grass or cluster inexplicably, in the middle of roads
like drunken conventioneers, stewed to the gills and weaving
away from the bar, party hats still in place.
They ignore approaching cars until the last
minute, then are swept into the updraft of the wheels, billowing
around the fenders
like the ruffles of petticoats or a scattering of sequins
off a lady's dress. I don't know why I think of them as female,
because it is the males that are more flamboyantly marked.
Perhaps I'm taken by the flutter of wings, coquettish as a
debutante's eyelashes, or how they arc and dip through sunlight,
their movements stirring the syrupy air. They are everywhere
along the coast, jewels glistening in the thick summer heat.

Don't get me wrong. When I think of Mexico, I don't think: *dreadful heat.* My affair with Mexico is much too complicated for such a simple-minded label. Although each of my trips into Mexico has been plagued by some combination of the weather, the water, or my traveling companions, the Mexico I know is more than tourist bureaus, cantinas, and mariachi bands. It is not just fiestas and the palm groves of a Club Med resort. It is not the smog of Mexico City, or that infamous gateway to the u.s., the Rio Grande— *Rio Bravo de Norte,* they call it. And despite all the celluloid glamour, it is not even the Mexico of sweet señoritas and mustachioed bandidos, although I confess to a lasting desire to have Zoro and Pancho Villa ride off the movie screen and into my neighborhood, where I will be swept up by a revolucionario who smells of saddle leather and gun powder. Too many movies, you see. So quite possibly the Mexico I know is a Mexico I've dreamed while awake, a kind of half-sleep that the heat pulled me into when I was on a bus from Tijuana to La Paz, or between Cancún and Chichén Itzá.

Perhaps I saw this Mexico in the slow deaths of bulls at the hands of matadors in Motul and Vera Cruz. Maybe it was in Mexico City on the

Calle de los Muertos, the Street of the Dead, where you cannot find effigies of the dead except for the ghosts of Aztecs trapped in advertising logos and street names. And because I am a writer, I am sure the Mexico I know has been captured in the stories of third generation expatriates, those who speak of the beautifully surreal world of Frida Kahlo and Diego Rivera, a world of artists and political intrigue.

Mexico is a place where the past rushes up to meet you as if you've been away for only a few days and everything has been kept as you left it. Whole towns have an air of dusty abandonment, an air that some have described as "sleepy," a mistake often made by people who have not bothered to look beyond the picture postcard surface that layers the country in the acceptable myth of our "neighbors south of the border." What I sense is watchfulness, as if everyone is waiting for the right time to take care of some unfinished business: the land that must be reclaimed, the revolution that will flare up again with as much fervor as it held five, ten, twenty, a hundred years ago.

In Ixtapa, if you ask the right questions, you may find your way to Paseo del Pescador and El Gumil, a shop of masks and silver where art and death are one and the same. It is a small shop, two rooms holding masks upon masks, all hanging in a profusion of shapes and colors, the worlds of the dead and the living blended in enchantingly bizarre configurations. Among the candles, effigies of goats, birds, crocodiles and snakes, cast their baleful eyes upon the living. They are waiting for the Day of the Dead, the ceremony when we, who are trapped behind the masks of life, will say to the ancestors: "¡Salga! ¡Salga!" "Come out! Come out!"

One afternoon in a cantina near the Museo de la Ciudad in Mexico City, I talked for hours about the whys and wheres of art and politics with a Mexican painter I'd met at an artists' colony several years earlier. I'll call her Estella. We drank for hours, Estella and I. Chianti with slices of lime floating in each glass. And later, when the heat allowed, she drove me past Frida Kahlo's bright blue house. She laughed about the gossip over Diego Rivera's weight. "They say the casket wasn't strong enough to hold his body," she told me. "It fell through and rolled down the hill." A few blocks later, we swept past the house that had been Trotsky's self-imposed prison before his assassination. And she told me how her grandfather had talked about Trotsky's death and the many plots against him that had failed. "He called them young Turks," she said. "They were dangerous, but they didn't much know what they were doing."

"Someone did," I said. "They finally got to Trotsky."

"Anything is possible," she shrugged.

I understood what she meant. All of it seemed the stuff of dreams and enchantment, florid and elaborate, what you read in history books rather than saw up close with your own eyes. I tried putting it all together, the history I'd pulled from books and from the old houses lining the Calle Londres and the villas along Morales. What would I write in my journals? As Mexico City sweltered under its apron of late summer heat, I began to understand why most of Estella's paintings were filled with flowers growing out of stone, out of brick and wrought iron, out of the very sky itself. But I needed more. I was still obsessed with all that was left unsaid, with a history that lurked right at the edge of twentieth-century luxury. I wanted what I thought was the true seasoning of Mexico: the pyramids, temples, and cenotes— the places that seemed as timeless as the cries of the flamingos and monkeys who still lay claim to parts of that sun-scorched country. I wanted to travel along the ancient routes marked by names full of sounds that filled the secret corners of the mouth: Quetzalcoatl, Kukulcan, Teotihuacán, Xpuhil, Zihuatanejo.

The present name of Yucatán originates from the Mayan's first response to the conquistadores: Ci-u-than, *which in Mayan means, "We don't understand you."*

In certain parts of the Yucatán, you virtually stumble upon pyramids. They are scattered like pearls from the Gulf of Mexico to the

Caribbean Sea. In two decades, I have visited sites at Palenque, Tikal, Uxmal, Mayapan, Chichén Itzá, El Dos, Tumba del Caracol, Tulum, and a dozen more smaller ones, each one set in its own fabled past: the Olmecs, the Toltecs, the Mayans, each leaving behind a bit of mystery, a trail that never ends. They are shadowed by the thickness of trees where the jungle reclaims the land, where snakes and howler monkeys inhabit the ruins. They are there where the land has grown soft and swampy, where cenotes take their natural course under layers of rock, where everything perishes except the mosquitoes. The pyramids wait, under a canopy of trees and vine growth, to be uncovered. And when we do uncover them, we never fail to be amazed that such splendid structures have existed without our knowledge. We ask: Who built these grand places? And how did they move such stones? And who gave them power? And who took their power? And most of all, were they people like us? Did they know more about the world and the universe than we have ever known? For two thousand years, some of these cities have kept safe their stories. Who knows, perhaps they still do.

My first visit was in the early seventies. My destination was the historical sites at La Venta and Palenque, near Villahermosa. In those days, Villahermosa wasn't much more than the Zócalo, a plaza where all business transpired, and rows of adobe houses rested along cobblestoned streets too narrow for most modern vehicles. Outside of a few cars for hire, and busses that seemed to favor poultry over human passengers, walking was the best means of transportation. While I had no choice but to take a bus when I was going outside of the city, in town my route was determined by the distance between ceiling fans. Did I mention it was hot?

Villahermosa was occupied by a mugginess that clung to the ground like the steam from an underground spa, which was not too far from wrong. The whole of Yucatán is dotted with swamp land and cenotes, the presence of underground pockets of water adding stickiness to the heat. On the very first day, I became aware that life in

Villahermosa centered around insuring the movement of air. Ceiling fans were everywhere, at least in establishments that expected tourist trade. The fan in my room did not exactly cool the air, but it left me with a fifty-fifty chance of catching my breath before the next surge of heat. I spent most of my visit rising early to get organized, then sitting out the belly of the day in the nearest cantina while the sun did its endless dance across the landscape. Evenings were hopeful. A breeze blowing off the Río Grijalva felt even cooler when I was holding a chilled bottle of Coca Cola—no ice. Ice would have been my undoing. In those first days, I paid attention to all the travel brochure warnings: BEWARE OF THE DRINKING WATER. It was only later that I relaxed my vigil and suffered the consequences. And that was caused by the heat. Alas, the heat. Along with drinking water and mosquitoes, heat can unglue even the strongest traveler. At first, I kept bug repellent and albeit tepid, bottled water at my side; still the heat never really let up. It ate at me, more than once causing me to change my plans, but not enough to veer me off course.

On the second day in Villahermosa, we set out with a guide provided by the national tourist bureau and the Sociedad de los Folklóricos. Carlos wasn't that bad if you didn't mind discussing Coca-Cola in the same breath as historical artifacts. Right away, he set the record straight. "You have asked to go to La Venta," he said. "The Olmec they were in La Venta many many years ago. Dos mil." He held up two fingers and made the gesture for several zeros. "Now there is nothing in La Venta. Now it is all in Villahermosa. And in Villahermosa we may have some Coca-Cola in the park where we can see these stones from the Olmec."

"We want to see the original site," two people in my group insisted. They were a team from Indiana "earning doctorates in anthropology," they had announced the night before at dinner. With that announcement, they'd set themselves apart from the rest of us mere travelers, those without a paid project: two students of divinity, a sculptor, and me. I hid behind the fact that since I already had a doctorate, I was exempted from witnessing the struggles of those who were trying to get one. They had their mission; I had mine. The park in Villahermosa held the treasures of La Venta and I was determined to see them. Besides, Carlos had promised he would go with us to the pyramids at Palenque, so he must have had a reason for refusing to go to the site at La Venta. I consulted my map of archeological sites. La Venta carried only the symbol for swamp lands and marsh. I did a little mental mapping of my own: swamp equaled heat plus mosquitoes.

"Why don't you boys go off without me," I said. "I think I'll stay in Villahermosa."

The taller anthropologist looked at me with a jaundiced eye—at least I think it was jaundiced. I could hardly be held responsible for seeing true colors through a blur of sweat that was beginning to build even under the morning sun. "Suit yourself," he said, and boarded the bus, his partner close at his heels. Only one of the divinity students joined them. Carlos leaned into the doorway and gave the driver instructions, then waved and stepped clear of the bus. The divinity student was the only one who waved back as the bus went crunching off toward the coast road. Chickens crated on top of the bus cackled into the clouds of dust whirling under the wheels. The other passengers looked at us with the impatience of those who wanted to get on with their trip. As the bus rolled out of town, the sculptor grunted and muttered his favorite comment, "Well, you can't get milk out of a stone." No one answered. That comment had prompted much debate the night before at dinner. "Es lástima," Carlos said. I wasn't sure whether Carlos meant the bus trip to La Venta or the stone without milk.

Alone with guidebook in hand, you could easily cover the Parque La Venta in Villahermosa in two hours flat. With a guide, the visit can take the better part of a day. Carlos was an excellent guide. As the saying goes: He left no stone unturned. And there were many stones in Parque La Venta, all of them excavated when an oil company was dredging the island that held the original La Venta pyramids.

"Most of the ruins are still covered by mud," Carlos said, gesturing in the direction the bus had taken. "But here we have the important findings." He pointed to a group of carved figures set in a semicircle. "This piece has jade," he told us. "And this basalt. In this part of the Yucatán we only have serpentine, so the stone must be brought for many miles. That is how we know the Olmec lived in many parts of the Yucatán."

Even the sculptor was so impressed, he didn't utter his favorite phrase for the rest of the morning. Carlos explained how the elaborate Olmec calendar might have been the basis for the more refined Mayan calendar, and as we moved through the park, I felt as if we were falling under the spell of some time warp. The carvings came in many sizes and shapes, depicting men and gods, jaguars and rattlesnakes. For a while, I did not think of the heat and only absentmindedly swatted at mosquitoes who were rude enough to want part of my face for their meal. The trees flickered shadows in our path, shapes lost in sunstreaks full of butterflies and colored sand, the earth conforming to the architecture of a culture that had left fragments of itself in the swamps of La Venta. I wondered briefly what the archeology students would find, then I remembered my real reason for staying in Villahermosa.

The prize that I had come so many miles to see was the great stone heads—the basalt carvings of warriors or priests whose origins seemed as unusual to the Yucatán as the Easter Island monoliths are to that area of the Pacific. There were four of them at Parque La Venta, massive round heads standing seven or eight feet high, their expressions as fierce as soldiers or as all-knowing as impatient gods. Under stylized hair shaped like helmets, even the pitted surfaces of the stone, eroded by weather, gave the appearance of rough skin.

"Notice the negroid features," Carlos said. I forgave him for the outdated racial reference since he seemed to be more impatient with European biases than willing to adopt them. "In these stones we see the broad nose and thick lips that have been called Olmec," he continued. "But who are the Olmec? We will never know, but they have left many pieces for our inspection."

The sculptor leaned closer to get a better look. "Fine work, if I must say so myself. Odd. Not from around here. What do you think?" he asked me.

"Not so odd," I said. It reminded me of pictures I'd seen of Nuba wrestlers in the Sudan who cover themselves with ash before each ceremonial bout. The Nuba wrestlers and the Olmec stones have the same round heads and large features. Then I remembered Bumpsy, the big-headed kid who had lived down the block from my grand-mother's house. I shook off that thought. It was too hard to put Bumpsy, the class truant from St. Louis, into the role of warrior priest in the middle of the Yucatán. Still, there were my Aunt Jennie's stories about the black folks who had fled to Mexico during the Civil War.

"Colored folks didn't care much where they went as long as they left the South. Come to find out, they weren't the first Coloreds liv-ing down there. Not Mexicans. Some Africans. From a long time ago." Aunt Jennie wasn't sure how many folks there were or how long "long ago" had been, but she was sure they were Africans. And as my grandmother had said, "They got some of us everywhere."

Who knows? Having grown up barely having knowledge of African diaspora, much less exploration, perhaps I had found a little piece of myself, a two-thousand-year-old ancestor who had been denied by my American-ness. I studied the Olmec face. ¡Salga!, I wanted to say. *Come out, come out and talk to me.* But instead I said to the sculptor, "Looks like a bully I knew back in grade school."

"Trying to say he's a friend of yours?" the sculptor sneered.

The great stone face kept staring off toward some distant point on the horizon. I leaned over for a closer look. "Could be," I said, "except it doesn't exactly look friendly."

Carlos shrugged. "He is Olmec. A great warrior perhaps. Maybe like me he needs a Coca-Cola to make a smile."

The stone face remained unchanged, but at least Carlos made us smile. As the sun flicked across the Olmec sculpture, we moved to a grove of trees at the edge of the park where vendors sold sodas, ice syrups, and bottles of warm beer. The vendors, all women, seemed impassive to both the heat and the tourists. They wore the traditional dress of peasant women, a simple blouse and brightly colored skirt, and about their heads, mosquitoes, drawn to the scent of fermenting sugars, mingled with butterflies.

In stretches of swamp lands bordered by nesting grounds of graceful
pink flamingos, there are groves of trees alive
with a multitude of butterflies. Nothing grows
in the mud flats. The putrid odor of sulfur assaults your nostrils.
And the bones of cattle, picked clean by turkey vultures and bleached
white by the sun, are sprinkled about like bizarre wild flowers.
The only things that seem alive are insect larvae
nesting in the bones. Everything else is still and hot
and odoriferous. The ground is sandy gray, mud leeched
almost blonde. It is Frida Kahlo's landscape without the colors
of her beloved flowers, but just as surreal, decorated with remains
of luckless animals: skulls, thigh bones, hip
joints, and hooves. In that wash of sunlight
bones take on different images. A skull missing one horn resembles
a stork standing on one leg. The rib cage and spine of a large steer
looks like a palm tree grounded after a windstorm. Another
pile of bones seems to have reassembled into a warthog digging
its way into the mulch. And the bones themselves devoid of connection
with any living thing, have become rocks, stones, carvings from some
world that no longer exists, remnants of something long past
so alien that it is strange to drive down the road twenty or
thirty miles, past reed grass and shallow water
where flamingos step as daintily as ballerinas
and butterflies flutter to music that
only they can hear.

In the summer, during their migration, the butterflies of the Yucatán dance among the pyramids. Sometimes they are nothing more than sudden shifts in light, like floaters on the corner of the eye; other times they are bouquets of color, darting in and out of the crevices of crumbling temple walls or between the tendrils of vine-covered trees as if they are slipping through cycles of time. Sometimes they venture into the cenotes, into the inner chambers once known only to kings and priests. In those caverns, their companions are bats, fine-boned and quick, dotted like onyx on moss-covered ceilings. The butterflies prefer the sun and ascend, in flashes of light, from the darkness of cenotes into the green shadows of chiclé and sacred celba trees, those places where iguanas sleep. Often they will follow iguana trails into openings in the walls of pyramids, emerging from those recesses where you least expect them. Sometimes you will find them resting on the bas-reliefs of sun gods or carvings of glyphs that mark the calendar of Mayan days. There, among the elaborate codes of Mayan ancestors, they are scarcely noticed until the movement of their wings, delicate as a pulse beat on a woman's wrist, causes you to take a second look. I have seen them feather-kiss the sacred frescos, only to take flight in a quirk of wind and descend, seconds later, onto the stone hoop of an ancient ball court, or soar into the temple of warriors where the great Chac-Mool holds a solar disc in readiness for an offering. They are everywhere. In the decaying cities of the Toltecs, the Olmecs, and the Mayans, surrounded by lush green woods, in temples built high on cliffsides, or amid pyramids in the heart of sunburnt plains or dense jungles. Butterflies dress up the place, the witchery of their movement and color bringing life to that which has been abandoned by its people.

When I visited the temple city of Palenque, I had no other sites to compare it to. I had not yet seen Tikal or Chichén Itzá. I had yet to go to Machu Picchu or to Egypt's Valley of the Kings. Palenque was my first, and I was awestruck by the suddenness of it—Cortés, it is reported, passed by without knowing it was there. That was easy to imagine. Palenque was almost completely obscured by the canopy of the surrounding forests and circumventing paths that seemed to disappear into scrub brush. That made the first sight of the pyramid even more awe inspiring. Later, on other journeys, I discovered I'd feel the same whenever I was introduced to one of the great wonders of the ancient world. But to this day Palenque holds a special place, not only as my first pyramid but also because I undertook that particular trip before that part of the world had been turned into a series of tourist stops in host cities full of four-star hotels.

We camped out. Now understand, I'm a middle-of-the-road sort, a city girl—ghetto, if you like. I was used to downtown traffic and street hustlers, indoor plumbing and showers not inhabited by gangsters from the insect world, ready to extract your blood in payment for lodging. The Indiana team had returned from La Venta puckered with insect bites and miserable. They spent the first couple of days at Palenque covered in calamine over sunburnt skin as pink as rosé wine. I swear, they looked as if they were readying themselves for some mysterious rite of passage. I layered myself in extra bug repellent and suntan lotion, making sure I doubled the bug juice at night. I was not, nor have I ever been ready for sleeping bags, outdoor toilets, and food cooked over fires that are best used to tan the hides of large predators. But there I was sleeping in the dirt. "Black folks had their lot of sleeping in the dirt," my grandmother had told me as she tucked me under the quilts on her four-poster bed. At Palenque, I was glad I didn't need to explain this turn of events to her.

While Palenque itself has been abandoned, it is surrounded by a living forest. All day, we heard rustles and tweets as something or another called to one of its kind. Nights were filled with the click-click of iguanas and the snap of twigs as top-heavy trees let go their weight. And despite Carlos's reassurance, one of the divinity students was sure that the snakes were massing to attack us at night. I was more concerned with mosquitoes, slapping myself silly at the slightest suggestion of buzzing until I was more bruised than bitten. There was the constant smell of vegetating decay mixed with the pungent odors of pollinating plants. When I climbed the seventy-two steps of the temple at Palenque, I was sure my asthmatic breathing could be heard for miles in all directions. Even at that height, the smell of the decomposing forest was everywhere. The air was like a sauna, the jungle stretching in all directions like a finely woven carpet. (No wonder Cortés missed the place.) Birds shrieked warnings as they dive-bombed insects, and the rustle of leaves signalled the presence of something foraging among the foliage. Butterflies pirouetted in the branches. In three days, as we covered the seven and a half miles of the temple city, we became familiar with it all.

What I remember most is the pyramid tomb of the ruler Pacal, Templo de las Inscripciones, and El Palacio, the site of the famous tower of Palenque. To descend into Pacal's tomb is like descending into the earth itself. The corridor is damp and steep, the walls so close that no one with claustrophobia should enter. Aside from the dank smell of earth, there is silence, as if the tomb was holding itself in homage to its lord Pacal. Like the god-kings of Egypt, Pacal was surrounded by what he would need in the next life: effigies of servant-slaves, and jewels for passage into the underworld. The place of servant-slave, god, and ruler is depicted many times in the frescos at Palenque. One, in the courtyard of the palace, shows nine slave figures posed in obedience to their ruler. Others were more complicated. One, in the Templo de las Inscripciones, drew special attention from one of the divinity students.

"No one knows what it says," the taller Indiana student muttered. The sculptor added his usual, "You can't get milk out of a stone." Carlos quickly interrupted him. "Many still know the signs of the first ones," he said. "The conquistadores destroyed the books, but what remains is in the stones. Not like words that you write with letters, but what is here." He gestured to his head and to his heart. "This says," he told us, *"I am a precious bird, for I make books speak."*

I looked up, startled. No longer was he just Carlos of the Coca-Cola fix, the hired help who recited by rote what the tourist agency gave him. He had gone from ordinary vendor to historian, a thread that would help us find the past if we would only listen. In a country where it was not uncommon to see waterwheels pulled by oxen, he was the caretaker of the ruins who knew more than any college-trained anthropologist.

We spent three days at Palenque. Every day was a new discovery, although I was hardly ready for roughing it, Mayan style. By the time we returned to Villahermosa, the town looked like a mecca of civilization. So much so I threw travelers' caution to the wind and, unable to face the heat unarmed, drank some iced tea—a mistake I later paid for with my first bout of Chac Mool's revenge. That was a struggle that I should have let the heat win. I left Villahermosa with a battle-scarred stomach, but in my three days at Palenque, I learned to say good-bye to my manicured nails, check my sleeping bag (I refused a hammock) to make sure I was the only living thing crawling into it, and figure out, literally by fits and starts, how not to wet my pant legs every time I had to take a leak. Well, actually I didn't quite master that trick right away. The cuffs of my jeans smelled slightly funny for several days, an odor blessedly covered by the many smells of the forest. At night, as the scent of copal incense mingled with smoke from the day's nearby slash fires, I fell asleep wondering what a "po' lil chile" like me was doing in the wilderness. But then, how often would a St. Louis girl get to sleep in a place where the Mayans said the Lord Sun drops into the underworld of night?

In the Yucatán, Chac Mool waits for me. Six times I have ventured into the area, and six times Chac Mool has turned a vengeful eye in my direction. His revenge is double-pronged: heat that keeps me always on the edge of sleep, and a direct attack that strips my intestinal tract and turns everything I eat into liquid. "Perhaps you do not have the intestinal fortitude for Mexico," a public health doctor once told me. I knew she was trying to make a joke, but somehow, slogans on moral courage and what was happening to my insides didn't equate, so I ignored her play on words and asked again for something to guard me against the revenge of Chac Mool.

"There is nothing," she said. "Your intestinal bacteria simply won't fight off the strains you find in Mexico. Go farther north. Get away from Chac Mool. Perhaps Montezuma is kinder."

Perhaps, I thought. Indeed, I had never buckled under the revenge of Montezuma. But then, Chac Mool's warnings didn't seem to extend to other parts of the world: not South America or Southeast Asia, not North Africa or Eastern Europe. My stomach rebels only when I have been to the Yucatán. More than once I have barely made it across the border, embarrassed sheets in expensive hotels, sequestered myself in the bathrooms of friends: *Hi, I've just come back from Mexico. Where's your bathroom?* My state of distress, I am convinced, was the work of Chac Mool or in his other incarnations: Chacmool or Chaac. Chac Mool, sentry at the Temple of Warriors, solar disc resting on his belly. Chaac, who waits for the sun, his face turned expectantly to the east. In some ways, Chacmool is a gracious adversary, allowing me a slight reprieve before he turns my insides to mush. But his aim is swift and sure, and once the heat possesses me and I let down my guard with an ice cube, a sweetly delicious tomato, or even a grape or two, he returns once again to remind me of who's boss.

The beaches along Mexico's coast are bleached white as bones. Dazzling white sand and ocean and sky so blue you need new words to make the colors real. The sands are truly clean, as if each night, the sea, like a broom, sweeps away the day's debris. But if you rise early, just as the sun peeks over the horizon, you'll see what keeps this illusion going: the bevy of workers combing the sand in front of hotels that are clustered in a row near the shore like bruised Legos. Although the beach itself remains government property, the hotel owners make sure there is very little to obstruct their postcard view of the sea. So each morning, workers rake the sands in that demilitarized zone of tourism between the ocean and hotels. They move in synchronized rhythm, like so many seagulls gleaning the ocean's bounty. But the source of their bounty, the debris left at the end of each day, does not come from the sea. It comes from hotel guests who buy and trade with vendors from nearby villages, an army of men, women, and children offering a thousand and one versions of the same souvenirs. They work the free strip between the hotels and the sea, their paths as regular as bus routes. They know which hotels are likely to bring in more guests at one time of year than another. They are persistent, hoping to time a sale for that desperate moment on the last day of a trip when the tourist realizes the plane home is only a few hours away. Most of them offer a spiel that is no more than a sound bite, an ad agency's thirty-second spot commercial. But a few will surprise you. If you are lucky, you will find more than a papier-mâché replica of the plumed serpent, or a factory-made statue of the sacred jaguar.

I was taking one last tour of the beach the day I met Pele. The wind was a mockery that merely stirred the heat without cooling it. Pele's wife offered me a straw fan in a woven pattern that apparently is commonly used around the globe from Baptist churches in the deep South to island churches in the Indian Ocean. I already had a fan, but for some reason I couldn't recall, I'd left it in my room. Pele's wife, who spoke no English, gestured to indicate that she'd made the fan, but I was already parting with the few pesos it cost, turning my hand to set the air in motion. Mine wasn't a polite fanning action, a lady's coy turn of wrist; mine was a get-down-to-business-and-scatter-the-heat kind of action that my grandmother had taught me, a rapid swish-swish like propellor blades. Within seconds, I'd cooled my face and neck, scattering a few sand flies in the process. I could see that Pele was impressed. He began to unfold rugs from the bottom of his bundle.

"Señora, for the home," he said, and spread them out on the sand.

Automatically, I began to shake my head. All morning, I'd fended off vendors selling the usual mishmash of turisto souvenirs, tent poles full of merchandise balanced on their shoulders, one after the other, like an army trying to find its commander, each one selling more or less the same souvenirs to what must have seemed like the same tourist. "I don't think so," I said, but from the way I studied these rugs pulled from the bottom of the pile, Pele knew better. We weren't bargaining: we were politely circling each other. As each rug floated toward the sand, heat rose up around my ankles. I fanned faster and wished for a cool breeze. Pele's wife looked amused. "Tropico veranos abrasadores," I told her, piecing together Spanish like a five year old with pieces of a jigsaw puzzle.

She smiled, but Pele answered as if I hadn't just muttered in bad Spanish, "Tropics summers burning up."

"Sí, sí," he nodded. "Here it is very hot. Even the ocean is hot." He pointed toward the water. Over his shoulder, the sky and ocean flattened out into one straight blue line. "You come to go on the boats for diving?" he asked.

I shook my head. "No, no. Too rough," I said, although the water was flat as a mirror. But I didn't know how to say "I'm aquaphobic" in Spanish, so I said, "Hace calor hoy." Yes, it was hot. The understatement of the year.

"Why do you come here during the summer?" Pele asked.

I shrugged. It seemed too much to explain that professors, like most school teachers, were locked into winter classroom schedules and papers to grade. While my classes were interesting, given that I taught what I loved most—writing, my body clock was geared to a calendar that began late September and ended in June. During the summer, I let my writing guide me, taking me to places I could not reach during the winter. Summers, I was encouraged to muse, fantasize, create, and wax lyrical, get silly, chill out, unwind, or, as my computer buff students said, "grab a little downtime." Why else would I be in Mexico in July, a season when the heat was a side dish for everything? I thought of the clouds of butterflies, Frida Kahlo's paintings, the bullfighters of Vera Cruz, and the pyramids at Tulum, Palenque, Chichén Itzá, and Uxmal. I held my face up to the thin breeze that danced at the water's edge, then answered Pele in my bravest gringo voice. "I don't think about the heat," I smiled.

Blood Kin

In Peru, I was looking for Machu Picchu, the fabled place of the Incas, the meeting place of condors floating on mile-high mountain air, the place where clouds nested on mountains that kept the secrets of lost cities of gold. But once I arrived, I thought only of how far I was from home and of how this earth is a map full of distances. I had not gone to South America expecting to enter a world of faces that would bring back memories of home and family, faces that seemed copied from cousins and neighbors straight out of my mother's photo albums. In fact, most of what I knew about South America came not from my studies of linguistics but from the movie *Black Orpheus* and its scenes of Brazil—the carnival and crowds of faces in various shades of brown, from licorice to red bone to sandy yellow, skin tones as familiar as any-town-downtown-USA. But that movie was about Brazil. I was still in Peru, in a place of mountains so high, everything seemed close to heaven. The narrow gauge railroad to Machu Picchu carried me along zigzag tracks past a moss-thick forest where the earth seemed woven out of fabric thick as pile carpet. We were heaven-bound to the place of gods and clouds and thin air, a place that would enchant me out of the writer's block that had held me captive for months.

We had been in Cuzco only a short time when my roommate Emilie and I met Igor Gonzales, a Peruvian student who wanted to share a drink with the beautiful americanos. We had met Igor the way meetings happen when you are traveling and circumstance makes room for instant friendships. In the heat of a Peruvian afternoon, Emilie and I had stopped for drinks and conversation. We were drinking pisco and warm beer in a café on one of Cuzco's twisting streets. The air smelled of old bricks, llama droppings, wild sage, peppers, coca leaves, and sweat.

Igor wanted to know what had drawn us to Cuzco.

"Machu Picchu," we told him. "Everyone goes there," we said.

His smile had rested somewhere between pride and impatience with turistas. I thought we had offended him until he reached across the table and took my hand. As his brown hand covered mine, I wondered which of us was more curious about our origins. "You come here together," he said. "One is black. One is white. Will you again travel together in America?"

Emilie laughed. I listened to fluted notes of "El Condor" ending in one cantina just as another record fell into place and took up the tune somewhere else on the plaza. What could I say? It was 1977, and civil rights still evoked images of riots. Travel together in the States? Probably not.

But in Cuzco, while the afternoon sun lost its warmth and slipped behind the crest of the Andes, where it would sleep among the ruins of the Inca, Emilie laughed, and I listened to "El Condor" and smiled at the man whose handsome brown face linked Spaniards and Indians forever to that country in the same way the faces of my family forever linked black and white in America.

"Our paths may cross," I told Igor.

I remembered watching my mother, who like many army wives had moved from military post to military post without ever really leaving home. In the cocoon of the post exchange, the commissary, and dependent housing, she had been surrounded by American products and American attitudes. Under the APO postal designation, it was the task of army wives to maintain some semblance of home. But there was a heavy price hooked to that lifestyle—a cocoon with a blinding effect that made it easier to assume that the u.s. was the center of the world, a cocoon where the great racial divide of black and white was always observed and any other place was foreign, no matter where the camp was located. For my mother, who was all too familiar with a world where black people traveled with a history of sundown laws and racism, every place was suspicious. My suspicions were not yet written in indelible ink.

Early the next morning, just as the sun winked over the rim of the Andes, Emilie and I headed for the new train station, bypassing the abandoned depot, the one that had originally been built to link Cuzco to Machu Picchu in the north. The tracks in front of the old station were clotted with the shanties and market stalls of Indians, Quechuas, who were the descendents of the great Inca worshippers of sun gods. On the way to Machu Picchu, we saw similiar makeshift shelters huddled all along the stretch of switchback tracks from Cuzco to the foot of the Inca ruins. Indians stared as we passed them on the train, their looks as quizzical as Igor's had been.

In the elbows of the zigzag tracks, women peered through the dense smoke of their cooking fires. Once, near the Inca Bridge when our train pulled onto a siding to let a local express plow through, I stood downwind of smoke filled with the scent of root vegetables, roasted goat, and peppers. The express train churned up the odors, and after the cars had cleared the bridge, an Indian family on the other side of the tracks watched as we reboarded our train. The man wore loosely woven pants and a ruana, the poncho's hem decorated in a pattern of geometic llamas. He carried a bundle of firewood on his back, as did the woman standing next to him. She wore a layered peasant skirt, blouse, and a scarf topped by a black bowler hat. The children stayed close to their mother, one so small, he clutched the hem of her skirt and hid from me when I waved to him. Under the rim of her bowler hat, his mother stared, unblinking.

"The bowler hat is the symbol of the conquistadors," Igor had told us. "In the old days, when the Spaniards have first come to this land, the Quechua woman who sleeps with a Spaniard takes his warrior's helmet to wear as notice that she is his woman and receives special favors. But many of my people did not think this a good thing, and the women have to fight their pride. But the women are not all ashamed. So then they come together and say: It is no matter who goes with the Spaniard and who will not go. We will all wear the hats and we will all have the favors. And so, today all of the women of the Quechua wear the round hat and none are ashamed."

"Do you think it's true?" Emilie asked.

I shrugged. "Do you think it's not?" I said.

I listened to the buzz of noise from the string of open door cantinas, the ever-present "El Condor" emanating from a jukebox, the crowing of chickens, and the flapping sandals of Indians scuffling along the quagmire of muddy cobblestone streets.

In the crooks of the railroad tracks ascending to Machu Picchu, Quechua women bent under the weight of morning chores, their ample hips draped in heavy skirts, their shoulders covered in shawls, and single braids of midnight black hair hanging beneath the rims of their bowler hats. What we present of ourselves, by language and custom, shows the world where we place our pride. History and family may be locked in a bowler hat, an apron, a dish of food, a necklace of beads and feathers, a ritual dance, a name.

On the train, I had tried to ignore the Englishman rattling off statistics of Indian deaths as if he were collecting mere scientific data rather than the tragedy of human existence. I ignored the Germans tightly repacking their hiking gear and the drawling Southerners who loudly declared they wanted to take pictures of everything, especially "those poor souls living in all that filth right there on the railroad tracks." It would certainly not be my first or my last encounter with those who "have" viewing the "have-nots" as curiosities. But on the train, I had not wanted to be American, and I had wondered at the strength of women who would don the hats of conquerers so that none would be ashamed.

At the foot of Machu Picchu, hawkers sell native goods of all sorts, most of them cheap replicas of tourist junk found in roadside stalls from Moyobamba to Arequipa: cheap jewelry of silver alloy, miniature llamas decked in miniature festival trappings, rough-woven ruanas and shepherds' hats, factory embroidered peasant blouses, hastily thrown clay pots, thonged slippers, and wall hangings emblazoned with tacky postcard scenes of villages and Inca gods. Stands offer warm Coke, bottled water, and shaved ice, or corn cakes and skewered meat. Under the bright pink and blue canopies, everything is a bargain. But here and there, village artisans sell authentically handmade goods.

I heard a voice softly call me, the accent more Portuguese than that of most Indians. "Madame, por favor." I took another step, my back still turned to the voice. "Madame, momento," the voice purred. "Madame es negra: ¿Quiere ver, por favor?"

Her face was dusky brown, almost the same color as her eyes, and not as round as the Indians I'd seen but a bit thicker than those of the mestizos. Like Igor's. She was from the east. Iquitos, maybe. Or Brazil. Río Branco. Negrita. Crava negra.

Without her accent, the mountains in the background, or the line up of vendors calling out similiar greetings in coarser voices, I could have been turning to greet my cousin Erma Jean or any number of girls I'd known in school. Hers was a face I'd seen in St. Louis as well as on the streets of Bogatá, or on a worker at the factory Fabrica Mesa Pan, or someone rushing past me in the airport in Tampa. That face, so close to my own, could have belonged to the person hastily closing the shutters when I'd passed through the village of Chirimaya. I was sure I had seen that face on the steps of La Catedral in Lima and on a mural of the Magi inside a church in Venezuela.

"Madame, quiere ver, por favor?" She gestured to the goods she had spread across the table. The usual ruanas, junk jewelry, wall hangings, and lumpy pottery. Then I spotted a statue of Bonifacio, the black king who in fables ruled the Bolivian Andes long after the Inca had lost their kingdoms. And nested under it, four Quechua burial dolls, their faces brown as the clay soil of the mountains behind us, their bodies wrapped in the rough woven cloth of peasants. The vendor picked up one of the dolls. "Para tijo, cincuenta pesetas, madame. Especilatas para tijo, madame."

"Too much," I said, beginning to bargain in my best tourist voice. Besides, I did not want the doll, not even at a bargain of fifty pesetas set especially for me. I pointed to the statue of the black king, Bonifacio.

"Bonifacio é para mijo," she said, and grinned at me, then at the women selling goods on either side of her. Their flat faces showed no reaction. She smiled and pulled her shawl away from her hair. Her braid was as kinky and thick as my mother's hair when it was freshly washed.

"Madame, es crava negra?" she asked. I shook my head. She laughed. "Madame es Esmeralda." Then she held up the doll for my inspection again. "Cincuenta pesetas. Especilatas para tijo." The doll was flat and stiff, as unyielding as the women I'd seen trudging beside the railroad tracks.

Later, as I climbed the mountain, I remembered how her skin was deeper in shade than mine and a richer brown than the doll I would take home with me. And I thought how strange it was to be so like someone yet so different, to be here and still be half a world away and in another language. But at the crest of Machu Picchu, all colors floated into green, a green that pulsed in sunlight, beneath clouds hanging at eye level. Behind me, Huayna Picchu, the tallest of the peaks, captured all light. In the right equinoctial pattern, the sun climbed down from Huayna Picchu through the Inca doorway to the sun and onto the altar, where young women who had not fought their pride had been sacrificed to the sun god. Left there, their bones would be picked clean by the condors. Now, those keepers of the sun god sold trappings to tourists.

"Crava negra," the vendor had said. "Esmeralda."

Without the military, or a tour guide to lead me, I can step away from tired old racist milestones and enter new territory by putting one foot in front of the other, while keeping an eye on the potholes of local customs. I am still discovering all those places where we found by birth, by stealth, or by choice.

At the crest of Machu Picchu, I circled the altar but did not sit on it as other climbers did. Instead, I walked to the far side of the peak and looked down at the ruins. They seemed so orderly, so close to heaven, following the geometry of the slopes and rises of the mountain, terracing each level with a pattern of chambers, passageways, gardens, and aquaducts that took advantage of light and air. A city so sculpted into the natural landscape, it rose out of stone and lifted itself toward the sky. At the crest, I was virtually standing inside a cloud, mist swirling about my head, air sharp and electrifying.

Who could have imagined living among all this without dreaming of gods? How many thousands of snakes had Igor told us were found trapped in the crevices of stone? And how many virgins sacrificed? In the dim distance, I heard the faint sound of a train. Somewhere out there, the Urubamba River wended its way through the mountains, and over there, another Inca ruin called Sacsahuaman, or "sexy woman," as Igor would have said. Pachacamac and Tunquelen rested somewhere under that distant lace of pale gray-blue clouds. And others: Palena or "cruel spider," and Llanquihue, "lost lake." Somewhere in that velvet green world there was Puyehue, "the place of arrival."

A sound reached me, a sound both sad and inviting, like the wail of a train late at night when you're in a hotel room dreaming of home. But I was in the Andes, place of gods and spirits. Tucked in a pocket of the mountainside, a shepherd was playing a flute, the notes so sweet and true, this time I didn't care that the tune was the ever-present "El Condor." I climbed down and sat near him, and on that slope, began writing the first poem I'd attempted in several months. "El Condor" wafted across the thick green carpet of the Andes—for once the right song for just the right place. Perhaps I heard traces of Pablo Neruda's poems caught in the strains of the shepherd's flute music, or perhaps it was simply that Machu Picchu was singing to me—whatever the case, that afternoon, sitting in the apron of mountains in air so thin it could steal your breath, your very senses, I began a cycle of poems. *These mountains are like women,* I wrote. *They will whisper strange stories of the moon and the stars.*

Weeks later, I arrived in Brazil. By that time, South America no longer surprised me with its array of faces. If I'd had any doubts about that, those doubts were dispelled the day I visited a bookstore in Rio de Janeiro. Casa do Livro was a small shop, dusty and so barely lit, its leathery handmade books seemed even older, more fragile, as if they were attempting to return to their original state among earth and trees. I pulled an oversized volume from a shelf of books on the history of Brazil. The one I decided on had been compiled early in the ninteenthth century by a Portuguese explorer named Joao Muricio Rugendos. It carried the Portuguese title *Viagem Pitoresca Atraès do Brasil,* in Creole French *Voyage Pittoresque dans le Bresìl.* I began thumbing through the pages. It was a beautiful edition of handpainted drawings done in sepia tones, each recounting what Rugendos considered the six major racial groups along the Amazon from Ecuador to the Brazilian coast, with notations on the subdivisions for each group. It was a meticulous job, painted in the way daguerreotypes were tinted, lips and cheeks rouged in pastels and every eyelash penned in place. Each page contained four drawings of head and shoulders, the figures clothed according to Rugendos' notions of ethnic dress. I moved from descriptions of Spaniards and Portuguese to those of Africans and Indians. *Biancos, 125,000 Homens livres de cor,* Rugendos noted. *130,000 Negroes livres; es cravos Negroes 250,000; es cravos de cor 4,000 . . .*

The owner watched me for a moment, then came over to the table. "What are you?" he asked. "Not Brazilian, I think."

What are you? There was that insistent question, I thought, but I answered simply, "I am American."

The bookseller grunted and gestured toward the page where the author had drawn the faces of Indian tribes from the Manaus. "Look. Here alone, Father Rugendos describes two or three hundred groups. All, as you would say, Indian. But none with a history that can be recalled by one name. In this country, history is mucho importuno."

Yes, I thought. Mucho importuno.

The worn leather binding creaked as he turned the pages. Pages opened to faces so much like the vendor's at Machu Picchu, like Igor's, even like mine. I nodded and let him guide me through the book. "Here," the bookseller said, "Father Rugendos includes many blacks. Angola, Mozambique, Dahomey." Again he turned the page. "And here. Pasalaqua, mulatto, mestizo, creole, garifunas, africanos. Es cravos negros. Is this how you say in American?"

"Es cravos negros," I repeated. "Mulatto," I said, "Mulatto." Esmeralda, I told myself. It is all American. But that was something I needed to tell myself, not the bookshop owner. How could I say to someone who was unfolding the history of his country that in this land, by some quirk of fate, I had found myself close to home even among the keepers of the sun god?

Tickets Please

I have never liked tours. Except on the first day in a new city, when a tour is the best way to cover a lot of territory and find my bearings, map in hand, I avoid tours whenever possible. There is a certain perversity about them, a perversity caused by that kind of organized attempt to instantly dish up history as if cultures were 57 Varieties spread thinly over some supermarket shelf. I tried explaining that to Emilie and to the others in our group, who, for the price of a ticket, had come together in South America to travel unescorted. I emphasized *unescorted*—the freedom to venture out on our own, free to make our own arrangments, collectively or alone.

Most days started with Emilie and me conferring on the best transit routes offered by the various maps we had. An agreement meant we explored together that day, but some days, I went with Helen, whose keen photographic eye might delay us while she waited for the right camera angle. Sometimes I joined Fred and Hubert, Haitians who, by some remarkable coincidence I have never been able to explain, seemed to have cousins in telegraph offices of each town we happened upon, regardless of the country. Or I tagged along with a couple whose passion was gem stones, or with the ladies from Kansas whose goal was to find bread dough figures of Christ, or with the judge who compared local judicial systems to those in

Chicago. Sometimes I went off on my own, helped by strangers who mistook me for Brazilian or Costa Rican, and were pleased to discover I was norteamericana. The pleasure of an unescorted journey was that we did not have to be hooked to a tour guide like a lineup of bedraggled schoolchildren or like those groups from tours-of-the-damned, huffing to keep up with the leader, some acting as if they had to please a teacher by gathering everything for show-and-tell, others trailing behind like luckless truants just waiting for a chance to vandalize something. And others, like me, just not wanting to be told where to go and what to think once we arrived.

A city tour is just a way to learn the map of a town, I told myself. That reasoning made it ok to sign up for tours on the first day in a city, when I didn't know any better than to let someone else tell me what's what and where's where. Or I saved them for the downside of traveling, some spot that's all story and no glory, but where I was sure the visit would be clotted with tourists because the place was listed in every guidebook in the world and anybody visiting that neck of the woods had to say they'd at least walked through its Number One attraction. Using that logic, I could say I didn't jump into any tours without first protesting. Some tours I turned down flat—"You won't get me on a bus with all those hicks"—but on my last day in Lima, I was swayed to sign on.

"By the time we hire a car, pay the entry fee, and have lunch, we could have taken two tours," my traveling companions said. "But we're unescorted," I said. "That means no tours," I said. And they said, "If we're leaving Lima tomorrow, we'd better not waste all day today trying to figure out a guidebook."

So I relented, swallowed my oath of independence, and signed on for the Royal Excursion/Grand Getaway tour of the church holding the remains of Franciso Pizarro in Lima, Peru.

If there is any requirement for a tour, one is that you must be dressed for the encounter. I put on my best walking shoes, tried to make my camera as inconspicuous as possible, strapped on my money belt for easy access, and when I boarded the bus, paid my fare and smiled when the driver called, "Tickets, please." But all the while, the tour guide's spiel left me feeling as if I'd just been invited into a stranger's house for a party, only to be escorted to the attic where the family idiot waited to drool all over me and someone's ugly brother was ready to chase me down a hall waving dirty pictures of angels.

It is no coincidence that my memory of La Catedral leads me to connect insanity and angels, saints and sinners. It is an easy association. Not only is the history of South America fraught with conquering fanatics and sacrifices to fanatical religions, but most of the countries are still rooted in that stifling reality. It is a rule of bloodletting sanctioned by belief in a supreme being. It works not only because the Spaniards were masters at that plan but also because the pre-Columbians—the Toltecs, Aztecs, Chemùans, and Incas— had laid the groundwork. Having done so, they left the country with a history so complicated, there would be endless jobs for tour guides forever. Tour guides seem to have a primary objective, a sworn duty perhaps, to rattle the complacency of tourists and to uncover the history of sinners and saints who provided the convenient, albeit, gruesome history.

"Look there," a voice intones over a crackling microphone. "That is the last hanging tree (or blood altar) in the city / country / territory of (fill-in-the-blank-of-any-place). You'll have five seconds to take pictures." Cameras whir, click, snap, hiccough, and ping, and the bus speeds to the next stop. "Here is the burial place of Saint What's-his-halo, and in that crypt, What's-his-sword the Great, two of our beloved founders." Click, ping, whiz, snap, and on to the next stop. Well, it's a job, so I ready my camera and prepare to do my duty.

The good things about signing up for a limited tour are one: you have precious little time to embarrass yourself by tramping around with a camera slung about your neck, and two: afterward, you don't have to go back to the hotel with the group and suffer through a recounting of how the sights compared to Duluth or Farmington or last year's trip to Greece or Egypt. And if you're careful, no tourists' faces will appear on whatever photos you've taken. I'm not always careful enough, and sometimes I catch an elbow or part of a profile at the edge of a snapshot, or worse yet, I lose the war of flashbulbs and prints show up with globs of color slammed in the corner of the shot like Venusian moons, or glassy reflections clouding the eyes of the subject the way a dog's eyes absorb the headlights of an oncoming car at night. A roll or two of photos like those is all I need to convince me that words are my forté.

But whenever I do relinquish my journal for my camera, I aim for some part of the scenery that is less likely to have been nudged out of a tour guide's summary. I want none of those pictures where poverty becomes quaint and arrogance becomes colorful, where every landscape is a romantic vista and everyone, from diseased beggars in doorways to old men in button-down suits, seem costumed for the occasion. I also avoid pictures of some statue, monument, cave, seaside, garden, scenic view at (fill-in-the-blank-of-any-town) with me stuck in front like graffiti—a tourist version of Kilroy-was-here. I want photographs to be a bit closer to Braille—or rather to a sighted person's version of it—allowing me to feel what I could not otherwise sight read without distance between myself and the subject. This means pulling myself away from the insistent shutter of another camera or from the tour guide's relentless voice. It means breaking my instinctive retreat into words and relying on my clumsy efforts at photos. In the first stages of a trip, at least, this seems easy. I have numerous photographs of roads, plazas, trees, doorways, and the outsides of places.

Now forget all of that grand philosophy. As we approached the Plaza Independencia, my camera clicked, snapped, and whirred with the best of them. Then the guide began her spiel, her voice crackling over the badly wired loudspeaker.

"Ladies and gentlemen, please to imagine the traffic," she announced. Her accent was tinged with a Castilian *s*, a slight lisp that seemed somehow appropriate for her formal Latina manners. "Each year this grows busier," she said. "We have had so many accidents, I wonder at the accuracy of accounting. So many die, no one can be sure." She paused, a lilt in her voice. I grew uneasy. This is where the attic door is opened and the crazies escape, I thought. And sure enough, as the guide proceeded to tell us about the intersection's traffic fatalities, I watched her transformed from a middle-aged matron into Lucretia Borgia in walking shoes, as if midspeech, she'd slipped into a tour guide's pitfall, her laughter full of life's little horrors.

"The traffic here is ruthless," she continued. "Forty-three people killed right in this intersection we at present occupy. Last month, a pregnant woman, and this week, two schoolchildren. Killed dead. Bodies tossed in the air and limp as rag dolls. When they hit, blood, teeth, intestines, and all covered the pavement." Her giggle was high and thin. "I think it is the curse of the Incas," she added.

I glanced at Emilie, but her attention was on the guide. Next to her, Fred and Hubert wore their usual expressions of bemused tolerance. The judge was near the window, all but smothered by members of Royal Excursions or Grand Getaway tours leaning over him to get shots of the street. They were recognizable by tags designating their groups. Their cameras clicked, whirred, pinged with the urgency of faulty life-support systems. I sighed and wondered again how it was so easy to be fascinated and repulsed by death. Even the judge who was bent on describing murder trials slumped in his seat.

I remember Otovalo, where I met Mico. He couldn't have been more than eight—an Afro-Indian with button eyes, a broad nose, and thick, curly hair. Out of school for a schoolmate's funeral he wouldn't attend, he hung out in front of the ice creamery, hoping his innocent eyes and dimples might earn him a cone. When I came along, he pointed to his face, my face, and smiled. It worked. With one brown hand in mine, the other holding a double scoop cone, Mico became my tour guide: the church, a backyard pen of goats and llamas, the revolutionary's statue, then bypassing the street where his classmates were forming a miniature funeral procession. Perhaps the sight of that small coffin had turned Mico's innocence to mischief, but suddenly he danced with excitment and waved me forward. We were on a one-way street—*una via,* the arrow said—and Mico's finger insistently aimed in its single direction. I turned the corner and almost stumbled over the severed head of a recently butchered bull placed on the sidewalk to signal the availability of fresh meat. Mico doubled with laughter at the look on my face. The back of the bull's head, fleshy and red, swarmed with flies, and its ears stuck out like handles. I tossed my ice cream in the gutter and stumbled back, another tourist thrown off balance in a country where death is always around the corner. And I thought, One day, Mico my boy, you'll make an excellent tour guide.

The Plaza Independencia is a monochrome of gray-brown buildings and Spanish bricks facing a narrow street. La Catedral is at the far end of the plaza, and adjacent to it, the monastery and the school. At the opposite end is a residential area of row houses with colonial balconies, their fronts not unlike barracks, which, reportedly, was their original purpose. Yet the plaza seems small and ordinary, and compared to its European counterparts, rather shabby and sad. The same sort of somber air had greeted me on another downside tour I had taken, a depressing look at the Salt Mine Cathedral at Zipaquirá, Columbia. On that tour, the bus had deposited us at the top of a spiraling mountain road cut into a low saddle of hills where the resolute uniformity of grayness marked both sky and ground. Zipaquirá seemed desolate, although the cathedral was a domed room with a thirty-foot ceiling, ridged like the palate of some geodesic beast. The Salt Mine was a cold place where dust gathered on my skin and filled the pores, the corners of my eyes, my teeth. Its smell was sharp and sour, almost metallic, almost fetid, most surely the rancor of an ancient fire, and with its soot black bituminous walls and lances of artifical light, the place was anything but inviting. Not so with the Plaza Independencia.

The plaza is locked into the heart of Lima, figuratively and literally. As soon as I step off the bus, I am pulled into that mixture of time and temperament that is special to South America. Someone is playing a hurdy-gurdy at the far end of the plaza. The noise of cars traveling along the outside road mixes with the echoes of footsteps ringing against the cobblestones. The plaza is clotted with people: priests in monk's robes, women on morning errands, children gathering for school, Indians clothed in the solid bulk of native dress, vendors selling straw hats, ponchos, rosaries. And, of course, tourists. Small groups cluster around stone benches at the periphery and near the fountain area. More are on the street beyond in shops selling religious items and artisans' wares.

But basically, the plaza has an unassuming air about it. The daily comings and goings of local residents is steady, as if to imply there is nothing extraordinary there. Don't believe it. At first glance, there is a certain gaiety about the Plaza Independencia, but in reality, it is a place of contrasts.

A fan of steps leads to the cathedral's thick Spanish doors, which are ornamented with iron rings and hasps, and curlicued spires. As we approach the steps, several beggars, all children, stop us.

Suddenly there were children everywhere. Children in rags, shapeless dresses, tattered trousers, bare feet, and faces of indeterminate age. All carried the paunch of hunger, legs bowed with malnutrition. These were the Indians of the city, some of them abandoned by families who could no longer feed them. Some, like a child I'd seen earlier in the week in front of the Museo del Oro, begging for a mother too weak to beg for herself. School bells signalled the beginning of classes for the day, but the beggar children merely stared at us, their hands extended in silent pleas.

"Don't give them money or you'll never get rid of them," the tour guide said. An Indian woman stepped from the shadows with a cardboard tray of votive candles. "For the dead," the guide said. "It is fitting to buy them from the Indians. Once these bricks flowed with their blood. The very ground was soaked in it." Her breathy giggle bubbled over.

The Grand Getaway tourists lined up like ducks, and the Baptist ladies from Kansas bought several. Fred and Hubert each bought one. I eased toward the church door, nearly tripping over a beggar hunkering in the corner, one thin hand extended from the folds of a gray-brown ruana. Fred held open the door as I dropped a few coins into the beggar's palm. In the quickening light from candles just inside the church, the beggar stared, unsmiling. I stepped inside, his face held in my memory.

During our first week in Lima, Emilie and I had spent the day at the Museo del Oro, a state museum holding a massive collection of pre-Columbian treasures, mostly gold, as the name implies. It was hard to comprehend the wealth of the Incas until we stepped into the vault room of the museum. That room could accommodate only fifteen or twenty visitors at most, and once we were inside, the doors were closed, locked with a ceremony of alarms and buzzers. For a few seconds, everyone was in total darkness, then the lights came on, and suddenly we were washed in a blaze of gold. The walls were glass cases filled with gold. Gold was trapped in the ceiling, gold under glass on the floor below. And all of it so bright my eyes ached as if they refused to take in what they saw. Gold everywhere and in every shape—goblets, rings, tiaras, coronets, cuffs, bracelets, vests, amulets, plates—the gold of sun gods and kings, chosen women and condors. The gold of a century. The guidebook claimed that the pre-Columbian period lasted only thirty-nine years. *Thirty-nine years,* I thought, looking around at a room that held only a portion of what the conquistadores must have found. My fingers itched to touch the gold, but at the same time, I began to wonder what sun could have allowed the descendents of those who fashioned so precious a treasure to become the beggars outside the building that housed their inheritance.

Those same thoughts crossed my mind as I stepped into the sanctuary of La Catedral, the memory of the beggar's face still clear in my head. La Catedral does not hold as much gold as the Museo del Oro, but its treasure is equally encased in glass. I sensed a certain opulence as soon as I entered the cathedral, an aura if not an actual abundance of gold. The walls were covered with religious paintings, each canvas rich with colors. For a moment, I was captured by a painting of the Magi. The Moor, black and splendid in his robes, his camel behind him, reminded me of the tapestry depicting a desert scene that had hung in my grandmother's living room. It was a while before I realized the others had moved toward the front of the church. When I heard a collective intake of breath, as if everyone on the tour had shuddered at the same time, I pulled myself away from the wise men and quickly moved past the Annunciation and Pietá to the area where the tour group stood. They were clustered in a niche and I had to inch my way forward to see what had captured their attention.

There was, no doubt, a faint echo of the Museo del Oro lingering in the light of the cupolas where gold leaf embellished the frescoes. But none of it was enough to make the whole group shudder. What they saw, gold aside, was the ultimate treasure of La Catedral, the coffin of Pizarro, conquerer and conquistador, embellished in glass and gold. At first, all I glimpsed was the coffin, glass with its gold rim encrusted with precious stones, enough to feed all the Indians from those begging in the Plaza to the those in the shanty town outside the old train station at Cuzco. I nudged another tourist aside. Then I saw the body. Or at least, what could pass for a body. Actually, it was more like a twig, an old strip of leather, a rotten banana. Francisco Pizarro, dried into a short, parchment colored banana. This time, I giggled. Saints and sinners, angels and soldiers.

"Pizarro," the tour guide intoned, "was a fearless explorer. When he was killed, the natives threw him in a vat of brine. I am not sure they realized this would be a natural preservative. They pickled him, as we would now say."

She tried muffling her laughter, but it was too late. We all expected it. "Jesus, he's so short!" I said. "But no doubt he looked better in real life," Helen added. Now everyone laughed.

"Come-come. Five minutes for pictures," the guide insisted. And as the cameras whirred, clicked, and snapped, her glare told us that she was the only one allowed to tell jokes.

Tourist brochures promise all sorts of wonders, from a view of model governments and dimly lit cafés full of artists to architectural triumphs and ruins. And if you read the guidebooks carefully, you discover that some of these sites are jammed cornice-to-cornerstone with dungeons, jails, prisons, insane asylums, and places of interrogation. With all that on hand, it is no wonder the macabre easily becomes the highlight of a tour, and tourists, like any other audience, are easily fascinated by the macabre. It holds the elements of tragedy, suspense, horror, and fear. It is as natural as curiosity, sympathy, love, joy and pain. Tour guides are no fools. They know the macabre can be the stuff of great literature, the stuff of soap operas. Movie makers rely on it; mystery writers traffic in it; pulp journalists exploit it; and tour guides make the most of it.

The school next to the cathedral was housed in a three-story building that had the look of a government headquarters or business center. The classrooms were small, like cells lined along the outside walls of every floor. There had been no middle section to the building since the core had collapsed during an earthquake years ago, so each floor was open to the next, and the lower levels, where we were entering, served as a courtyard. On the walls between each room were statues of saints, and in the heat, most of the classroom doors were open. As we looked up, we could see a series of saints and open doorways, saints and open doorways. We could hear the children intoning their lessons in that exacting way I've come to associate with Catholic schools. There was an innocence about the sound of the children's voices, a devotion to the regularity and rhythms that religious obedience brings. I suppose this is why I was so unnerved when instead of walking up the stairs toward the school, we descended down into the catacombs, where the guide promised us a glimpse at the secret history of Peru. Everything changed so suddenly. When the door to the lower passageway opened, the hall filled with a rush of air that carried the scent of stagnant water and pocked earth. The light was dull, as if it had been depleted of sun for centuries. In places, the tunnel walls seemed too smooth, like shiny scar tissue clutching an old wound, but a few feet away, tiny markings were visible: rough hieroglyphics, partial cuneiform shapes, patterns of parallel scratches in rows like a calendar. I didn't need the guide to tell me that the place had been a prison, but this one was bent on giving us perfect details.

"During the Inquisition, the Indians who would not renounce their pagan gods were sealed in this place." She gestured to a recess in the wall that was less than four feet by four feet. "They crouched in each of these holes," she said. "They were asked once, twice. Do you renounce your pagan god? Do you renounce your pagan god?"

She paused, tested her audience. We were waiting for the other shoe to drop. Satisfied, she smiled. "Some were determined to remain heathens," she said. "And so they died heathens. Old men, women with children. Boys and young girls. They all died here. Entombed."

Her laughter was thin and high. For once, the group was silenced by the presence of death. I thought I heard water dripping against the stones. I knew I heard the children at their lessons. The only real light in the passageway came from windows in their classrooms. If I turned, if I pushed my way back to the entrance, I would be able to see the floors rising above me, doors opened to recitations.

"At the end of the corridor, we will see the Inquisitor's room," the guide said. "In that room we will find all the records and paraphernalia of the Inquisition. How many of you knew the Spanish Inquisition had come to South America?" No one spoke. "How many know how long it lasted?" Silence. "Well, every school child in Peru knows that answer," she laughed.

Cameras clicked and wheezed. My obedient side stood near Helen and watched her trying to adjust her lens to the dimness of the tunnel and the angle of available light. Her movements, usually professional, seemed clumsy. Suddenly, I had to get out. Something was choking off the air. The children's voices seemed to turn from dull repetition to laughter. I felt a headiness to escape, to dislodge this awful reality and its gruesome history. I leaned against the wall. Above me, the children resumed their recitations again, while all the saints stood silent, their arms outstretched in gentle benediction.

Emilie caught sight of the pinched look on my face. "You want to go back to the bus?" she asked. I nodded and turned, shoving my way past "Royal Excursions" tags. I could hear Helen following me. She said something I didn't really understand, but I'd found the door and stumbled into the sunlight, Helen directly behind me. I heard her lens cap click in place and the camera case snap shut. We reached the bus at the same time.

"I couldn't stand it," I said.

"I know," she said. "It's like Auschwitz with mariachi."

"Lord," I said, "I'm glad this is the last stop. I don't know why I even bother to sign up for these damn tours. They never really go where I want to go."

Helen grunted. "Well, kiddo. You buys your ticket, you takes your chances."

The bus door wheezed open with a rush of artificially cooled air, and we climbed aboard.

To Market To Market

In Lima, on summer afternoons, rain can come down thick and
viscous and wash the cobblestone streets clean of the day's traffic.
On those evenings in a certain part of Lima, after everyone has
had supper, after the sun has released the city and let it rest,
finally, under a curtain of warm air, Catalina Luna comes
to life. Under this tapestry of heat, the midnight market
beckons all those who can not sleep until the heat
breaks in those final hours before dawn. Once
a thieves' market, the Catalina is
now a market for villagers
who have traveled from
Huancavelica and Pisco
to sell to wholesalers who will,
by day resell the goods at higher prices
elsewhere. Some have traveled from as far
away as the Bolivian border, or Tacna in the south,
or Cobija, north, but most come from dozens of small
villages skirting Lima. And others, lovers and tourists, have
traveled no farther than the heart of the city where in afternoon
heat everyone gathers to delay sleep until it forcibly overtakes them.

They arrive in the lull of early evening, after the rains, after the
streets have been swept and washed until the cobblestones look
almost new. In the afternoon when the vertical sun is a spear
of heat, the fresh air market ends its business for the day.
Housewives and maids finish their daily shopping and the
people of Lima take their sensible siestas. Those who
venture out—mostly Indian servants running last
minute errands—walk stealthily from one shaded
doorway to another. Quiet softens uneven stone
paths, cracked stucco, and chipped facades.
Only a few insects swarm in the drugged
laziness of heat. Lizards doze in crooks
of trees and dogs drag themselves
to patches of available shade. Everything seems ready to sleep, even birds in
tourist hotels, desultory parrots who lazily
spent their waking hours crapping in elaborate wrought
iron cages. In those hours, between siesta and evening,
shutters are closed but with little imagination you can
still hear ancient incantations of some Quechua high priest
sprinkled like dancing dust motes in shafts of bright sunlight or
the clatter of Spanish horses with their polished leather saddles and
bright silver trappings hobbled under overhanging verandas inside
closed courtyards.

But after the vendors have arrived,
after the market goods are spread under bright canopies,
no imagination is needed. *Market* could never be a proper name
for Catalina Luna. It's a carnival, an eastern souk, a fiesta. When
I ventured into its confines with Emilie, I was swept into a stream
of pedestrians. The market was just beginning to gain the momentum
of evening. A scant two hours before midnight, the peak of evening
Peruvian time, but the heat of afternoon had refused to follow the sun
to the Andes. Night insects had replaced those that had plagued the

street during the day. They sought light, flesh, food, any rot redolent
with odors. Clouds of bugs swirled around whatever was warm and
inviting. Waiters quickly cleared sidewalk tables, but the bugs
gathered inside lingering smells of tapas, peppers, empanadillas,
frutas, carne, cerveza. Half a block from the hotel, I draped
my bare shoulders in a shawl of Ecuadorian lace. The movement
scattered insects and attracted the attention of two passing
Latinos who kissed their fingertips and seductively
called to us. Emilie and I laughed, but at a nearby
sidewalk stand, grew bold and bought flowers for
our hair, pink blossoms heady with fragrance,
the petals tipped in darker shades, almost
violet, with centers, darker still, pale
stamen like secrets, like the sweet
night air which seemed filled
with delights of Spanish wine,
wild flirtations, and
Catalina Luna.

The street was lush with colors, sounds, smells, everything
to satiate the senses. Villages were celebrated by patterns
of woven and embroidered blankets, rugs, skirts, shirts,
and shawls. Here: a pattern in a woman's skirt copied
the flow of water. There: the neckline of a peasant
blouse embroidered in patterns of sunlight, river-
washed stones, wind-blown thistle, the sleeves stark
white against the undertones of red highlighting
brown skin. The men wore loose pants and white
shirts open at the throat where knotted leather
thongs followed the curve of the neck.
A perfect frame for medallions:
a coin, a polished stone,
a carved amulet.

In the street lamps of the night market, skin tones seemed
burnished even browner. In that flickering light, everyone
assumed varying shades of brown. My own complexion
was tinted a darker shade under the lace crochet of
the Ecuadorian shawl I'd bought. Even Emilie's
skin, after two weeks of Peruvian sun was
reluctantly losing the last of its New York
pallor. Light glistened against burlap sacks
heaped with maize, beans, and seeds.
Adjacent stalls offered the bright
plumage of birds, or the birds themselves—
yellow macaws, red, blue, or green parrots.
Wealthy Peruvians from Miraflores, dressed in leather
and heavy linen, cruised the market for bargains. Tourists
wandered past, seemingly dazed by the colors. Two Indians
wearing rough cotton guayaberas sold shark bones, jaw bones
and teeth all polished and ready for whatever use a buyer
might have. And to the side, chickens tied to a pole by
their feet. squawked protests. Squawking birds hung
over a pen where three suckling pigs rooted in a
dark corner as if trying to hide themselves in
grunts and shadows. A man selling tallow
passed us, his wares smoothed into
yellow shapes like fat teardrops or
altar candles. But a candle maker,
several stalls down, had added dyes
to the fatty wax, and her candles
hung like stalactites:
red, green, blood-brown, and orange.

Ducks honked and parrots shrieked.
A woman stopped us for ten minutes with
an urgency to sell wall hangings, hemp that felt like
cactus, the scenes poorly dyed, so fuzzy they seemed

ready to fade back into the coarse fiber. Behind her,
turtles thumped against the sides of a crate. Snakes lay
dormant in wire boxes. All of them—the turtles, pigs,
ducks, eels, mottled snakes, and fish with wicked faces
and teeth like machetes—all would become someone's
meal in a day's time, each dish complemented by
mangoes, soursops, avocados, red bananas and
green plantains, hanging like the candle
maker's tapers. Emilie and I drank
orange Fanta and ate tapas of
cervice, and spicy meat
rolled in thin dough.
We ate fried plantains
washed down with rich coffee. The air
grew even thicker. Overhead, constella-
tions of stars I could not name glittered
above puffs of oily smoke. We passed stalls
filled with serapes, ruanas, green-flame beads,
mosquito coils, sage, coca tea, trays of butterflies piled
on a counter. I studied the trays. Lovely blue aphrodites,
wingspans so wide, I could almost imagine them soaring
like condors. Their colors were iridescent, other-
worldly, shimmers of blue and deep violet pulsing
in candlelight as if the butterfly could free
itself of display pins and sail toward the
starry sky above us. The butterfly seller
spread out his trays, calling each
specimen by its Spanish name, his
fingers gently, almost
lovingly, tracing
patterns of wings.

I have always been shaken by the sight of living things
trapped for display. Caught in the wonder of Catalina

Luna, I was saddened to see them forever in midflight.
Who had said: *Man kills the thing he loves?* I
quickly turned,examined embroidery on
huipiles and guayaberas sold by women from a
village near Paraná River. But before I
could select a shirt, a knife seller
walked by leading a monkey. The man
poised a knife on the tip of his
tongue, then flipped it,
catching it, tongue-tip
like a juggler with pins.
His tongue was calloused
to the weight of the knife, but
each time he demonstrated the blade's
awful sharpness with a slight cut on his arm.
The knife seller's arm was striped with scars, but still
the monkey yelped each time the blade drew blood. That's
the way it was in Peru: beauty and death existing side
by side, each taking a bit from the other. Hot breezes
sweep across the plains of Nazca carrying the scents
of mountain flowers and high clean Andes air where
virgins were once sacrificed on the stone altars
of Machu Picchu. There was always the sense of
human sacrifices and conquistadors and cities
lost in their own bone-chilled deaths.

When those smells reached Lima, they were heavy as the lingering
scent of animal fat clinging to cloth woven from the wool of llama,
vicuña, and alpaca. One look, one sigh, one slight twitch of
muscle, and the present merged with the past. Everything
spilled over as scores of people surged into narrow paths
between stalls. A child with the face of an old woman
and the rounded belly of hunger begged for coins. I
gave her some. She asked for more. A young boy

leading three goats pushed past me, his eyes
bright saucers of light in a sweet brown
face. Then he winked and vanished into
the crowd, goats neighing after him.
People called to one another
in Quechua, Portuguese, French,
Dutch, or Spanish. A few argued in
English, which marked them immediately
as tourists. All sorts of sounds drifted
toward me and away: words or bits of phrases, some
merely hoots, some screeches, howls, and whistles. We
eavesdropped on two American women, their voices full of midwestern twang as they complained about bargaining for prices. "I
know she overcharged me," the first woman said. "They all do, you
know. They take one look at us and they cheat us. They all hate us,
no doubt." "No doubt," her companion sighed. The first woman
agreed. "I think everyone hates us. But then people say we all hate
each other. It's the way of the world." "So what's the difference?"
her companion asked. "Sad," the first woman answered. "When
they have so much tradition."

Emilie and I moved through endless
piles of goods. Stacks of glazed pottery,
earthenware, large rugs and hammocks swaying under
their own weight, skeins of wool drooped over lines
in front of stalls that held hand-embroidered patterns,
the dye of threads already bleeding into the fabric. Jewelry
was slung over the wire of another stall: silver bracelets, golden
Inca earrings, glass beads, feathers, amethyst, and turquoise. And in
another, dozens of pots, glazed and unglazed, with designs from the
Incas, Mayas, and Aztecs. I had one in my hand the first time Silas
spoke to me. In his safari suit, he could have stepped out of some
grade B movie, but with his thick English accent and the shadows
cast from a potter's stall all but hiding his face, the whole

encounter might have been pulled from a grade B movie. Once
he realized I was staring at him, he said, "G'd evening,
Miss. Silas here. The last name is of no concern. But
I think I have something you want."

I tugged my shawl tighter and glanced at Emilie. By my calculation,
her look had reduced him to customs clerk, like the ones we'd
encountered at the last border crossing. "Ah, I see we're a bit
the wary sort," he said, his English accent even heavier this
time. "Fear not, m'lady, Silas is the last of the honest
tradesmen in these parts. I'd present my card if I had
one. I'd present myself to two lovely ladies like your-
selves if I weren't so down on my luck." He paused.
Emilie and I did not respond. "And lovely you are
too," Silas added. "Lovelier than the night itself.
And here I am with only luck to hold me. But luck
or no, I do have a bit of goods that might be of
interest to you. Not tourist fluff," he said,
dismissing the clay pots we'd been examining,
"but the real thing. Authentic Quechua.
Pre-Columbian even, if you're
of a mind. And I'm thinking
you are of a mind."

Emilie and I waited.
We knew whatever Silas No-last-name
had on his mind was not on ours. "And where
you be keeping deese theengs?" I asked, falling
into the lilting accent I'd learned for high school
theater—an Island-girl accent I now used in a pinch,
one I'd adopted ever since a jive Jamaican historian had
asked if I was one of those poor unfortunates who spoke only
one language. I'd resolved back then to stumble through whatever
language was on hand, but when in doubt, fall back on that fool's

brand of Island English. Emilie stared but Silas picked up on it right away. "Well, Jamaican, eh. Right-o," Silas said. "My wife's brown. Sisters under the skin," he winked. "We'll see what we have and the wife will make tea."

I suppose his mention of a wife allowed us to follow him. Why would two seemingly intelligent women trail a seedy dyspeptic Englishman at two o'clock on a hot, muggy morning in Peru? "How long had you been watching us?" Emilie asked. "Oh, I can see most of the street from my flat," Silas said. "A prime view, you might say." Emilie and I nodded, and glanced at the window. Even with the thick dusty drapes pulled back, there wasn't much view from Silas's flat. From where we sat, the noise of the crowds was reduced to a murmur, and through the dirty windows, colors turned muted and somber. The street that had been so alive a second before now seemed like a dream, part of a play, some place we'd been years ago and brought back to life only because we had so carefully recalled it. But the flat was right on the street, a second floor walk-up at the top of narrow stairs. Each step had shuddered with our entry. "As if the house was telling us to turn back," Emilie said later. But we hadn't turned back, and sitting on the tattered damask sofa, there seemed to be no reason for ever having considered turning back.

Silas's apartment had all the goods the street offered and some
thing more. It was an archeologist's dream, or a nightmare. The
rooms were more Mudéjar, Moorish, than Limeño, all available space
filled with a miscellany of old pottery, rugs, weavings,
jewelry, statuary—the flotsam of centuries of Peruvian
life gathered like debris washed into the cul-de-sac of
Silas's flat. Chifforobes and wardrobes were crammed
to overflowing, and in corners, stacks of unopened
crates stood ready for inspection. Every available
space was taken. Emilie and I moved shards of
tapestry from the sofa so we could sit down,
the weavings so fragile that once we touched
them, they left the dander of fiber and
earth ground to a fine brown dust. Like
everything in the flat, the sofa was
coated with this patina. Dust
whispered of tombs and
graveyards, moon-
light raids, and
plans to outrun
the militia and
customs agents.
Dust proclaimed
Silas's livelihood: *guaquera,* graverobber.

Silas was perched on the edge of a bishop's fladstool not unlike one
Emilie and I had seen behind the braided visitor's ropes at La
Catedral. "I'm damned lucky to be so centrally located, don't
you think." "Lucky," Emilie repeated. She was watching
Silas's wife. The woman kept herself entirely in shadows
all the while we were there. I saw part of a face:
one eye with dark thick lashes, the line of her
cheekbones caught in a wedge of light, her skin
olive brown and weathered. Or turning: part
of one nostril, full lips, chin, a tiny gold

loop winking in a pierced ear. She was
Indian, that I determined and Silas
confirmed. "My wife's from
Leticia," he said. "Near
the Amazon River. I like
strong women," he
laughed. But the-silent-one,
as I'd call her later, must have
shown her strength when we weren't
there. Silas never introduced us, only
referred to her as "my wife." She brought us
cups of tea in English teacups, Staffordshire or
some such, and though I promised I'd take a close
look at her face the next time she entered the room,
I never had a chance. We were always busy, distracted
by Silas's chatter and endless stash of trade goods. Cups
of sweet tea just seemed to appear, always at the right temperature.

Silas was teaching us how to spot bogus antiques. "It's all in your
spit," he said. "Take your finger, wet it, put it against the clay.
If the moisture vanishes almost before you remove your finger,
there's a good chance what you're holding is the king's truth.
That is, unless you're spitless at the moment. Happened to me
once, eh? Dry as a widow's thigh, I was. So I slid my fingernail under the ridge, and by glory, the sliver came off
ragged. Another test. If it's a clean cut, more likely
it's a new firing of clay you're holding. 'Course the
chaps these days are wise. They've got methods
to make the old look new and the new look old.
Native boys. Running the likes of me
straight out of business, I tell you.
Got the courts on their side when it
comes to who goes to jail. Can't
touch 'em and can't trust 'em."

97

Trust. An odd word for Silas.
But I sipped tea and listened as he
led us through the catacombs of his artifacts. He showed us finely worked silver from
the upper Andes, bone carvings from the Amazon, straw
fishing baskets of coastal villages, and of course, bounty
from graves: burial detritus, some so badly decomposed, we had to
take his word for its original shape. And the problem was his word.
He said, "In pre-Columbian days everyone was a potter. From the
time a chap learned to walk, he learned to throw a pot. Crude at
first, to be sure, but after a while, you got the hang of it. Then
comes the day when you're full grown, and you pick the pot that
most says you've walked this earth. That one you keep with you for
life. The others are broken, melted back for new pots. But that
one is buried with you. Tells the gods what kind of soul
to expect, so t'speak. And that's what I've got here.
Pots of the soul, so t'speak."

He held up a small vessel in the shape of a cup, but sensual,
more mythical than real. Bodies pulled away from the sides:
an arm here, a leg there, a knee, a face held serious at
its task. Turn the lip and it clearly depicted a couple
having intercourse. Another showed a ménage à trois.
And a bowl with eight, no nine figures intertwined
over the rim with the last one curving to the inside of the dish to form a lip from which liquid
could be poured. Silas chuckled. "Busy little
buggers, eh? Not what you'll find out there on the
street. Out there, you'll see imitations. Cheap stuff.
And safe. Mothers feeding babies, a young lad playing his
flute. Family stuff. Sure, you see some with idiots, or hare-
lips, but these . . . Chichén, they are. Best of the lot. Make me
an offer. We'll deal." He nodded toward his wife, the silent-
one wi her ever-present cups of steaming tea.

Years later, in Uwajima, Japan I would bargain for a woodcarving
while plum rain pattered on a tile roof. By that time, I would this
know way of doing business—the man to explain the craft,
his wife to come in at just the right time and collect the
bounty—but that night in Lima, I only assumed Silas's
wife was sullenly quiet, resenting our being there,
Emilie and me, resenting her husband's trade on
her ancestors' bones.

I held up a drinking cup.
A woman's body curved along the outside of the vessel, her lover assuming the
shape of the handle. As I turned it to pick up
the flickering light from the street, they seemed
to smile. Another turn, and they were absorbed in each
other once again. "One of a kind," Silas winked. "Something
wondrous from a time that will never see this sun again. Something
beautiful for a beautiful lady," he said in a voice soft as a velvet
glove. I turned the cup once more. The woman's broad face was
sweet, naive, despite the fullness of her naked breasts and hips.
The man was lean and muscular. Where the glazing still held, a
medallion clasped by a knotted rope, winked in the cusp of his
neck. The
cup seemed to grow warm in my hands. Without thinking, I
reached for my tea. It was fresh, although I'd emptied
it only moments before. I looked up. The-silent-one
was turning back toward the kitchen, but I glimpsed
the one eye that was visible to me and caught
a slight smile playing across her lips.

The tea was heavy and sweet. Emilie made soft noises to signal
she was ready to leave. I realized the muffled street below had faded.
Light from the window had begun to soften all the shadows in
the room. By someone's calculation, dawn was fluttering at the edge
of the skyline. Perhaps it was the sense of imminent daylight bringing

99

reason into that shadowy room, or the guidebook's caution to
travelers to be aware of charlatans with phony relics, or
perhaps it was that I could never really trust anyone who
seemed to have stepped out of a grade B movie. But I was
young and whatever the reason, I walked out of Silas's
flat and left thatdrinking vessel with its ancient
lovers. "A time that will never see the sun of this
earth again," Silas had whispered. It is a decision
I have always regretted. For one evening, I had
visited a place that was like no other. In that
evening, time had grown liquid, passing
only when we paid attention to it. In
that apartment, with its clutter of
graveyards and tombs, I had put
time in a corner, and believed
what I saw before me. With
that cup, I had held; for a
moment the magic that might
have brought the past into
my present.

It was only when I once again became aware of daylight approaching
as my way of measuring time that belief failed. But for me,
the cup will always be real, and always sitting on a trunk in a
dark flat that smells of dusty earth, weeds, treebark and tea.
And in my head, Silas is still perched on that rickety
fladstool, the-silent-one pouring him a fresh
cup, one part of her face accepting light.

The Moon and Malaysia

There are some who will tell you dragons guard the moon. If you have any doubt, go to Malaysia on the night of any full moon and watch lizards try to resume their ancient positions of importance. Under the lip of rooftops, where cool air circulates between rafters and walls, lizards wait for the moon. And when the moonlight falls tangerine bright into this space between house and roof, lizards sing their moonsongs in tweets and riffles.

There are those who doubt this tale. They say that in the tropics, walls crackle with the trails of lizards and beetles, spiders and worker ants. Sounds separate, disappear, and return. The doubters say that when the heat of the day evaporates in the air space under the roof, lizards come to eat mites and nightcrawlers passing by, and that is why you hear them clacking triumphantly, smacking down their latest meal. I only know that sometimes, wide-eyed in my bed, I could hear the music of their laughter after the moon reached its peak.

"It is good luck to have lizards take up residence on your walls," my friend Bee Bee said. But I only thought of enjoying the luxury of time suspended and imagined them as dragons come to save the moon for me. And it must have been true because the moon

seemed to wink its approval.
In Malaysia, the moon appears closer, perhaps because you are
so near the equator, but even without this sense of the moon,
my introduction to Malaysia would have been special. Bee Bee
had been after me for years to pay her a visit, and for years
I had hesitated. Now the country seemed more than ready
to help me shed my reluctance.
It was all that Bee Bee had promised—and more.
It was a country of beautiful extremes, an array of people
of color, a profusion of flowers, birds, butterflies, and
traditions as varied as the climate that ranged from mountains
to seashore. A land as glorious in its delicacy as it was
in the clutter and filth of its urban back alleys. Even as my flight
circled in a landing approach to Penang, I glimpsed from my window
the beginning of some of the contradictions that awaited me. The
resort island of Langkawi rested at the tip of the mainland like a
lush green pomelo in a backwater pool of silvery blue ocean that
was sadly
unfit for swimming. And to the south, verdant mountains rose above a
thin layer of gray smog.

"It's beautiful, isn't it?"
my seat partner said. I answered yes, but why not?
We were the Ferenghi—the foreigners come to taste
for a moment a bit of this country. I did not see him again
for several weeks, the next time by chance
in the airport lounge at Kuala Lumpur. And by then,
he would not recognize me. By then, I would be
only one more brown face lost in a range of skin colors
from ebony Tamils to ivory-complected Chinese. And I would stare
at him for a full five minutes, thinking him just another Ferenghi,
another blond American sampling the world between college
and the promised career. In the larger towns, outside
the posh hotels and resort enclaves, I saw

them everywhere—English, Swede, Australian, American,
more native than the natives below their streaked blond hair.
We began our reacquaintance with his surprise that I had seen a side
of the country not opened to him. "These are beautiful people,"
he said. "Exotic. Different.
But I feel like such a foreigner here.
Nothing like it at home."

What could I tell him?
How an East Indian cleaning woman in the train station
had passed me three times before she sat down and spoke?
She called me "sister" and seeing my books,
asked where I had learned the "trade of reading."
I showed her the photo of the writer Gloria Naylor,
an African American. Our skin tones were the same—
hers, mine, the writer's—
and though she was younger, her dark skin was mottled, drawn
around the corners of her mouth in the same attitude
I'd seen on the faces of my grandmother's friends in the States
who'd worked as day help in the white suburbs. The woman
told me she had seven children, three grandchildren,
and another on the way. She wanted to know how long
I'd been away from home.
"More than a month," I told her. She smiled
and leaned heavily on her broom. "Here," she said,
"I have the day to myself and my children only at night."
When my train left, she waved good-bye
the way an old friend would.

The woman in the Central Market at Kuala Lumpur
was convinced I should buy something of Nonja silver.
"They were women of letters.
Like you," she said. "They made their own way." She was part Malay,
part East Indian. Because I am black, she asked me

103

about America and what to expect if she would move there.
I told her how color was still a simpleminded distraction in the u.s.,
and how far we have yet to go. She pulled out a canvas bag
of silver belts, told me the history of each, reducing them
below the market price for every story.
Her daughter, she said, had moved to Singapore
where dark skin was not always an advantage.
"Because there are too many Ferenghi," she said. "She needs to
come home where she is wanted."

Some mornings, Bee Bee and I would visit one of the temples
in the heart of town, where the Buddhists were on one side
of the street, the Moslems on the other, and in front of each door,
flower vendors sold offerings of joss sticks, incense, and blossoms
to the passing crowds. The heavy smells of sandalwood and spice
drifted into the street. Holding offerings of jasmine and frangipani
and wearing wreaths of flowers in our hair, we joined
the lines of people going in. In the darkness of the vestibule,
with my bare feet on the cool stones, I remembered island temples
of Hawaii, and my friend Makaleia,
who had been dead for twelve years when I went to Malaysia.
My memories of Hawaii are full of the heady smells
of plumeria and maile leaves and watching Maka, a master teacher,
lead students in her hui in the graceful
movements of the hula. She and I had walked
under palms as heavy as the cassurinas lining beaches in Penang,
and we had watched lizards, long sticks of curious eyes, follow us.
Makaleia, like Bee Bee, so full of laughter. The flowers I
threaded through my hair when Bee Bee and I joined the morning
procession into the temples were my tribute to her.

"I want to be a writer," a young Tamil student said to me. "But
when I read about women writers, they do not have such happy lives.
What is a woman of color like me to do? I want to have a happy life,

but I want to be a writer. I don't want to be lonely and alone."
"We are never alone," I told her. "We nag each other. We cry
together. We keep in touch."
Bee Bee, at the other end of the table, laughed knowingly.

During those first days of my visit to Malaysia, everything
seemed to be in motion: the crowds, the smells, even the melody of
languages—a dozen, it seemed, syllables playing against each other
in a canopy of sounds. And the sounds themselves played and replayed.
Early in the morning, the ping-ping of bicycle bells began
the day's deliveries of laundry, fresh produce, newspapers, and
mail. Diesel-fueled buses fumed toward the center of town, and
trishaw drivers took up their posts along the main roads. Some
trishaws carried their morning pickup of uniformed schoolchildren,
some so small, they occupied only the middle sections of
narrow trishaw seats. Other trishaws ferried office workers or simply
circled the block, pedaling slowly in front of
buses and cars as they cruised for passengers.

By midmorning, downtown streets were stamped with food vendors'
stalls, their woks heated and ready, the clop-clop and swish of knives
and chopsticks mixed with the scent of rice, pork, noodles, cuttlefish,
bok choy, and peppers. Knowing my penchant for hot peppers,
Bee Bee
would select a portion of the spiciest food, which we'd eat
at one of the metal tables cluttering the edges of the sidewalks.
In the heat of the afternoon, we cooled our thirsts with shaved ice
or melons. But mornings were the time for sweet rolls and coffee
made thick, Turkish style. Mornings held the last cool air
of the day trapped in the shadows of trees, dark corners of temples,
and antique shops. That was the time when thousands of birds
sang their praises of heat: calling and cawing, whistling and squawking,
tweeting, chirping, trilling, and caterwauling—creating
their own songs and imitating a dozen others. Even in front

of the arcade mall, a bird seller's shop echoed with songs
of caged parakeets, yellow headed cockatiels, and brightly crested
mynahs. The noise followed us into the hubbub of the modern shopping
center, where the old world slammed into the rudely efficient
new world,
and the sounds of birds and trishaws were replaced by blaring
loudspeakers and pilfered hits from the latest American pop music
charts, along with a cache of designer jeans
and some version of Kentucky Fried McDonald's.
On the street of tailors, where Chinese shops advertised
their skills in ideographs, a single piece of English graffiti
declared: BEWARE OF GOD!
Nearby was a Sanskrit equivalent, a filigree of warning
scrawled like dragon's fire.

Quiet is not a word I readily associate with Malaysian cities.
Each street held the sounds of half a dozen languages.
From dawn until well past midnight, people gathered to noisily
eat, work, drink, flirt, dance, and gossip. Malaysians ate five
times a day, maybe more: a quick bowl of noodles, sweet
melon, or rice
cakes, an order of satay, Indian bread, or curry. Or a late night snack
along promenades like Gurney Drive, where moving past kiosks
of pirated audiotapes was like being trapped inside a radio
that never held to one station for the length of any song.
The voices of other strollers became the static in between, and the sea,
an arm's length away, amplified everything. I had no choice
but to flow into the mood of the day, whether I was on Guerney
or at the Thieves' Market, where you could find anything
from ornate Chinese pipes and ladies' leather
gloves to boxes of dolls' heads, no bodies,
crates of uniform trousers, penny nails, or handheld eggbeaters.
Lines of people squirmed around stalls like conga dancers,
the whole line stopping if somebody caught sight of an item they

just had to have. Anyone need three hundred rubber bathtub stoppers?
And at the end of the market, the usual array of cubbyhole eateries
with a few tables set at curb's end.

I began to expect the myriad of sounds, so much so
that on the day Bee Bee and I saw a boatload of Burmese monks,
I was stunned by the silence that swept the crowd. We were
at the ferry terminal purchasing tickets to leave Penang,
when the street, normally awash in a babel of noise, fell quiet.
Suddenly, I saw a surge of saffron robes
extending from a boat ramp onto the quay. But the only sound
I heard was the whisper of sandals.
Everyone moved to let them pass.
"No one touches a priest, especially women," Bee Bee whispered.
I watched the monks glide by, the line punctuated, now and then,
by motorcycle policemen coasting beside their charges.
Within minutes, the group extended without pause
past three docks, nearly six city blocks.
We waited a full five minutes, maybe more, but I never saw an end—
just a procession of men in saffron robes, faces clean shaven,
boyish, almost expressionless, but not submissive.
In that honored space accorded all holy men,
they simply moved through the crowd without the need to
acknowledge anyone else. When Bee Bee and I left, they were still
moving in a silent procession, in complete uniformity
as if they moved as one: one brown shoulder exposed,
one saffron robe fluttering in the humid air,
one head, shaved and slightly bowed.

It is hot in Malaysia, and between the humidity and the noise, there is
no sense of quiet until you reach the mountains or the sea.
The quiet of the hidden valleys in the limestone mountains near Ipoh
demanded the same reverence those monks had held over the dockside
in Penang. The mountains were mysterious and restful and offered me

my first glimpse of the real beauty of Malaysia. And it was there
I met Lau Soo Chye.

The day after we reached Ipoh, Lau Soo Chye
strolled into a tea house where Bee Bee and I
were spending the better part of a sweet afternoon with one of her
students, a handsome master of the tea ceremony. Lau arrived
late, bringing with him bags of fruit, seeds, and berries, which
he immediately spread upon the table, a bounty full of fresh
odors and clean air. Even before he told me his name, he
had begun to peel a lily seed, his fingernail quickly
slicing the seed's green sleeve to expose the sweet
white pulp nested in the pockets of stems, like
marbles on a Chinese checkerboard. The fruit,
he said, had been gathered on a trip he'd just made to
help a friend harvest melons. Within seconds, I was eating
the seeds of lily pods and slices of sweet mango, knowing neither
their names nor his. And it was with that kind of trust that I went
with Lau and Bee Bee on an excursion into the mountains of Ipoh.

After the noise of Penang, even the smallest rustle of leaves or
soft thrumming of insects seemed loud. At an orchid farm, I
watched lizards scoot through the sawdust around pots
holding plants called Queen's Lip and Jane's Story. Row
after row of delicate blossoms exuded scent. Lizards held a pose
that extended the stem of the plant into its shadow, and sometimes I
made the wrong choice the way I had in the Yucatán when I'd mistaken a giant lizard for a fallen tree limb until the click
of my camera sent it scurrying away, taking its smaller,
more photogenic kin with it, laughter trailing
behind them. In Ipoh, I had no better luck
"Quickly, quickly," Lau instructed while I tried to
capture the lizards midflight in my camera lens. Everything seemed
to move rapidly: the light filtering through palms and vines,

the scent of blossoms, the swirl of insects. At a stream, water
rushed over rocks with such force, I failed to hear the
whine of mosquitoes until after I was bitten. Lau
gathered sprigs of thick grass and rubbed
their juices across my skin. In seconds,
the stinging had vanished.

The mountains of Ipoh rise like the cliff dwellings of Taos,
except in Malaysia, mountains still hold their primoridal state.
When I looked up at the shale cliff sides
of Ipoh, bats swirled from their caves into the first rays of dusk.
It was early evening, and the movement of their wings hummed
in the cavern openings. Then they took to the air, circled,
floated, and in a single wave returned to the silence of stone.
I counted at least six caves on one cliff—openings
filled with the swirl of wings like pepper flung into the sky.
At the base of another mountain, Lau took us to a monk
who told fortunes and another who offered sanctuary for those
in need of a time of peace. Their retreats were carved out of the
mountain itself. The walls of lime-washed rock seemed safer
than any room I'd been in for months.
Outside, Lau showed me trees that rained winged seeds.
Their pods were gossamer and floated to the ground around my head
like butterflies or the shadows of stars.
"A gift," Lau said,
and offered them to me the same way he'd offered
the sweet seeds of water lilies the day before. I think he said, "It
will cleanse you,"
but I can no longer remember if he meant the lily
pods or the winged seeds from the limestone caves of Ipoh.

More than once I thought of Maka and Hawaii, especially when
I went with Lau and Bee Bee into the caves. In Hawaii, I had
scrambled over stony cliffs, one hand-hold away from tumbling into the

Pacific, to take rubbings of petroglyphs that recalled the ancient gods
of the Islands. At Ipoh, my cave exploring was a bit more subdued
until I came upon a breathtaking valley on the hidden side of a grotto.
Caves have always been somewhat magical for me
(especially after the caves of Majorca, where Moors
and Nubians once took refuge and Jules Verne
was inspired to write *Journey to the Center of the Earth*),
so it was only fitting that when Lau pulled me, hand over hand
to an outcropping where stalactite deposits had percolated into
wondrous forms, I felt myself moving into the sudden unveiling
of something magical. The cave opening formed a picture window,
and in the overhang of stalactites, I immediately recognized
the curve and cup of dragons.
"It is from the rainbow," Lau said, tracing the arch of the
stone. "All the patterns are ancient patterns of earth staring from
the heavens. Bending down." I saw multicolored deposits layered
like rings of a tree. "The shape is the rainbow," Lau continued. "In
my language, the rainbow is called Dragon-coming-to-take-the-waters."
When I touched the rock, my palm was filled with moisture.
Above us, a few white clouds scurried by.

Malaysia seemed at once distant and familiar. Everywhere
the lattice of sounds and smells seemed to
double and redouble. Night brought the scents of tropical
forests closer to cities. The air held the waning aroma of acacia
and cassurina, and foul odors of overripe breadfruit and prickly
durian, fruit bearing heavenly tastes cloaked in the smell of sewers.
"There are durian addicts who are outcasts," Bee Bee said.
"There are laws against office workers eating the fruit at lunch."
At night, half-asleep, I could smell the raw earth
of backyard gardens, and pools of water turned mildew-green
with twigs and leaves. Under the locked awnings of shops,
there was the lingering scent of dye from silk factories, spongy
wood from the drying shed, rings of salt crusting

the edges of the tubs. In the temples, snakes
awoke from their drowsy daytime stupor to suck the eggs left
by worshippers. Behind the fresh air markets, ripe smells
of vegetation and fish blended with fine dust sifted through
bags of rice and sharp traces of sweat drying on the leather seats
of trishaws parked nearby. Sidewalk arcades along Gurney Drive
reeked of oil from roast duck, crispy fish, sautéed mushrooms,
and broccoli. A sudden shift, and the night air was
bloated with the dander of feathers from plucked birds
on their way to market, squids salted for the next day's sales,
or the lingering smell of incense for kitchen gods
burnt low and fragrant as roasted cashews.
And always there was the smell of flowers: delicate
mimosa, the lacy scent of lilacs, a dazzle of orchids and wild
lilies. And caught in the current of rivers that untwisted from dense
trees somewhere in the heart of the country, flower petals
sometimes found their way past cities and into the sea.

On the last day of 1990 in the last decade of the twentieth
century, I stood in front of the colonial railway station at Ipoh and
watched the moon rise just beyond the edge of rooftops. The night was
heavy with sounds, and the full moon hung low in a sky so balmy, birds
seemed unable to sleep, and flowers barely closed their petals. The
moonlight fell across the flagstones of the promenade,
onto the shoulders and arms of lovers and onto families
sauntering in the heat of that Malaysian
night. I was strolling a few feet in front of Bee Bee, lost
in the laughter of everyone about to enter the new year,
when I came upon a couple of vendors advertising something
they called elixir. They were gypsies. Or at least they said
they were. With the moon that low, it didn't matter. Nor did it
matter if their elixir really was an aphrodisiac.
What could be more propitious than walking beneath a
full moon hanging low over a public square on a night so balmy?

"It will make your lover miss you even more," the handsome
vendor assured me, his smile as inviting as gypsy smiles I'd seen
in half a dozen other countries. How do they know that smile
and how its magic transcends all language?
I took the elixir and dreamed
of my lover.

"How could you drink
and not know what it was?" Bee Bee asked.
I smiled the gypsy's smile.
"So . . . how did it taste?" she asked.
"Bittersweet," I said. "Like a purge."
A lizard darted from the base of a tree and crossed the brick
pathway in front of me. One more step, and I would have been directly
in its path. "That's good luck," Bee Bee said. The lizard peered up
at me, judged my size and its closing distance, then darted away.
"Every time I see a lizard, you say it's good luck,"
I told Bee Bee. "There are lizards everywhere. How can they all
bring good luck?"
"Well, you're here, aren't you?"
I laughed at her logic, but still, there must have been some
truth in it. I was there. It was midnight, New Year's Eve, and the
moonlight was falling across the rooftops of Ipoh, Malaysia.

Journey to Ulcinj

No matter how you cut it, you can't get to Ulcinj from here or anywhere. On the map of Yugoslavia, all the roads are full of conflicting
directions, all referring to some prehistory that only the Slavs understand. Ulcinj, I'd read, had been one of the harbors used by Turkish
slave traders, and in the last days of the Ottoman Empire, the slave
trading enterprise had simply been halted, "abandoning several hundred persons of Afric descend in Turkish ports all along the African and
European coasts." One of those ports had been Ulcinj, located on what
is now the southernmost tip of Yugoslavia, and according to travelers
in that area, including my Serbo-Croatian language tutor, still contain-
ing descendents of Africans abandoned on those shores. I looked at a
map. That explained the location, but nothing explained how all sense
of roads had been abandoned. "Everyone has their reasons," my lover
had once told me. And since he was a writer, living off his imagination,
he said all I had to do was create reasons where none existed. Therein
lies madness, I'd thought at the time. But that was before I needed a
road to journey to Ulcinj. So I told myself: McElroy, use your imagination. Simple enough, except when I had to consider that you can't
always get there from here, especially when here is Yugoslavia.

In the case of Ulcinj, all the maps were full of fuzzy lines. At first, I
made formal inquiries—the polite American way—but I was in

Eastern Europe, not America, and travel, by some inverse logic, seemed to become more difficult the closer my destination was to Belgrade. I spent weeks trying to cultivate the idea of time and motion with people who used time as a measure of determining what was due to them.

"Ulcinj?" they said in Belgrade. "That is in Yugoslavia?"

"On the southern tip. Near Albania," I said.

"Ah," they said. "Albania," they said. "But there is nothing there."

"Not in Albania," I began. "Near Albania. Montenegro. An old sea port for slave trade. When the Turks . . ."

I stopped. Their eyes had clouded over. I had crossed invisible borders—not once but twice. At the mere mention of the Turks, Slavs automatically replayed the five-hundred-year-old Ottoman invasion. Everyone was willing to talk about the invasion, but no one wanted to talk about the Turks. And as for Albania, no one talked about that—period. Somewhere in the middle of all that silence was Ulcinj.

"The problem," Nada Obradovic said, "is simply this town that you wish to visit is in Montenegro."

"Yes," I said. "Montenegro. Crna Gora, the black mountain. Go tell it to the mountain. That be the place," I said in my best ghetto English.

Nada smiled brightly. "James Baldwin," she said. "Richard Wright, Langston Hughes, Gwendolyn Brooks."

This time, I returned her smile. Nada Obradovic was my translator, self-appointed before my arrival in Yugoslavia. I was flattered but disturbed that she'd bypassed all the copyright laws and provisions for intellectual property rights (a problem in many instances when a writer's work is translated without permission of the author). What it meant, simply, was that my work was being read in Eastern Europe, in towns where long names held two vowels and history was tied to men called Ivan the Terrible and Vlad the Impaler. And Nada, all apricot and peach and round as a plum, with a shock of red lipstick and bleached hair and nails like jeweled talons. At our first meeting, she had swooped me away from the male enclave of the Writer's Club on Avenue Vuk to her apartment several blocks away. That apartment more than equaled any dowager's flat on Park Avenue. French antiques, neoclassic Italian baubles, Victorian lamps, Austrian silver, Russian carpets, and an abundance of modern and expressionistic art walled between an overflow of books, floor to ceiling on some walls. One room alone held the works of African and Caribbean writers.

And all this in a country where nobody seemed to know how to get to Ulcinj.

"I will take you to visit primitive painters in Korvacja. I have some of their works here," Nada said, waving a plump arm toward a nest of paintings on the wall behind her. "These artists are very famous in Yugoslavia. But Ulcinj is of no importance. And Montenegro, never. We have heard nothing of the literary life of Montenegro which holds any importance." She leaned forward to pour the coffee, her eyes filling with anticipation of a literary discussion. "Montenegro is no place for you," she said. "You should be here or in Zagreb, where many people will read your work. I know here a publisher who is anxious to speak with you. Yes, Belgrade is full of those who would translate your work." She offered a plate of chocolates. I declined. "Ulcinj. Interesting place," Nada continued. "But no one goes there."

"Obviously someone has," I said.

Nada sniffed.

I decided to try my own route. After all, I had been in the country for several months. I would simply book passage on JAT. My American friends in Belgrade had dubbed the airline Not Yet, and over the months, I had slowly learned why they harbored complaints about Jugoslav Air Transport. I placed a certain faith in any airline, believing it would generally go where they said it would, believing its comings and goings were regular, almost ordinary occurrences. Based on that, I ignored my previous JAT experiences, bought a ticket to

Titograd, and triumphantly waved it in front of my doubting friends. Ulcinj, I told them, was now within my grasp.

"A ticket is easy," my friends said. "But the problem is finding the plane to go with it."

JAT lived up to its nickname. I lost count of how many times the departure was announced, how many times we were escorted to the gate only to find no plane, and how often I could walk from the newsstand to the lavatory and back without losing my seat in the waiting room. Six hours after the scheduled departure, we were finally in the air.

We landed at dusk when the sky was still cast in a pearlescent blue light. I was sitting in a window seat just forward of the wing, not a particularly safe seat, but given anyone's chances of surviving modern jet travel, as safe as any. From that vantage point, I could see a bus pulling away from the airport parking lot just as the plane descended. The bus wended its way down the spiraling road from the terminal and turned onto an access road. We bumped ground. The parking lot looked empty. I checked my watch and twisted in my seat. Surely those faint red taillights could not belong to the last bus to town. Forget that we were six hours late—even Balkan logic could allow some variation on schedules. I cursed JAT's inefficiency and for good measure glared at my seat partner, who had unbuckled his belt while we were still in the approach pattern, 10,000 feet off the ground. "Damn Slavic fatalism," I muttered. The plane swung toward a loading ramp, and I saw a set of stairs standing stark, like some dinosaur's spine, against the backdrop of the low slung terminal building. As we pulled closer, lights flickered off inside the terminal. One by one, the windows dimmed until there was only the yellow light over the entryway. For a second, the scene was too poetic: the taillights of a bus disappearing into the approaching darkness, stairs leading to nowhere, and now, the darkened terminal. Dreams of Ulcinj flickered with the lights.

"Your departure will be orderly," the cabin attendant said. Except that everything was already out of order with the terminal closing before the plane had landed and passengers plummeting into the aisle, frantically calling to each other and grabbing bags from the overhead bins as if we'd been ordered to life rafts right before some impending disaster. I rose from my seat with the sinking feeling the disaster might be mine. I reached for my bag. It was soaked with bad country wine leaking out of someone's poorly wrapped parcel. The canvas L.A. Gear pack would forever smell foul. I sighed. Yugoslavs looked at me with sympathetic eyes.

"We have three possible routes that might carry you to Ulcinj," the travel agent said. "The first route takes you from Titograd to Cetinje. And from Cetinje you proceed directly to Budva. From there, you might find a local bus to the town of Ulcinj or possibly a taxi. The second route takes you from Titograd directly to Petrovac. From there, of course, you might possibly hire a car. The third route takes you to Herceg-Novi, and you may catch the express bus to Petrovac, provided the bus to Herceg-Novi isn't full with passengers returning from Medjugorje. In which case, you may come back to Cetinje and proceed from there. But of course, you have arrived too late for this today."

She seemed really pleased with all of her "mights" and "possibles." I watched her trace the routes on a map, her red line jiggling through mountainous passes on the other side of Titograd. My heart jiggled along with it. I had already been on highways where the carcasses of cars were piled in cul-de-sacs like toys left to rust in the corner of some kid's room.

"We only put them there after the accident," a taxi driver had told me. "Then only to clear the road. Someone will take them away later." He'd shrugged when I'd asked him when, exactly, was later. But this was the same taxi driver who "saved on fuel" one night by turning off his headlights and coasting down the narrow road into the valley after discovering his gas gauge registered nearly empty.

"Tomorrow?" I asked the travel agent. "Can I go tomorrow?" She looked confused. "Do the buses run daily?" I asked.

Now her look was that of a kitten startled in the act of unwinding a ball of yarn. She gathered up all of the loose timetables scattered on the counter. "The buses south leave in the morning. The buses north leave in the evening. Unless you are leaving Titograd, then you may go north in the morning, provided you are going by express to Dubrovnik . . ."

"Can I purchase my bus tickets here?" I interrupted.

"I can only provide you with time schedules which reflect the arrivals and departures posted in each terminal."

Somewhere near Cetinje, I fell asleep, which was remarkable, considering how the motion of most Yugoslav buses seemed fixed on a sprung rhythm of bumpity-bump-hiccough. At least when I was asleep, I missed several dozen hairpin curves and villages the size of cowsheds. But I also missed my connection to Budva. I was awakened by a nudge from my seatmate and opened my bleary eyes wide enough to discover half the bus passengers had been staring at me while I slept—open mouthed, I was sure. What startled me all the more was that my seat partner was Japanese, and for one wild second, I thought I'd traveled back in time and was once again in Japan, lost and with no language referrents. I forced myself from the twilight of a strange dream, one in which I'd been dancing to the music of a crazed string quartet under a canopy of palm leaves and rotting coconuts. Several people were eating goat's cheese, which explained the rotting coconuts, and the squeaky bus cushions explained the strange music, but I no longer knew what country I was in, much less where I was. I scrambled to find words. What came out was retarded German mixed with some sort of otherworld-Serbian: "Uh, Da li je ist moj?" I sputtered.

My seat partner smiled. Then slowly, with perfect diction, he said, "I am American. Do you speak English?" I nodded vigorously to show I really did, when I could speak at all. "I hope I didn't startle you," he continued, "but you've been asleep for a long time, and I wanted to know if you'd be going with us to the shrine of the Virgin?"

"Un-uh. I'm going to Ulcinj," I said. He frowned. "Ulcinj," I repeated. "On the other side of Budva."

A woman in front repeated "Budva," and the word spread throughout the bus. "Budva, ne," the woman said. People nodded. Even Ken Matsu, my American seat partner, nodded. "Budva je put sudje," the woman said. The mole on her upper lip danced into a smile line.

What did she know, I thought. So I asked again. "Koji je put Budva?"

Everyone, as if by command of some invisible captain of the guard, pointed south toward the back window of the bus. Meanwhile, we were climbing north, away from Budva, away from the mountains of Crna Gora.

"We are going to Medjugorje to the shrine of the Holy Virgin Mary," Ken said. "Have you seen the Virgin?"

I shook my head. "I haven't even seen Ulcinj," I muttered.

As one village dragged into another, I began to realize it would take twice as long to double back to Cetinje as it would to continue north to Mostar. In Mostar, I might catch the express to Dubrovnik rather than be stuck in Budva or Petrovac overnight. Besides, if I stayed on the bus, I'd have a chance to see what was being called the Miracle of Medjugorje, and that beat an overnight in a one-horse town any day of the week. I was beginning to think like a Slavic tour agent. And worse, my decision had a slight drawback: I was stuck in Medjugorje. The Christians, especially those who'd been on missionary assignments in Africa, took turns trying to save me, and even as we pulled into Medjugorje—a dusty little village where four teenagers claimed to have seen the Virgin Mary—my fellow travelers seemed undaunted by my stubborn refusal to embrace their beliefs

"I am as fascinated by Biblical stories as you are," I said, "but these are teenagers, kids. Look, they keep saying Mary told them not to dance and watch television. You mean to tell me the Virgin Mary came all the way here to warn them away from the evils of television? Doesn't she have something better to do?"

"It was a sign for all of us," Ken Matsu said. "There are people here from all over the world. It is truly a holy place."

"Dusty, too," I said, and contemplated the sandy uphill trail to the site of the visitation. A hawker passed us selling maps, postcards, posters, souvenir statues, and bus tickets. I took a shuttle to the top of the hill.

The land rolled out like a worn carpet, patterns that had been worked and reworked by feudal rules, invasions, makeshift governments, and centuries of desperate peasants. It was a thought I frequently had in Europe, a feeling that the land was sagging under centuries of wars and constant change from ruler to ruler, language to language, and all the endless fighting that attempted to hold it still and in one piece. Europe was full of history, yes, but the burden was taking its toll. I only needed to look at the grim, unsmiling faces of people in Belgrade, or the forced joviality of Germans or the carefully constructed mannerisms of the French and Italians. Like the pilgrims at Medjugorje, they all wanted that divine tie with the gods, a reason to keep it all going. Perhaps that was the difference between the Old World and the new one: In the States, there was a clear-cut definition of the conquerors and the vanquished, the country's history so new, those lines were still connected by the blood of Indian tribes and African slaves. The ties to the land were simpler: possession, bare knuckled and may the best man win, provided we approve of who that man may be.

But looking out from that Medjugorje hillside, I could see that the ancient grudges were still there, rooted like those Inca markings I had seen on the Plains of Nazca in South America, fantastic animals of gigantic proportions, rising up the sheer walls of the cliff and carved ten feet deep into the bedrock of the plains—a strange code that had become a part of the soil, clearly visible from a distance but reduced to erosion cracks for anyone at ground level. Maybe I was too close to the ground at Medjugorje to see the big picture. Maybe

I was simply distracted by my own journey to understand why so many had come so far on the strength of a rumor to see hillsides that were brown and webbed as sepia photographs.

If I looked really hard, I could almost imagine the purple mountains of Montenegro in the distance, and somewhere well beyond them, but still elusive, Ulcinj. All I really saw was a checkerboard of small wheat fields and dairy farms, a few scattered farm houses, and the town itself, with its lone church and cobblestoned streets, lines of pilgrims trudging away from it like worker ants. The grainy soil was shallow, a fitting complement to the downcast eyes and lackluster sales pitch of some of the more enterprising townsfolk. There may have been only a handful of them, but they were vigorous, and at the top of the hill, they pressed their advantage by offering both audio- and videotapes of three thin children kneeling on the grassy slope, their faces turned in beatitude toward the sky. Those tapes were our only chance of seeing the children that day.

"Isn't it wonderful," a woman said as we boarded the evening bus to Dubrovnik. "I feel so privileged to get a chance to visit the place where the children saw our Blessed Lady."

"What children?" I asked. "I only saw souvenir vendors."

"Well, two of them are married and don't have visitations any longer," the woman whispered. Her tone was as confidential as an *Enquirer* columnist's. "The others are visited only on the weekends now."

"Weekends? How does the Virgin know it's OK on the weekends?" Silence. "There's a book on visions. I think it's called *Salem Revisited?*" I continued. "Those girls in Salem had visions too, you know. Different kind, but according to this book I read, it all has something to do with the way the wheat was stored. You know, a hallucinogen off the wheat germ. Mother Nature's LSD. That and puberty. All those hormones. Maybe that explains why the married ones don't get visions any more."

"I'm sure I don't know," the woman said, then pulled her lunch of bread and cheese from her rucksack of souvenirs and left me to my thoughts.

I told myself: McElroy, ease up. Each of us is chasing some spirit. Yours is just in Ulcinj.

It would be equally true to say I arrived in Ulcinj by way of Medjugorje as it would be to say I finally made it on the magic of a Turkish carpet. Indeed, the Turkish carpet came as a result of my visit to Dubrovnik, but the only magic was how one quick look at Medjugorje could send me scurrying off to Dubrovnik to recover from the pilgrimage. Dubrovnik was a wonder city, an Adriatic Disneyland of castles, seashore, and tourists, where the sound of laughter, so foreign to Belgrade, was often heard. After months of wandering through the gray smog of Serbia, where dimly lit restaurants promised no more than boiled meat, clumps of radishes, and conspiratorial conversations, Dubrovnik offered succulent scampi turned pink with spices, black risotto steamed in inky squid, roast lamb, rich red wine, Turkish coffee, and some of the best desserts south of Austria. All of it served under bright umbrellas in outdoor cafés pocketed, table against table, along narrow streets and cobblestoned stairwells in the old walled city, the Starigrad of Dubrovnik. There, even the waiters smiled, and the competition for customers was carried on in loud, friendly echoes throughout the little nooks of the castle walls. But the life of the city was not exclusively in the castle, shops, and public square of the Starigrad. Dubrovnik was blessed by sun, sea, mountain air, and an overflow of foreign visitors. Under its mantle of sunlight and medieval glitter, the city carried its past as some modern members of royalty assume their crowns—to be admired without all the bother of wearing them every day. Its cachet of urbanity welcomed me as no other town in Yugoslavia had.

Dubrovnik was no Medjugorje full of suffering children who lived through visions, nor did it mirror Belgrade's impolite ruffians who had stared and taunted me. I discovered that difference earlier in the spring when I'd gone to Dubrovnik to attend a meeting of the International Congress on Women. Almost every country in the world had been represented at the conference, including America, and luckily for me, several of the writers were black women, two of whom I knew. The day I saw Geneva Smitherman and Angelita Reyes walking up the stairs of the University Admissions building, old home week had come to Dubrovnik. We greeted each other as if we'd been lost in the desert and found an oasis. Geneva and Angelita, along with four other black American women, were presenting papers at the conference. That first day, we had lunch together. The word spread: Black women have come to Dubrovnik. Had there ever been so many, and American, in town at the same time? Tongues wagged, as the gossip columnists would have said. Eyes followed our progress down the street. Not that we made any effort to be inconspicuous. Rosalind Griffin, a psychologist from Chicago, had me help her interview several young men who sold their bodies to tourists from Western Europe. "Ask them if they have a union," she insisted. "And what about health insurance?" The young men tried to answer, but it was easy to see that they were more fascinated with having a conversation with black women than they were with the questions Rosalind proposed. That was the contrast of Yugoslavia: the religious visions of Medjugorje, the political shortsightedness of Belgrade, and the ease of Dubrovnik, a city that had attracted every tyrant since Attila the Hun because of its access to the sea. All those invasions had made Dubrovnik cosmopolitan, more open to the world outside of Yugoslavia. The best shopkeepers in Dubrovnik were Albanians. Geneva and I visited a rug merchant in the Starigrad who held us in conversation so long, we almost missed a dinner appointment with the other women.

We met at one of the outdoor cafés in the old city. There were five of us, and as we waited—too long it seemed, for waiters to notice us, I began to think that some of Belgrade's coldness had reached the coast. Ten minutes passed. Twenty. This would have been slow even in Belgrade. Finally, a waiter came over. In a Slavic dialect heavily accented in Serbian, he began asking about a purple book. The women looked at me. "What the hell is he talking about?" Geneva said. I had understood knjiga, the word for book, but little else. "I don't know what he's talking about," I said. The waiter grinned. "I speaking English," he said. "Who is writing the purple book?"

"Purple book?" Angelita repeated.

Then I understood. "He wants to know which one of us is Alice Walker," I said.

The women laughed. "Get out," Anita said. "We don't look like Alice."

"Well, think about it," I said. "There's the conference, and here are five black women in one place at the same time."

"That doesn't mean one of us is Alice," Geneva said.

The waiter held out a battered book. The title was *Ljubicasta Boja*. "Well, until he holds out a menu instead of that book, one of us had better be Alice," I said.

"No problem," Rosalind laughed. "You're the writer."

I signed the book: LJUBAV, ALICE, in scrawling letters. And let me tell you, that dinner was the best one I had in Dubrovnik.

Later, when I returned to Dubrovnik after my failed attempts to reach Ulcinj, I headed straight for Rafi, the rug merchant I'd met when I'd been with Geneva. The visit was old-fashioned, neither of us getting to the point until we'd had a bit of conversation. "Sit. Have a cup of tea. We will talk," Rafi said.

We talked about his collection of James Brown, and rock 'n' roll. "We have heard much of your music," he said.

I said, "Yeah. On my first day in Belgrade, I heard Terrance Trent D'Arby blaring out of a shop on Revolutionary Square. But I still had to go through six people before I could buy one grapefruit."

Rafi laughed. "But it is that way for everyone. Here in the state store, you have someone to select for you, someone to weigh for you, someone to price, someone to bag, and so on. Then everyone has work."

I looked around the shop. "You're the only one working here," I said.

"Yes, but you see, I have the work permit for selling to foreigners. Turkish rugs, Albanian rugs. I sell them all. It comes down through my family through the generations. That is what we have been doing for hundreds of years." He paused. "Where is your friend?" he asked, referring to Geneva.

"Gone home to the states," I told him.

"Pity," he said. "She never buys from me a rug." He shook his head.

I bought a rug. Then we talked about my perceptions of Yugoslavia. I bought a tapestry. Finally, the conversation moved to history. I bought several pieces of embroidery, and Rafi talked about Ulcinj. "I can get you there," he said. "I know many people in that town. A cousin of mine lives there."

I said nothing. I had once traveled with two Haitians who claimed every telegraph office in South America was manned by one of their cousins. And I once left a traveling companion on a lonely road in the middle of a country about to erupt into a civil war. He too was going to visit a cousin, although all I saw from the rear window of the bus was him standing in a swirl of dust and no houses for miles in any direction.

"How far from Ulcinj does your cousin live?" I asked.

"Oh, he lives no more than two kilometers from the center of the town," the rug merchant said. "It is easy to find his house."

"Good. So, how do I to get to Ulcinj?"

"That is not so easy," he sighed. "You must decide if you will travel by the bus or the boat. By the boat, you arrive six, seven o'clock, and next morning, you take the return boat. Or you may go by the plane or the train. Then you must take the bus. But I prefer the boat. Then you only need to take the taxi to my cousin's house."

Boat, bus, plane, train? There were too many memories of the bus to Medjugorje still fresh in my head, but in the end, I had no choice but to trust Raji's route and his cousin.

The beach at Ulcinj was anything but inviting. We entered at high tide under the shadow of the old medieval fortress. From a distance, all I saw was sharp rocks rising abruptly from the water into clumps of bushes that trembled under the force of the wind. Down the beach, there were thin patches of white sand among the rocks, but the day was overcast and blue sky was a distant dream from Dubrovnik. The air was sharp with the smell of salt and diesel fumes from passing fishing boats. Aside from myself, those few passengers who had come this far south from Rijeka, Split, or Dubrovnik were Germans and Swedes who seemed to relish the brisk air and swift current. Those on shore under the shadow of the fortress ruins, greeted us with the sour looks of people who had battled the weather all too often. Even in cloudy weather, the shadow of the fortress fell on everything, the skeletal shapes of Venetian, Turkish, and Slavic architecture looming like something left over from Mary Shelley's novel. At the end of the boat dock, I took a careful step, but land was elusive and the planks slippery with years of accumulated algae. My foot slipped, and the motion began to carry me back toward the sea when someone grabbed my hand. I looked up into the face of Rafi's cousin, and behind him, an older man whose features were so familiar, he could have been my own cousin, or uncle, or neighbor from any one of a dozen places in the States. And I knew I had finally reached Ulcinj.

What I remember most about Ulcinj was once there, time settled into place the way it does when I return home. Slobodan Tresic welcomed me into his house the way my mother's friends would welcome me home. His wife, shyer, never left the kitchen except to greet another neighbor come to see the "mala crna amerikanischa." Only the language was different, although after a while, no one really needed Rafi's cousin to translate for us. Neighbors dropped in to see the homesick wanderer, and like my relatives in the States, everyone brought food for the visitor. We ate. I ate far too much of everything. Some brought small gifts. Almost all brought children. Babies sat in my lap and looked big eyed and confused. Some fell asleep, their pale brown faces nestled in the crook of my neck. Others cried, burped all over my dress, and caused general distress for their mothers.

Young children played with my finger rings, measuring their smaller hands against my long thin ones, all the while haltingly counting the number—jedan, dva, tri . . . each time surprised that my fingers and their vocabulary ended on the same digit. Women showed me their family heirlooms and needlepoint. I showed them pictures of my children, my books, my home in America. I listened to old men tell stories that I only half understood, but their laughter told me enough to understand that only half was true, anyway. And when the stories turned to war and hunger, I heard about young people who had been killed and others who had moved away to better jobs or schools. And how the Germans had taken scores of men during the war. How the others had hidden in the hills. Who trusted the Yugoslavs or Albanians or Turks. And who counted back far enough to find home in Africa, where faces like mine, Rafi's cousin said, were locked in some family albums. And toward midnight, when all the children were curled inside sleep, the singing began. An old man played a violin. I remember a particularly sad song about the sea, and how it always tries to return to land, only to be pulled away again. I remember the voice of the old woman who sang it, her weathered face brown like the sturdy trees near the cliffside. Several days later at Ohrid, Yugoslavia, I had my morning coffee under a striped umbrella by the lake facing the distant shores of Albania. And I swear that woman's voice was singing still.

How not to Cross the Border

1964, the Mexican border. Nogales. It's hot, of course, and I've got all the windows open. The car still smells new, an overpowering smell despite dust billowing behind approaching traffic, and the inevitable odor of human sweat and fruit gone bad from all the cargo trucks. I'm sweating, but I'm wearing my coolest smile.

"¿Habla español?," the agent smiles back.

"¿Qué pasa?," I mutter.

"¿Dónde vive?," he says slowly, as if he suspects I'm slow witted. In a bad movie, he'd twist his mustache, and although I feel as if I'm in a bad movie, he merely looks at me impatiently. I wonder how early he had to report to work that morning. He looks tired. He looks exasperated.

"¿Dónde vive?" he repeats, articulating carefully.

"¿Adónde?" I answer, just as carefully.

He opens the door. "Get out of the car, señora."

That I can do. I lean against the car, a Caddie, powder blue. I'm wearing a dress and heels, sling pumps. Obviously I have no plans to run.

He walks around to the front of the car, checks out the Kansas license plates. He shakes his head. Great. Now he thinks I'm a K.C. gangster, a black woman in a pimp blue Caddie. He looks me over and I'm wearing just the outfit to confirm his suspicions: fuschia dress, tight around the hips, and three inch heels to match. Nails, long and lacquered red. My hair in the latest Kansas City curls. "What business do you have in Mexico?" he asks.

"I have no business in Mexico," I say. Little does he know, that's exactly what my mother had said when I left the kids with her. "You've got no business in Mexico. You oughta be here with these babies."

"What brings you to Mexico?"

"This car," I say.

Now he thinks I'm a smart ass. I want to correct myself, to say that I am delivering the car for someone else. I want to say that he's as scary as all the Southerners I saw working in gas stations when I was driving through Texas, places that kept the NO COLOREDS signs on the walls with the old license plates and posters for Dr. Pepper and Nehi Grape Soda. I want to say I don't know what possessed me to drive to Mexico in the first place except a free trip away from Kansas City and Swift's Packing House, a getaway from a job where my patients were more likely to fly to the moon than recover language functions. I want to say that I drove down with Shirley. She's in the next lane over, black Caddie. We're both divorced, and it's a vacation. "A chance to get out of Kansas City," I'd told my mother. "It will do us good." I want to say this to the agent, but before I can figure out how to put any of it into words that will help me slide across the border, he says, "Papers, please."

I stop myself from answering, "I don't got to show you no steenk-ing pay-pers," but the agent is not Alphonso Bedoya and I'm not Leo G. Carroll and this is not a movie, despite the locked trunk that has kept the Caddie riding low all the way from Kansas. I show him what papers I have.

He looks at my driver's license and at the car registration. "This car does not belong to you?"

"No, my car is at home. I'm delivering . . ."

"Open the trunk, señora."

I gulp. "I don't have a key to the trunk," I say. Did he actually unbuckle his holster? I want to throw up my hands, scream: *Don't shoot!* and surrender immediately. "She has the key," I say quickly. I point to the car one lane over, where Shirley stands, sunlight beaming down on all of her six-foot blondeness.

He eyeballs her Cadillac. Same model, different color. "Señora, I would like you to open this car. The car you are driving."

I stare across at Shirley. She smiles and waves. The agent she is talking to looks in my direction. He is not smiling. "Ask her for the keys," I say. "I don't know nothing."

"This also is the car of the blonde señora?" he asks.

This is getting really bad, I think. "No, her brother's. When we finally deliver it."

"And where is the brother of the señora?"

Really bad. "I don't know," I say.

He's resting his hand on his gun. "Señora, please pull the car into the waiting area. Go into the office. Leave the keys in the car."

I step back into the Caddie, gentle it into a parking slip in the neutral zone between the u.s. and Mexico. As I get out of the car and head up the stairs into the customs office, Shirley waves at me again. But I am gallows-bound and have no friends. Two hours later, I am convinced that I will become the Woman Without a Country. Twice they've come in, asked me my name and Kansas City address, my place of employment, and marital status. But then suddenly, it is over.

"You may leave, señora. Your friend she is waiting."

At first, I think he must be talking to someone else, except I am the only one in the room. I have been the only one in the room for two hours. I almost trip at the door. Without chicken wire covering a window, the sunlight is bright, almost surgical. Shirley is wearing sunglasses. I put on my sunglasses. We drive to Nogales and I sulk all the way to the hotel. She chatters as if we're heading home from a shopping trip at the mall. Her brother now has the car, she tells me. "Next time, he can drive his own damn car," I tell her. "Was the trunk still locked?" I ask. She doesn't answer. I never see the blue Caddie again.

Blaine, Washington, five years later. I've crossed this border a hundred times or more. "How long do you plan on staying in Canada?" the agent drawls. I wonder what joker has sent this southern transplant to the Canadian border. All he needs are reflector glasses to complete the picture. On the other hand, all we need are love beads and incense to make us full-fledged hippies. I figure that means we're already in trouble.

"How far is New Wes?" Don asks.

"About half an hour," I remind him.

"About an hour," Don tells the agent.

The agent leans over and looks into the car. He doesn't say anything, just pokes his head in the window and takes a look-see. Don's wearing a fringed suede vest and jeans. He has just left a theater rehearsal and there are traces of stage makeup near his ears, but it's too late to tell him to wipe off the stuff. I'm wearing bell bottoms and a halter top, my midriff bare. I pat my Afro into shape in case there are dents in it. Don reaches over and turns off the radio. He pats my arm. I give his hand a squeeze—my black hand over his white. The agent raises his eyebrows. He sees we're both wearing wedding rings. "You two married?" he asks.

"To each other?" Don laughs. I laugh, too.

I think of my husband, off flying planes somewhere near the Arctic Circle. And Don's wife at home, bossing their two kids, who are smart enough to be inventing weapons that will blow us all to Kingdom Come. Fortunately, Don is trying to keep them interested in theater, a safe, penniless career. I'm hoping some of his enthusiasm will rub off on my kids, although my daughter is the only one who has taken the bait so far. That is, if you don't count me: I hang around Don because he is in theater and I'm willing to beg my way onto the stage. We're simpatico, but married—no.

"Are you married?" the agent repeats.

Don says "No" and I say "Yes." Don says "Yes" and I say "No." The agent says, "Step out of the car."

Obediently, we open the doors.

"Let me see your driver's license," the agent says.

"For this I had to get out of the car," Don says.

I kick him. It's not the time to be a comedian. With all the Vietnam war objectors heading across the border, it's not the time to be anything but a u.s. resident on a couple of hours of R & R, unless you have reason to be running. And if we were running, we'd have our act together better than this.

"You have a driver's license, too?" the agent snarls, except it sounds as if he's asking for my criminal record.

I'm almost tempted to flash my television press pass, but all we want to do is buy a couple of bottles of Canadian Fifth and some Indian smoked fish in New Westminister to take to the cast party tomorrow night. So I'm not ready to make a federal case out of it. Yet. I hand over my license.

"You don't have the same last name," he says.

We both say: "No." Don winks at me.

"But you're wearing wedding rings."

We both say: "Yes."

"Open the trunk," he says.

Don begins waving his hands, talking fast. His speech is eloquent. I don't know if he's doing Hamlet or Puck, but it's something Shakespearean. The agent stares as if Don has just lost his mind. I can't tell if he's listening or wondering how long it will take to subdue this Looney Tunes and handcuff him. I'm wondering why Don doesn't just open the trunk. Instead, he's describing the theater, the art of making drama, of making an audience believe they're somewhere else instead of in a room, in the dark, with a lot of strangers. It's not a bad explanation, fit for a beginning drama class at the college where we both teach, but Don's doing this for the benefit of an overweight customs agent whose uniform shirt barely buttons up.

"What are you trying to tell me?" the agent says.

"Yeah. Just open the trunk," I say.

Don glowers at me. "Look, you don't want me to open the trunk," he whispers in a voice that's like Iago plotting Othello's downfall.

The agent whispers right back. "Open the trunk." There's doom in every word. I decide the agent is definitely doing Hamlet.

Don shrugs and takes the key from the ignition. "Don't say I didn't warn you," he announces, and clicks open the trunk.

At first, all I can see are naked bodies, fleshy pink arms and legs jumbled in every direction. Three arms going one way, four in another. A leg missing a foot. A foot coming out of the pile at an impossible angle. The agent groans. What must he be thinking: the gruesome remains of mass murder? A storehouse of body parts? A gull screams and passes overhead. The wind whispers in the evergreens, then flees toward Birch Bay. I have nowhere to go. Then I notice a head, the eyes staring and blank. Mannequins!

"You're crossing the border with stage props?" I ask. My eyes are stuck open as wide as the mannequin's.

Don grins, playing Puck again.

"If you have an explanation for this, I don't want to hear it," the agent says.

He makes us unload the trunk, but after a few hollow left arms and a foot or two, he's had enough. "Next time," he says, "take that crap out of your car before you get here."

"There's a man who doesn't appreciate theater," Don says, as we drive toward New Westminister.

"And you're the master of understatement," I say.

I had decided to take three days from the steel mill grayness of Belgrade and head for Budapest. "Budapest," they told me, "is beautiful like Paris." That's all the incentive I'd needed to battle the red tape of making train reservations. "You can fly," they said. But Air JAT was my last resort. I figured I'd rather spend my waiting time on the train than hanging around an airport watching the departure schedule change with every half hour of delay. JAT had been six hours late on my last flight out. Sitting on a train had to be better than that. There was one little thing about trains that I had forgotten, but I was working so hard to put Belgrade behind me, I wasn't thinking about how a train was made up of many cars hooked one to another. I just found a car that had a sign for Budapest and hoped the train was as strong as the one in that children's book, *The Little Engine That Could*.

It was an old train—wood panelled compartments with two cushioned benches facing each other behind sliding doors. Not the Orient Express, but a reasonable facsimile. My compartment filled and emptied, filled and emptied, as we crept toward the Hungarian border. And *crept* is the word. That train was slower than the milk run on the Baltimore & Ohio. Each time we stopped at a town, the conductor asked for my ticket. I showed him the same ticket he'd punched before we left Belgrade. He just reread it and handed it back, but at least his intrusion broke the monotony. I couldn't fall into my usual airplane pattern of sleeping and reading, letting someone else make the decision for getting me where I was going. Each time, I asked the conductor if I was on the right train to Budapest. And each time, he'd nod yes and point toward the front of the train, which indeed was heading in the direction of Budapest.

I spent the next six hours estimating the ages of my traveling companions—working-class men in faded brown pants and flat-brimmed caps who got on at villages with names that had very few vowels and left the train at other villages with similiar names. And stocky country women with string bags full of produce and baguettes, their faces flatly curious as they inspected me, inch by inch, between one stop and the next. And the students, with their worn leather book bags and equally worn blunt-toed shoes. They stared at me. I stared at them. Each time they entered the car, the compartment was filled with the foul air of smoke from the engine and the raw tobacco of Yugoslav cigarettes.

At each stop, the train would burp, roll forward, hiccough, and jerk into gear, but never gain any real speed. This seemed to suit the pace of the countryside, the farms seemingly as tired and dissipated as the people who boarded the train. It was a train of the dull, a train of plodders and stoics who seemed unable to recognize the passing of time. I tried to understand how they'd come to accept this snail's pace of travel, the tedium of slow. I became so involved in thinking of them as characters, I didn't realize how far we'd gone until I heard someone say, "Hungary."

I looked out the window. The train wasn't moving. At least, the part I was on wasn't moving. Along the curve of the tracks ahead, I could see the engine and a line of cars creeping north. At first, I didn't quite understand that the train had split into two sections. I leaned out the window. "Hungary," my seat companion said again, and pointed in that direction. That's when I remembered that the conductor for once had not checked my ticket.

"Budapest?" I asked, and pointed toward the moving cars. Everyone nodded. "Da, da," they said in chorus. I grabbed my bag and scrambled for the corridor.

The conductor was standing on the platform not far from the exit door. I jumped off the train and walked over to him. "Why do you get off the train?" he asked. I answered him in my best Fulbright language class Serbian. "Is this train going to Budapest?"

He bobbed his head up and down like one of those birds people stick in the back windows of their cars. "Budapest," he said, and pointed toward the moving section of the train.

"My ticket is for Budapest," I said, waving the ticket under his nose, the same ticket he'd checked at every station except this one. He grinned and pointed to the northbound section of the train again. My Serbian fled and I resorted to basic English. "Shit! Why didn't you tell me I was supposed to be on that part of the train?" He grinned again. This butthead understands English, I thought. I pointed to the car behind me. Several people were hanging out the windows, watching us. "So where the hell is this train going?"

"Belgrade," he grinned.

"I just came from Belgrade," I yelled. "I want to go to Budapest."

"Da. You must take the bus," he said in perfect English, then pointed to a dilapidated bus sitting at the train crossing—on the Yugoslav side.

"I don't want to take the bus," I said. "I have a ticket for the train."

I pointed to the northbound train that had now come to a stop on the other side of the railroad crossing on the Hungarian side. He pointed to the bus. By this time, we looked like traffic cops giving directions to invisible vehicles. Several people on the northbound train were also hanging out the window watching us. They waved to me. I pointed to the conductor.

"The train is now in Hungary," he said, pointing to what I imagined was the borderline between Yugoslavia and Hungary. "Now you must take the bus."

"When does the bus leave?" I asked.

"In three hours," he said.

"I'm not waiting three hours for a damn bus. I have a train ticket," I said, waving my limp passage to Budapest for all to see. The folks on the Budapest train cheered. The folks on the Yugoslav train sucked their teeth.

"I'm catching my train," I said, and picked up my luggage.

"You cannot just walk across the border," the conductor said.

He pointed to the Hungarian side, where two border guards were moving slowly to the train crossing. Now the windows of the train into Hungary were filled with people, mostly men, giving me directions in languages I couldn't understand and gesturing for me to hurry. The engine was hiccoughing again, and from the looks of the smoke, it had every intention of moving away—to Budapest.

"I'm outta here," I said, and brushed past the conductor.

He said something in Serbian that I couldn't understand. How could I when folks were yelling: Dama! Dama! Fraülein! Mädchen! beckoning me to walk faster.

The engine belched. I walked faster. Behind me, the conductor yelled what sounded distinctly like an obscenity, but I'd been numbed by comments like that from men loitering in downtown Belgrade. Yugoslav men had leering down to a fine art. He'd have to do better to keep me off that train. The two border guards watched my progress. They had combat weapons slung over their shoulders, guns that seemed as compact as a woman's purse but steel gray and evil-looking. If one goes for his gun, I'm a dead woman, I thought. I walked faster so that I'd fall on the Hungarian side if I got hit. Folks were waving to me, gesturing with bottles of wine and loaves of bread. Whatever happened, it would beat the sullen looks I'd caught on the Belgrade train.

"Halt," one of the guards said.

He couldn't have been more than eighteen or nineteen, and although a teenager with an automatic weapon was scarier than anything I could think of, his order to halt wasn't very commanding. He didn't move from where he was standing and he didn't unshoulder his gun. I waved my ticket. "Don't start with me," I said.

I reached the train. A hand reached out and grabbed me. Another took my suitcase. They pulled me onto the train just as it started moving again. Even the folks on the Yugoslav side cheered. Finally, I was on my way to Budapest. Without so much as "Hello," I was hustled into a compartment and handed a glass of country wine and a hunk of bread with onions. With gestures and laughter and a lot of misunderstanding of languages, I learned that my rescuers were from Greece—kicked out of their homeland because of their political leanings. They were immigrating to Hungary to be with their comrades. I'd been saved at the border by Greeks bearing gifts.

Thirty-five thousand feet over Tahiti and the toilets begin to fail, one by one, like a string of Christmas tree lights going out. First the rear coach cabin, then the middle, then forward, business, first class, and bingo—the whole plane is in the soup. "I should have flown United," my seat partner, a man from Boston complains. Kids, sensing the danger, need to go potty every ten minutes now. They clog up the remaining reservoir with toilet tissue. "When are we going to land this shithouse?" a voice from the back yells. Everyone grows surly. None of us look at the extra movie, thrown in free to calm the folks in coach. It doesn't work, but the cabin attendants tell us they're ready to try anything. "Hang your ass out the window," the voice in back suggests. We land, finally, in Vancouver, B.C., but only the cabin crew can disembark. The passengers have no entry visas for Canada and the plane is British Air, so red tape requires a change of crew for entry into U.S. airspace. "What? Are they still mad about that tea party?" the man from Boston asks. The new crew comes on board to find three hundred-plus passengers ready to mutiny. Even a promise of free bottles of champagne don't help. "Stuff it, guv," the voice from the back yells. We drag our tails to Seattle. We're late and smelly and ready to kill wild bears. When the doors open, we all run for the toilets. The guys at customs shake their heads.

1991. The flight from Malaysia seems endless, but after lunch, when the second movie ends—something senseless that never made it into the theaters—the flight pattern appears on the screen. The radar image of our plane darts into position like a dancer caught in a disco strobe light, one movement slightly out of synch with the next. The screen shows the sameness of the ocean and little specks that I assume to be land, but from 40,000 feet, they could be the shadows of Capt. Nemo's submarine. The plane's image moves forward, then back, losing ground as the map shifts to coincide with our position. Something ought to stay the same, I think. The map or the plane, I don't care which one. The artificial image dances in scheduled intervals. I squirm in my seat, business class, thanks to Steve. My motto: *The travel agent is your friend.* I ask for another mineral water, my fifth. It arrives in a real glass. The cabin attendant is all smiles. I toast her and Steve. The map is magnified on a scale of one. The radar image falls back a hundred miles or so. That's how it goes. The map gets bigger and we lose ground while moving forward.

"We need a tail wind," the cabin attendant says. The businessman in the window seat recounts a journey when the pilot outmanuevered the weather. The radar map shows that we are inches away from the American coast. Translated, that means several more hours. At the very edge of the screen, the Pacific Northwest is beginning to take shape. I've been away for nearly a month and begin to think about home, that touch of nostalgia I get when I'm returning. I must admit, my nostalgia is low key. I have been on flights heading for Yugoslavia or Fiji when half the passengers began singing the national anthem of their homeland as the planes entered the airspace of those countries. It's hard to imagine Americans doing the same except at a baseball game. But as the plane carries me closer to the Pacific Northwest, I am filled with the thoughts of my family and my friends, people who are there when I call. In the air, everyone at home is a friend, and all I want to see are the snow capped mountains and glittering lakes bordered in lush green. The view from my living room window. That's my dream postcard of home. As we pass over the Olympics, I salute the view.

Then it's reality. Baggage claim and customs check. I'm unloading one of my three bags off the carousel when an agent approaches. "Is this your bag?" she asks.

I'm tempted to drop all twenty pounds of it on her feet, but instead I mutter, "Yes. And I see the other one coming."

"May I see your ticket and passport?" she asks.

Maybe she didn't hear me say my other bag was in view, I think. I lean forward to snag it off the carousel.

"Your ticket, passport, and customs declaration," she insists.

This time, I do drop the bag. It misses her feet by inches, but she gets the sentiment. Her eyes narrow. I hand her my papers and a wicked little smile. Around me, passengers from three international flights are scrambling for their luggage. I see the Christian group from Ohio off the same flight as mine. They look so clean—I wonder if they took baths in the aisles while I was strapped in my seat, sipping glasses of mineral water. No one is asking them for papers. In fact, the agents are only questioning the fringe element: people of color, women traveling alone, guys in Birkenstocks. I'm always questioned at customs, even when I'm traveling with someone. There was the time I came home from Mexico with Johnnella. We were the only two black women professors on the plane. They waved her through, but detained me with endless questions, even demanding the credit cards I'd used to purchase my ticket. "You keep that passport too busy," Johnnella said. "It looks suspicious." I wondered, then, why they gave me one with so many blank pages if they didn't want me to fill it. On another trip, my lover—bearded, burly, and dressed in a leather motorcycle jacket—whisked through while I was asked to open every bag. I think maybe it's simply my face, an expression that gives away my intolerance for petty bureaucracy. Whatever it is, I know I'll be questioned. This trip is no exception.

"How did you pay for this ticket?" the agent asks.

"I beg your pardon?" I answer. Wrong move. Her eyes grow narrower still.

"Are you employed?"

"I'm a professor," I say. "I've been on a lecture tour for USIA." I pull out my faculty ID card, my driver's license, my letter of introduction from USIA to contacts in Malaysia and Thailand.

She looks skeptical, but she hands back the documents and waves me on. I load my luggage cart and get in the U.S. citizens' line. The agent's delay has thrown me at the end of a line behind at least one hundred people, but the other lines are even longer. Ten minutes later, I've moved a foot. Another agent approaches.

"May I see your passport, please?"

I wonder why she hasn't asked for my ticket. I look over her shoulder. The first agent is watching us. I point to the second agent and shrug. The first one turns away as if she hasn't seen me.

"What was your business on this trip, and how did you pay for this ticket?" the agent asks.

I am getting testy, but I know the spiel. "I'm a professor," I say. "I've been on a lecture tour for USIA." I pull out my faculty ID card, my driver's license, my letter of introduction from USIA to contacts in Malaysia and Thailand.

"Do you have any other proof of employment?"

I pause. Twenty years at the university, and no one has ever asked to see my contract. "I don't generally take my contract with me," I say.

"Perhaps you should."

"Why? Don't I look like a professor?"

The agent hands back my documents and walks away.

By this time, the line is moving faster. The Christians from Ohio are whisked through with no questions. The agent inspects each page of my passport. A nuisance, since I've had pages added to accommodate an array of visas after ten years of travel, the life of one passport.

"Where do you live?" the agent asks.

"Seattle," I say.

"Do you have anyone to vouch for you?"

"Not in this line," I say. I hand him my faculty ID card, my driver's license, my letter of introduction from USIA to contacts in Malaysia and Thailand. He doesn't even bother to look at them. He merely slams down the entry stamp, folds my passport, and hands everything back to me. "Don't you ever stay home?" he asks.

Not if you'll be here, I think. I smile and keep moving.

I'm in baggage clearance. This agent is a black woman, but I can see that sisterhood died when she put on that customs officer's uniform. I hand her my papers before she can finish asking for them.

"Open the suitcase," she says.

"Which one?" I ask.

"All of them. Including your handbag and briefcase."

I watch the Christians laughingly skip toward the exit doors. In the next bay, an Asian woman with three kids is trying to open suitcases and juggle the baby, who's crying. Beyond her, a blond kid in a pony tail is untying one of the biggest duffel bags I've ever seen. Welcome to the fringe, I think. I sigh and begin opening bags.

"Can't you move any faster," she asks.

"It's a combination lock," I say. "That way, I don't have to worry about losing the key." I laugh. She doesn't.

She pokes and prods and lifts. But when she picks up a book and sniffs it, my patience breaks. "What are you looking for?" I ask. I try straightening out the mess she's made so I can at least close the suitcase without shredding my clothes. This move irritates her. She motions with her hand and another agent appears. The other agent takes my ticket and passport.

"Come with me," she says.

"What for?" I ask.

"We need to ask you some questions."

"Ask them here," I say.

"Don't make a scene," they say. One unbuttons her holster.

"Damn," I say, and begin closing my suitcase. The black agent reaches over and starts stuffing things inside. "You damage it, you pay for it," I warn. She withdraws her hand. I make sure everything is secured, put it all back on the luggage cart, and follow the agent with the unbuckled holster. The passengers waiting in line begin to murmur. I can almost hear them say: *Illegal.* But the only thing that is illegal is the thought I'm having about separating customs agents from the shelter of their jobs.

I'm escorted into a room. "I'll be right back," the gun-toting agent declares. My patience is oozing away fast.

A second later, she enters with another woman. "We need to search you," the agent says. "I want you to see that I have a gun and to know that this search is legal." The second woman nods.

Now, I'm pissed. I may have acquiesced thirty years ago, but meanwhile I've crossed too many borders to be jerked around without reason—and in the u.s. This is my hometown, I think. Not Turkey or Czechoslovakia, where lint on your collar can get you stripped. And I swore it wouldn't happen again after being strip-searched in Berlin when I was playing hookey with Wilma Hessel back in the fifties. "I'm American," I say, "and you don't search me without my lawyer."

"We can leave you here," the agent says.

"As long as you don't put me on a plane or anything else that's moving, I don't care. What are you looking for anyway."

"We have a right to search you," she says.

"You have a right to ask me," I say. "And my answer is: not without my lawyer. I believe I get a phone call."

"If you have nothing to hide, you won't mind being searched."

I've gone from pissed to enraged. "What do you mean, nothing to hide? I just came out of a country that has a big sign over the door in customs that says POSSESSION OF DRUGS IS PUNISHABLE BY DEATH. Now why would I risk death in Malaysia to give you a chance to search me in Seattle?"

"Are you refusing to let us search you?"

"Not until I'm advised by my lawyer."

"Did you go to Vietnam?" she asks.

I try to hand her my USIA letter. She refuses it.

"Have you ever been to Vietnam?"

"Do I look like Jane Fonda?"

"Take off your shoes, please."

"What?"

"Your shoes. I want to see the soles of your feet."

I flip off my shoes, snatch off my socks, and stick my feet as close to her nose as I can.

"Why didn't you search all those Christians?" I say "They're probably bringing in contraband Bibles."

"This is serious," she says.

"This is outrageous!" I say. I realize I'm getting loud when I see her hand move toward her holster. But that doesn't stop me. False courage. I've stared down eighteen year olds with automatic weapons. I'm just about to throw a St. Louis hissy fit when the door opens. A man walks in. The women slip out of the room as if they have never been there. So much for that big old gun, I think. The man nods at me. I don't nod back. SUPERVISOR, his tag says. He smiles, then hands me my passport. "I hope we haven't caused you too much delay," he says. I guess he doesn't see the flecks of anger foaming at the corners of my mouth. "Welcome home," he says.

Island Hopping: Fiji and the Dragon Caves

Let me set one thing straight: the ferry boatman at Toberua in the Fiji Islands did not work the underground lake that is nestled inside the Dragon Caves of Majorca. That boatman only knew the waterways between Toberua and Suva. In my memory, I simply collapsed geography to suit my own ends, the same way the early mapmakers centered Europe, drew it larger than the African continent, and moved Egypt into the Middle East. (Quite a continental drift, if you think about it. But the strangest map of the world that I've seen is the Shobunsha's guide for Japan where Europe all but disappears and Anchorage is slam-bang against the Texas Panhandle.) For me, it was reasonable to make a direct connection between the Fijians, who look like the descendants of Africans, and the Moors of North Africa, who rendezvoused in the caves on the island of Majorca. Not that I saw any Moors in Majorca, but I found many look-alike brothers and sisters in Fiji, their righteous Afros putting the brothers back home to shame.

Over the centuries, the Fijians have fared a bit better than the Moors. For one thing, they're still called Fijians. (Seen any news flashes about a Moorish detente lately?) For another, the Fiji Islands are off the beaten path. On the other hand, the Moors were messing around in major sea lanes between the Spanish coast and North Africa when things heated up for them (so to speak). Fiji hangs out there by itself, just waiting to be taken, or so many people have thought. The Japanese tried for years, but it is rumored that during World War II, when Japanese soldiers found themselves cut off from the rest of the troops, they would sooner surrender to the Allies than be taken prisoners by the Fijians.

On the other side of the world (and a few centuries earlier), the Spaniards gave the Moors a hard way to go and a short time to get there. The Moors might have been better sailors in their lateen-rigged ships, but they hadn't figured on Spanish vindictiveness. (These are the folks who brought us the Inquisition, remember?) The Spaniards simply dogged their attackers across the Mediterranean, and at one point in history, wiped out the invaders by pouring hot tar into the caves on Majorca where the Moors were hiding.

The way I remember it, I chose Majorca because it had one of those names that sounded like someone lazily plucking the strings of a flamenco guitar. (These days, if you ask P., he might have another story, but that's how it is when lovers are no longer lovers.) I dreamed of paella and gauchos and star-studded beaches. "We're going to Majorca," I said. "Off the coast of Spain. Just hang a left from Cote d'Or and look for the nearest flamenco bar. You'll find us."

P. said, "We're going to the Balearic Islands. An interesting place because it has both Spanish and African influences. Lots of color," he said, "and sunshine." I thought: leave it to a fiction writer to ferret out details. Not that I objected. Influence was good as long as it had bright sunny beaches and plenty of paella.

When we landed, a bit dazed and out of sorts as always after a long plane trip, P. maneuvered the rental car onto the main road through the city of Palma. It was night; the road was narrow, unlit, and we weren't getting a lot of help from the map (as always, made by some folks passing through, since locals knew where they were and how to get there). I left the driving to P., who had the patience for stick shifts and traffic that fit the wrong side of the road. As we drove through Palma, I concentrated on the obvious landmarks, at one point catching a glimpse of Majorca's prize bit of real estate, Bellver Castle, bathed in spotlights like a monarch or a saint. Then we plunged back into corkscrew turns and narrow streets before reaching the beachfront road to Illetas and our hotel.

We slept late and rose to the sound of Germans romping in the pool. That's one of the enigmas of seaside hotels the world over: While the ocean beckons on one side of a line of palm trees edging the beach, on the other side the pool glitters chlorine-blue. In Majorca, despite the invitation of the Mediterranean, hotel pools were standard along the coast. That was great for people who were afraid of deep water. (I have dozens of pictures taken before the eighties where I'm posed coming out of the ocean as if I've been swimming, but if you look really close, you'll see that my ankles aren't even wet.) The pool, with its designated depths, offered some comfort to aquaphobics like me who were nervous about the endless ocean, but from my vantage point on the balcony, the pool looked as dangerous as the glittering water on the other side of the trees. "Fraülein! Fraülein! Kommen Sie. Kommen Sie," the Germans shouted as I stared into what I believed was my greatest nightmare: death by drowning.

Understand, when I was growing up in segregated St. Louis in the fifties, inner-city ghettos didn't have pools, and black folks didn't yet live in suburban ghettos with community pools. The closest thing we had to a pool was when we played in water from the fire hydrants in the summer or when the gutters backed up after one of those midwestern downpours. (As a child, I was terrified of the whirlpools that churned in front of the huge storm sewers that always filled with water after the rains.) Besides, I'd already tried drowning twice—once at Girl Scout camp, then at the Y. Down I went, once, like a rock, and never came up, so don't let anyone tell you I was trying to swim. I was an aquaphobic, confirmed and certified. (I couldn't even hold my face under the shower.) But with the chance of island hopping on the horizon, I figured I'd better get acquainted with water. So at the age of forty-five, I'd enrolled in a Seattle adult swim class for aquaphobics. That first night, I'd walked around the rim of the pool and recalled my life story. The instructor had said, "McElroy, next time we'll have to get wet." I almost didn't go back. But I stuck it out and by the time P. and I went to Majorca, I was ready to master the float.

I waited until the dinner hour, and while the Germans were chowing down in the dining room, P. would come with me to the empty pool. I had it all to myself—competition length with a fifteen-foot depth at one end, deck chairs neatly arranged with their little cocktail tables beside them. The chairs were tempting, but I stepped into the pool instead—the shallow end. And there I stayed. P. swam several laps while I stood in waist-deep water, letting my body get used to the idea. (I swear, that water was saying: *Gotcha! Gotcha!*). Palm trees rustled against the starlit sky, and the Germans murmured behind the plate glass of the dining room. P. would swim over, wink, and swim away. It was good to know he was there. I remembered my instructor saying, "Trust the water to hold you up," so finally, I gripped the side of the pool and let my legs float to the surface. Then, head tilted back, I'd see how many stars I could count before I panicked and lost my balance.

It was nearly a week before I could let go of the pool wall and float on my own. Under the smell of the sea and the ever-present aroma of orange and lemon blossoms, I drifted beneath the Mediterranean sky. That night, the Germans cheered me on, their voices muted by the glass.

Two years later, I was scuba diving in the ocean off the Fiji Islands. In the time between Majorca and Fiji, I'd tried my first dive in Hawaii. (Thirty feet down and I couldn't swim a lick. But all you need in the water world of the deep are fins and an oxygen tank.) Fiji was water country, dozens of islands strung out in the Pacific at the edge of the Coral Sea. Each day (with the tide), the beach appeared and disappeared. Some of the smaller islands that were our diving launches disappeared entirely with the tide. But I was ready. After graduating to deep water, I had discovered that through the miracle of scuba gear, I could keep my landbound lungs in operation. (*Control your pulse. Breathe. Breathe,* my diving instructor had said.)

Without my instructor, I was still timid as we descended into the blue ocean of turtles, sea snakes, coral, and fish. Ten feet, twenty feet, and I gave up my references to the sun, its light nothing more than an inverted spot in the blue rush of water above me. When I followed a line of brightly colored fish, I even lost reference to which way was up in the excitement of discovery. The direction of the air bubbles from my snorkle was my only clue to the horizon, but for nearly an hour while I traveled in that sea world, the horizon didn't matter. I cruised the edges of coral castles, diving down and circling, checking out the paths of golden fish or blue ones or reds.

My attention was caught by eels and octopi, by clams disguised as coral and coral imitating rocks. I hovered at the edge of sea grass swaying like lost hula skirts and watched turtles swim among cuttlefish, while monkfish as big as one hundred pounds darted out of sight at warp speed. P. spotted a reef shark. The diving instructor in Hawaii had told the class that flipping a shark on its back would make it go limp. (Of course, he'd lost an arm to a shark. Never trust a one-armed diver to tell you how to handle a shark.) I watched the reef shark glide out of sight and wondered again why anyone would try flipping one. (Ten years later in Belize, I landed a fifty-pound nurse shark at the end of my fishing line. I battled that shark for nearly fifteen minutes. It spun, twirled, flipped, but didn't once go limp. On deck, it snorted like a poor muzzled dog until I took out the hook and let it go home.) In the Coral Sea, P. tried taking photos with an underwater camera. I tried feeding the fish to get them closer as he focused. Bright yellow butterfly and angel fish billowed around my legs until it looked as if I were wearing a ballroom skirt. It was better than dancing at the prom. In the water, the world was all fins and flutters and the magic of light. Kini, our Fijian guide, had to coax us to the surface. As I climbed back into the boat, I realized how far I'd come since that chlorine-filled pool in Majorca.

The flight from Seattle to Fiji is thirteen and a half hours, but after you leave the plane, you must give your body to water. When P. and I arrived, we went to Nakelo Landing, where we hitched a river taxi heading east of Suva and the Coral Sea. We were all at sixes and sevens, or nines and tens—whatever numbers best describe the feeling when there are parts of you still humming along at 30,000 feet while your body has found ground level. We arrived at the tiny isle of Toberua around teatime. (Teatime because Fiji has a reluctant shoulder-rubbing acquaintance with Australia.) Toberua was thumbnail size: palm trees, thatch covered huts or bures, and all the coconuts we could eat. Each meal was exquisite: fish baked in palm leaves, coconut rice and yams, mango purees and pastas. (Italians are also in Fiji.) But regardless of whether the food was Italian or Australian, there was always the flavor of Fiji. Flowers adorned everything—orchids and camellias on the plates, the glasses, the beds, the wash basins—and tropical breezes to bathe it all in the charm of the South Seas.

In Majorca, the food was no-nonsense Spanish. At the resorts, I watched ladies drinking pink Campari in tall thin glasses. (That stuff might have been pretty, but it tasted like mouthwash gone bad.) The tapas made up the difference—grilled lamb with skewered vegetables, and olives, olives, always olives. (Some olives even made anchovies taste sweeter.) I went straight for the paella. For that, we had to leave the Illetas resort area where the English could find fish and chips, the Germans schnitzel, and the Americans hamburgers. (Fact is, I spent far too much time looking for my ideal serving of paella.) We drove into Palma, down the boulevard El Borne to the Plaza Pio XII. The architecture of Palma was a mixture of Spanish and Moorish designs, some church towers so much like minarets, I could almost imagine the muezzin calling the faithful to prayer. Even the doorways of Spanish palacios were embossed with Moorish designs. But the layout of the streets themselves was more European—wide boulevards, crooked cobblestone lanes, lots of plazas, and plenty of cathedrals. On the benches along the tree-lined

El Borne, old men commented on the constant changes in the city. When I passed by, I swear they commented on me as well—except when I turned to look at them, they muttered, "Signora," and slumped as if they were too old to do anything but doze in the sun. Restaurants had that same Old World flavor: table linens and bored middle-aged waiters who'd just as soon flick away the last customer's cigarette ashes as change the tablecloth. The food was nearly always worth the hassle. I discovered my taste for paella had been Americanized, but I fell in love with a soup of fish, tomatoes, almonds, and garlic stewed in wine and spooned over a thin slice of bread. Cervice became the side dish I'd have with fish—fish with fish, Majorcan style: fish à la plancha, fish à la romana, fish marinera —and always with a glass of Majorcan wine.

Palma was our jumping-off point for the rest of the island, although it took some maneuvering to get out of the city. In fact, there weren't any roads on Majorca that didn't require careful driving. Majorcans didn't seem to understand straight lanes. The road through the olive tree groves near Soller was so famous that it was used for practice by bicyclists heading for the Gran Prix in France. (At the time, my son was racing bikes, and I couldn't help but imagine him spiralling down the road toward the sea on that fiberglass thing he referred to as a bicycle. But then he thought the thirty-mile round trip ride from Seattle to Long Acres race track was just the ticket for a morning pick-me-up before work.) All along the road, groves of olive trees stretched for miles into the countryside. The olives had been harvested and the trees were bare, so instead of the thick leaves that accompany that oily fruit, there were only naked limbs, twisted into grotesque configurations like some Gothic nightmare that Mary Shelley or Maurice Sendak would have found marvelous. I shuddered as P. relished every hairpin curve, gesturing toward the bizarre symmetry of the trees as we headed toward the coast where the Mediterranean glittered like a neon sign. We had lunch on the terrace of a hotel at Miramar overlooking the blue blue sea.

The sea surrounded us in Fiji. Toberu, at its widest point was no more than a mile or so across, and the resort dominated the center of the island. That left us with the beach. We ate on the beach, slept on the beach, explored the beach, and watched it grow and shrink with the tide. Back home on the beach at La Push along the northern tip of Washington State, the incoming tide brings in souvenirs: glass weights from Japanese fishing fleets, a dead whale, tons of leaves stripped from trees due to a forest fire somewhere else along the coast, the bones of birds or cows that have strayed too near the water. Beachcombers have to take home their finds before the outgoing tide, like a well-trained housekeeper, sweeps the sand.

On Toberua, the sea was fastidious and allowed for only small treasures. The current from Moturiki Channel carried most of the debris to the ocean, but the Fijians wasted nothing. Water was their home, their angel gateway between heaven and earth. To them, Moturiki was a sacred path, so Kini did not speak while the boat was traveling through those waters. He gave us clues about what to watch for in the tides. The color of algae that signaled a change in current, or shells of one sort that meant marauding fish, while another sort meant it was the mating season. When I was gathering stones along the beach, I came upon a skin recently cast off by a sea snake. The skin itself told me much about the size of the snake, its age and general coloring. Kini filled in missing information about battle scars and nesting habits. "Leave it there for the sea to take back," he said. I followed Kini across the beach, his footprints so large, both of my feet fit into the print of one of his. We traced the snake's trail, a small impression in the sand that vanished and resurfaced in a grove of trees, only to vanish again near the water's edge. "There is only so much to say about what is left behind," he told me, "and we can only guess where it has gone." At dusk, I watched snakes trailing toward Bird Island for a fast-food fix of eggs—the oldest ones in front coated in black-and-white second skins, the youngest skittering behind like speckled pups or ducklings. In the water, they swam past us like surfers riding the currents to the next island.

For the Fijians, water was a road with traffic patterns above and below its surface. In the mornings, fishermen set out to catch the evening meal. Water taxis carried workers to their jobs and children to school. Housewives shopped for staples that couldn't be grown on the island or found in the sea. And every weekend, the family went to church. On the big island of Viti Levu, a Black Christ reigned over the banks of the Wainbuka River. Some of the women who worked at the resort had three crosses tattooed on the back of their hands, a combination of Christian and ancient religions. (I had seen those tattoos once before at a condomblé in Brazil.) "Come with us to church," they said. "Receive salvation." When Kini took us through the channel past Cagalai or Ovalau, I could hear the sound of church music, its gospel rhythms so familiar that I had to remind myself that I was in Fiji and not on some bayou in Louisiana.

On Sundays, in river traffic of the Fiji Islands, you can see church ladies in flowered dresses and wide hats sitting stiff-backed in outboard water taxis, fanning themselves righteously. They are full of grunts and groans these women who pass judgement on all they know, these women who can find their duplicates in black communities all over the world. I've heard them in the South, in Brazil, in Zimbabwe, in Madagascar. They know the currents of life, these women. Maybe it was true that Fiji was the spore of some distant migration from Africa. When I was in the market in Nadi, vendors called to me in the same voice that boys back home had used to get my attention. I was reminded even more of boys back in the States when we went to see the fire dancers. With ashes smudged under their eyes and their enviable Afros, they could have been members of a high school football, except this ball team defied fire, walking barefoot on the hot coals as if they were high-stepping down the beach.

Fire walkers exist in many cultures around the equator, from India around the globe to Africa. Maybe it's the heat, the sun so directly overhead, that makes men feel as if there's nothing left to do but conquer it. They paint their faces with the shadows of flames and adorn their bodies with the amulets of warriors: bicep and ankle bracelets, girdles of puka shells, necklaces of polished conch. And they walk, barefoot and blessed, over the breath of the gods. After the performance, P. and I saw the fire dancers changing into street clothes. They looked at me and whistled, calling, "Hey," like any teenager flexing his muscles. (Who said those warriors weren't scattered far and wide?) Even after we'd left, taking the river taxi home, echoes of the drums stayed with me.

In Valldemosa, the music of Chopin played constantly against a background of bees droning in the gardens like motorcyclists. We had headed east from Palma because I wanted to see Valldemosa and P. wanted to see Deyá, where Robert Graves had lived. But Valldemosa was the romance of Chopin and George Sand in all of its melodrama. I couldn't miss it. Neither could hundreds of other tourists. The town was full of winding streets, most of them clotted with huge tourists buses, the German models that are like hotels on wheels. (In Yugoslavia, one driver had tried to maneuver a German bus around a corner and down a set of cobblestone stairs that served as a street. "Malo ulice! Velike autobus!" he'd shouted to the people sitting in their houses not more than twenty feet away. From the stunned looks on their faces, I knew they didn't have to be told that the street was narrow and the bus was big. There might have been an inch of room between the bus and the walls of the houses. We were so close, they could have invited us to join them for dinner.)

The buses in Valldemosa took up most of the road, the roofs almost brushing the flowers hanging in pots from the patios. The town was ablaze with bright flowers, and in the monastery where George Sand had been cloistered with the ailing composer Chopin, the town's gardeners had gone mad with vivid blossoms. Flowers, bees, tourists, and piano music boxes tinkling Chopin, Chopin, Chopin. (I don't think my daughter has ever forgiven me for not buying one for her.) Every day, someone from the village placed a single rose on Chopin's piano centered in the apartment he shared with George Sand. And they talk about the baleful nature of Sand's daughter, the mischievous Solange, as if they'd lived there while she was still alive. Even though the villagers have taken those stories from their grandparents, they say, "Tourists are nothing. We have lived through Solange." Each story sells more trinkets.

In northern California, there is a gargantuan statue of the missionary Junipero Serra that stands on a hillside near the Pacific Ocean. The highway dips on either side of the site so that you see the statue suddenly as you come over the rise—Fra Serra, his arms extended in supplication before the freeway traffic that races beneath him. P., who lived in California, wanted to go to Petra, Serra's birthplace on Majorca. It was a nice stopping-off point on our drive west. Petra was a provincial little place that smelled like goat's milk and thick rain off the sea. The stamp of the missionary pervaded the landscape, but the Fra Serra statue in Petra was not as impressive as the one in California. I stayed in the car while P. photographed yet another church. (Why is it that travel guides detail visits to every church, mosque, synagogue, and temple in the area? Do mapmakers believe all travelers need redemption?) After awhile, several children gathered around the car and stared at me. They simply leaned against the wall and watched me, all the while smiling. Then an old man joined them. We all stared at one another. Finally, to break the tedium, they consented to let me take their picture. (In the photo, their faces have turned neutral, neither hostile nor friendly, just curious.) I was just as happy when we left Petra, especially because the town was on the direct route to the coast, where we could visit the Caves of Drach, and its twin, the Caves of Hams. But it was the Dragon Caves that I was interested in.

After I completed my collection of poems *Queen of the Ebony Isles,* which included a series of poems for the "Dragon Lady" from the old comic book series, *Terry and the Pirates,* I had adopted the dragon as my totem. (Or perhaps the "Lady" adopted me?) So I looked forward to seeing the Caves of Drach. I had imagined them to be spectacular—after all, they had inspired Jules Verne to write *Voyage to the*

Center of the Earth—but I had not expected such immense grandeur. Our descent was not unlike diving into the ocean. It took nearly an hour to navigate the series of platforms and flights of stairs into the main labyrinth. All around us, the rock formations took on phantom shapes: fluted stalagmites and stalactites in the shapes of fish or ferns, fossils or amphibious creatures. I think of amphibians because of the ever-present water. Each step seemed to take us deeper into the stomach of the earth, the walls damp with moisture. Colors were at once both clear and muted, like the piece of pottery I'd bought in Palma from Castaldo, one of Majorca's famous artists. The clay in Castaldo's pot was streaked with colors: pinks, lilacs, aquas, as if he had duplicated the tide leaving its salt deposits on rocks.

In the Dragon Caves, I saw the image of the sea mirrored in the patterns of the cave. As we took the spiral descent to its center, we moved away from and toward the sea. In one opening, the sea was a step away at high tide, but we were told that at low tide, the mouth of the same cave would be at the top of a sheer cliff, the water some twenty feet below. (There, the Spaniards got their revenge on the Moors by scaling the cliffs and trapping them in the caves.) The treasure of the Caves of Drach waited for us at the very end of the labyrinthine descent. After traveling through grotto "rooms" at various levels with such names as Cueva Blanca, Cueva Negra, Venus de Milo, and Indian Pagoda, we arrived at Martel Lake, a grotto lagoon with an auditorium that could seat 3,000 visitors. The surface of the lake was flat, the water so without color that in the reflection, reality and mirrored image seemed to merge. This gave magic to the torch-lit procession of rowboats, one big enough to hold an organ. Barcaroles—boating songs—echoed off the cave walls, but barely a ripple was made in the still waters as the boats passed. Eerie, I thought as they slid silently along that ghostly lake. "Everything is constant," the guide said. "The water has no tide, no oxygen, so only microscopic organisms exist here and they are blind."

I had read how astronauts felt removed from the earth when they were in orbit; in the caves I felt consumed by the earth. I thought about the Moors and how they must have believed that in the bowels of the earth, in the heart of the dragon, they were safe from the trouble that raged toward them from Spain. Retreating to North Africa, they had pulled themselves and their boats into the caves to wait out their pursuers. The illusion was still there. As I watched the pageant of son et lumière, the world above me seemed far, far away.

I have always found caves mysterious and a little scary. The Midwest is dotted with them—Meramec, Onondaga, Cathedral —each one invested with the unspoken secrets of the Native American people who once owned the land. I remember being taken to Onandaga Caves by a teenage love. What I felt was not exactly claustrophobia (because the caves were beautiful, their walls like an artist's canvas), but the more I was told about the Onondaga Indians who had lived there, the more uncomfortable I became. My grandmother would have said I had walked too close to ghosts. I also may have walked too close to the ghosts of Moors in Majorca, but in the end, it was the sound of water that saved me. Even though that might seem an odd statement for an aquaphobic to make, for me the ocean is a cradle song. And after a year of being land-bound at a university, I need to hear the ocean, to say: I'm alive and the ocean is still out there moving with the tides.

Perhaps that need to touch the ocean explains my obsession with learning how to swim. Certainly I could have continued to rely on fake photos of me as a mermaid at the edge of the sea. But water calls to me. Despite my fears and my earlier failures, I had to learn how to swim. (Before I joined the aquatics class, I heard from more than one white person that my inability was genetically linked to dense bone structure, which prevents black folks from swimming. Perhaps they'd never visited the South or countries in Africa and the Pacific, where black folks take to water like dolphins, dense bones and all. Kini's dives were effortless, graceful.) In Fiji, where water is greater than the land, tapa cloth designs mirror the cycles of the ocean. In our bure, there was a length of tapa hanging on the wall that reminded me of the coral we had seen when Kini took us diving.

I guess I was still thinking of Kini when P. went shopping for a set of Fijian spears. He waited until the evening before we left Fiji to make his purchase. Had I been interested in spears, I would have bought them, boxed them, and had them shipped home long before flight time. But since P. was carrying the heavy luggage, I became the designated carrier of two six foot long warrior's spears. (They were long enough to be just right for Kini.) I boarded the plane with them—stretching, of course, a cabin attendant's last bit of patience: the passenger who won't check her spears. (Come on, how far could I throw a six-foot spear inside a plane?) She looked at me, shorter than the spears, my hair growing into dreads after too many days in sun and saltwater, and she finally agreed to let me put the spears in the garment bag section in first class. I thought that was more dangerous than the cabin section, since the first-class section on that flight was filled with the Fiji National Soccer Team. When those guys stood up in the aisles, they blocked out all light.

On the flight home, I used up most of the thirteen hours when I wasn't sleeping unbraiding my hair, but when we arrived in Los Angeles, I had finished loosening only half of the braids. The hair recently freed from its braided confines stood out in all directions and made me look like a mascot for the soccer team. We waited for them to leave the plane (an extra half hour, it seemed), then I retrieved the spears from the forward section. The cabin attendant gave me the smile of someone who'd seen it all but still managed to be surprised. I offered her the same smile in return. In the airport terminal in Fiji, I'd seen a sign that read: *Is your attitude on straight?* Damn straight, I thought, smiling at the cabin attendant.

"You'll never get those things through customs," she said.

"Watch me," I said.

P. went ahead of me, certain that I would face the usual round of unnecessary questions I often had to answer when clearing customs. (Where do you work? How did you pay for this ticket?) P. sailed through the procedure, as always. Then it was my turn. This time, fate was with me. The agent was tired. He stamped my passport, checked the visa, marked my bags—then he looked up. That's when he saw my hair and the spears. "What the hell is that?" he growled. I gave him my fiercest Fiji imitation. "My spears," I growled back. I don't know what answer he expected, but he waved me through. Never mess with a black woman when she's trying to get home with her spears, I thought. These days, I hope P. still has those damn spears hanging on his wall.

In the Season of Plum Rain

In Japan, everything seemed to run hot and cold, old and new at the same time. No matter how I tried, I just couldn't seem to find the right fit. I felt as if I were traveling through the story about the three bears, always looking for the right sized chair, the right bowl of rice, the right house on the right street. No, I wasn't Goldilocks, but think about it: I was very different from everyone else—tall, lanky, and black. The three bears business didn't mean I went around smashing teacups and breaking furniture, but in a country where language constantly failed me, I sometimes got lost between one breath and the next. Still, let me set the record straight: the idea of bears really didn't start with the Japanese; it started with an American couple who were living there.

P. had been invited to celebrate the Japanese publication of his novel, and I was taking advantage of the visit to meet with Japanese poets. The chance to stay with P.'s friend, a professor from California who was with his lover on an exchange program in Japan, was supposed to make our trip easier. P. and I arrived in June, toward the end of the couple's year of residency. Ideal, right? Two couples from the West Coast catching a glimpse of Japan. We assumed that knowing someone there would ease our introduction to the country, make us feel a little less like we were lost on an unfamiliar landscape of customs and language.

They picked us up at Narita Airport and we caught the commuter train to Tokyo. At first, I wondered why we hadn't hired a taxi instead of being bundled onto a crowded airport express with three suitcases and a duffel bag. The train was packed, no luggage compartment and no rules about what would fit in the overhead bin. Whatever came off the airplane went onto the train, and I swear, some of those folks traveled with *all* of their household belongings. And they were all smiling. The more we bumped butts and tilted dangerously over suitcases, the more they smiled. It took a visit to a Tokyo English language bookstore to find an explanation. In a book about Japanese customs, the authors explained that in traditional culture, a smile could indicate pleasure or be a cover for negative feelings. The smile might be an outside appearance, *tatemae,* they called it, but *honne* was the inner thought. I had learned how to function in the hustle of urban America where folks rarely smiled, but the courtesy smile of the Japanese had me unnerved. Chalk it up to gaijin insecurity.

Still, it didn't take me long to understand how useful a smile was in a land where everything was compact and space was at a premium. We moved from being crammed on the train from Narita to being crammed into a tiny flat in Ikebukuro, a suburb of Tokyo. (The duffel held our traveling futons—that cut out the time of finding just the right bed.) Anytime we wanted to go into Tokyo, we had to catch the Yamanote train, which meant braving the subway where each ride was body to body and hanging from straps as if we'd been caught in an Ionesco play about rush hour New York—except we were all smiling. And all the shops were crowded, small and large, especially the department stores in the Ginza or Shinjuku, their wares stacked to the ceiling and leaving only narrow aisles for shoppers. And by the end of the week, P. and I discovered that the two of us couldn't fit into one taxi with our luggage, even minus the duffel bag, which we had shed. But in that week, we shed a lot of baggage, including the American couple.

I can't say that I sensed something was wrong on the way from the airport, but I did notice that the woman from California was full of cautionary remarks about Japanese living. "Don't trust these people on the street," she said, when we passed a fortune teller on the corner near the flat. As I marveled at all the wondrous new food in the grocery, she said, "That's too hot. That's too bland. That's too salty," for each item I admired.

The next day set the pace of their litany. At breakfast, we heard a musician tuning a stringed instrument, a delicate sound that butterflies might make if they could sing. Before the music took shape, the man from California put a Wagner tape in the player and turned it up, full blast. "The Kabuki theatre has a damn practice hall across the lane," he said. "This is my only defense." P. shrugged, and I made myself remember that we were guests and drank down my clichés of the "ugly American" along with my morning tea. But the image never quite left me. Sometimes it rose up in a casual way. The couple's dislike for Japanese sweets, for example. "They can't even make a decent cake," the woman said. Or the ever-present complaint about furniture not built for bulky Western bodies. "I'm too old to squat on the floor like a monkey," the man said. Or simply the lack of respect. On an afternoon walk through the neighborhood, we happened upon a small building behind the inverted arch of a torii gate. "A temple," the woman from California said, and without removing her shoes, walked down the middle aisle and, in a loud voice, began to explain the architecture of the building. It was as if she had not seen the altar of small white candles and two people kneeling on cushions that had been placed in rows along the floor. I rushed her outside.

"They don't mind," she said. "They just go in there to get away from the crowds."

"Maybe they're praying or something," I said.

She grunted. "It's not like a church," she said.

"How do you know that?" I asked as she walked away.

I was reminded of my mother, who never left the confines of the military, no matter where we traveled. But this wasn't the fifties, and unlike my mother, that woman, in all her blondeness, never expected to be excluded by bigotry. On the contrary, she'd brought her biases with her, defending them by saying, "You don't know these people." She was right. I was forever gaijin, a foreigner. What I knew about Japan I'd pulled from popular books published in America. Any real information could have been put in a thimble and I would still have had enough room left over for my thumb. I didn't always know what I was seeing, but I kept looking.

Later, after P. and I left Tokyo, I visited the zen garden of Ryoanji in Kyoto. The garden was a landscape of fifteen stones placed in a bed of sand, its beauty captured in the simplicity of the fine white gravel that was raked every day into a pattern spread out in an infinity of parallel lines. (That garden has become so popular that miniature Ryoanjis are commercially produced, complete with miniature rakes. You can meditate at your desk—get it?) At first, I counted the rocks, but no matter where I was, one of the fifteen was always hidden from view. "Did you meditate upon the pattern?" my friend Tetsuzo asked. I had met Tetsuzo my first week in Japan, and he had kept me sane with shiatsu massages, so I felt obliged to tell him the truth. I confessed that for me, Ryoanji was as its nickname suggested: a garden of nothingness, just sand and rocks. "You are too Western," Tetsuzo said. "You think only in that reference. You must meditate beyond the pattern. You must look beyond what you see."

When I arrived in Japan, I had a list of things to see: Kabuki theatre, the museum at Hiroshima, the city of Uwajima, the north country. Fortunately, my list coincided with P.'s list. Originally we had planned to make excursions out of Tokyo, spending only a few days at the flat in Ikebukuro, then traveling on the superexpress train through the country. Between trips, we'd meet with P.'s publishers. But as best laid plans often do, these went slightly astray. Our stay didn't last the week. The break came in a restaurant in Tokyo after P. and I had been to the Kabukiza Theatre. We'd spent the day at the Kabuki, enchanted by dramas pulled from the ancient world of Japan. When we reserved our tickets, the couple from California confessed that they had not yet seen Kabuki. "I understand some people spend all day there," she said, "but I don't know why. That music drives us crazy." If I had not already been enthralled by the idea of Kabuki, her comment would have been enough to make me a devoted fan.

We'd arrived at the Kabukiza, Tokyo's oldest Kabuki theatre, at ten in the morning. The theatre was crowded, as everything was in Tokyo. Lines were already forming at the food concession stands— light refreshments, sandwiches, Japanese-style dishes. From time to time, I caught the scent of oranges and green tea. No one would go hungry from 11:00 to 6:00, while the Kabuki unfolded. There were even lockers for those who wanted to bring a change of clothes, and the young ladies who came, immaculately dressed and mincing like geishas, must have made use of those lockers. If Kabuki meant high society, they were there to prove it. And if they wanted envy, they had mine. (How do they walk like that?) P. and I settled in, food in one hand and an English language program guide in the other.

Kabuki was grand theatre, classical drama on a royal scale where, in the three-hundred-year-old tradition of that art form, all the actors were male. The stage sets were breathtaking, and I had full view of the orchestra that I could now hear in its entirety, rather than in bits and pieces between pauses in Wagner: the ryuteki and biwa flutes, the stringed koto, the lutes, gongs, and drums. I wept along with handmaidens draped in yards of embroidered silk. I cringed when the Fox God, with his flaming red hair, bounded onto the stage. I fell in love with the samurai strutting stage center, padded and armed with great pomp, shoulders like a football player or a gladiator—my favorite character, but no doubt that was a holdover from having been a military brat. As we applauded the drama of the feudal code of honor, P. said, "It's like King Arthur, only more bloody." That was true. Characters died left and right as foul play abounded, and goodly deeds saved the day.

My only comparison was opera, the lavish sets of La Scala or the Met. Kabuki held the same majestic costumes and stylized movements, the easily identifiable models of good and evil, innocence and avarice. But unlike most staid opera audiences, the audience at the

Kabuki hissed and applauded, laughed and groaned with each dramatic change. "The actors seemed to stay on stage forever," I told the couple from California. "They pranced and leapt and died a thousand deaths. And the singing and screaming. Seven hours, but they never seemed tired. And that theatre was hot, let me tell you. I was sweating."

"Japanese people don't sweat," the woman said. "They're built differently." "Yes, and their vocal cords are built differently," the man added. "It's a genetic thing." I felt my patience begin to evaporate. I think I was launching into a long speech about the human anatomy and its universal similarities when a waiter showed up with another pot of tea. The woman from California said, "Domo" —Japanese for "thank you"—then without blinking an eye, added, " . . . Dummy." The waiter hesitated for a moment, surely understanding her slur, then continued placing the tea on the table. I didn't pause. I couldn't have moved faster if I were being arrested.

"That does it!" I said (or something to that effect), and within seconds, I was on the sidewalk and heading for the nearest traffic light. Only then did I realize I didn't know where I was going, nor could I read any street signs to know how lost I was. Also, I was carrying P.'s passport. I stormed back to the restaurant. It took five minutes of subdued screaming to extricate myself from the "ugly Americans," and another hour or so for P. and me to get our things out of the flat and move to a hotel. (We left the duffel bag of futons, and still it took two taxis to transport us to a hotel across town.) But I know that for a moment in that restaurant, I must have looked like a character out of the Kabuki, gesturing wildly as I raged against bad manners and bigotry. I think the only thing that brought me to my senses was that my behavior was so un-Japanese. I was already Gaijin Da; I didn't need to prove it. So I'd calmed myself, turned to the waiters, and smiled. I guess they accepted my smile as a sign of embarrassment and anger, but by then, I knew the proper etiquette was "smile regardless." The waiters bowed. I bowed. Then P. and I beat a hasty retreat, leaving the couple from California to finish their disagreeable meal. In truth, I can't say that my noisy exit was the only rift between me and

P., but I do know that our discontent would only have been exacerbated if we'd stayed with that couple. I was in the wrong house, and no matter how I tried to make things fit, it just wouldn't work.

Throughout Japan, I was struck by the inventiveness and deliberateness of the Japanese compared to my Westernized expectations of instant food, disposables, and clutter. I'm not saying that Japan was not full of junk food and plastic trash like the rest of the world—in fact, much of the world's plastic trash was designed in Japan ("nifty items" the guidebook calls them)—but I spent a great deal of time learning how to deal with time: how to move at warp speed on the Bullet Train, then slow down for the luxury of a twelve-course meal once I arrived at my destination.

The first time we took the Shinkasen, the Bullet Train, I began to think of our trip as In Japan Without a Clue. Moving through Tokyo's Yamanote commuter line was difficult enough, even with the ever-present help of the locals, usually students who wanted to practice their English. But as soon as they left us, we were lost in a morass of signs in Japanese characters and a thousand people milling about. The Bullet Train meant we could get lost at 210 miles per hour, instead of on a local at some reasonable speed where our ears didn't pop and we didn't have the sensation of flying without ever leaving the ground. I kept wanting to fasten my seat belt. Then I discovered that if I sat facing where I'd been instead of where I was going, I had less of a feeling of weightlessness and motion sickness. Seated that way, I could enjoy the ride and the goodies on the tea carts that went by at regular intervals. But my big pleasure was seeing stretches of land that weren't crowded with people. Traveling in reverse, I saw farmers with ox-drawn carts moving toward me as I sped away from them. Country women dressed in getas and kimonos barely had time to look up before they disappeared from my sight. Schoolchildren in parochial style uniforms would be always frozen in my memory, forever in the act of getting off a bus. A line of rice planters grew longer as I moved away, their movements growing indistinct until they abruptly vanished from sight. For a second, a farmhouse at the foot of an arched bridge looked as if it might have been pulled off the nineteenth-century Hiroshige print that P. had bought in Tokyo. Then we sped away and the scene blurred into an abstract. In fact, much of the countryside looked out of place from my vantage point on the Shinkasen. The faster we traveled, the more life maintained its sensible speed.

Each stop on the Shinkasen was an adjustment. Usually, P. and I went from the rocket-speed world of the Bullet Train to the world of the ryokan. The ryokan was strictly traditional. There was no more telephone room service or the buzz-buzz of elevators. (I could almost hear one of those TV ads: *At the ryokan, you leave your speed at the door.*) The first ryokan P. and I visited was on Miyajima Island. Our room was defined by pearl-white shoji screens, tatami mats covering the floor, paper lanterns with calligraphy designs, and blue-and-white cushions painted with Japanese flower prints. And everyone was smiles, making sure they took care of the strange gaijin couple who had descended on them. This time I assumed the smiles were real rather than mere politeness. They accepted my feeble efforts at what few Japanese words I had, and called me, Missy-san.

But my eating habits became a great concern at the inn, no doubt because I was overwhelmed by so much food. That first night, after P. and I had bathed (in the hottest water this side of Hades), and put on yukata lounging robes, we waited for dinner, drinking the saki that had been left for us. We had a lot of saki. Thirty minutes passed. I was beginning to think there would be no dinner when the outside shoji slid open and the waitperson placed a low table in front of us. Another waitperson came in with napkins, chopsticks, and more saki. (I hesitate to call them waitresses, these women who could fall to their knees and rise without losing balance or composure. I was already beginning to have doubts about how I would get up from a cross-legged position without orthopedic assistance. I've always had my misgivings about American-bred gracefulness. We clump around on our heels, tearing out tendons and gathering maps of varicose veins.

Nothing is articulated and fluid by the time we're in our teens. No wonder I was having doubts about sitting so long without a chair.)

Before the women left the room, we all bowed—P. and I more to the gracefulness of the women than anything else. Then the screen closed and we were left alone for another twenty minutes. I was becoming very familiar with that saki. The first course—something round and white and crisp. Bowls of miso soup. Some tea. More bowing. I don't think P. and I tasted much of that first course. That was hard to do while we were inhaling the food. Second course—something round and soft and yellow. And sweet spinach with sesame. Radishes and carrots like spring blossoms. Rice and more tea. More bowing. Now things are getting interesting, I thought. My stomach had stopped growling and was purring. Third course—something pink and gelatinous, shaped like a chrysanthemum. Some rice. Spicy fish with ginger. More bowing. "Have you tried the pink stuff?" I asked P. We stopped asking what a dish was called by the fifth and sixth courses. More bowing. Something that tasted like eggs, except eggs had never come in that color and shape. A thin, clear noodle that looked like gossamer. Chicken, with baby mushrooms. Something doughy the size of my fist. More bowing. I belched. The waitperson giggled. "Have you tried the purple stuff?" P. asked me. By the ninth or tenth course, I said, "I know why they don't have chairs. It's so when you're too stuffed to move, you don't have far to fall." More tea. Something sweet. Something sour. And oh, I forgot that second bottle of wine. I'm sure that's what put me off food the next morning.

The next morning, I felt as if I had a hangover. That wasn't going to stop ryokan hospitality. "Some of those old inns have been in operation for a thousand years," we were told. I think the one on Miyajima had a little more recent history than that, but they had tradition down pat. They took pride in making sure their guests were properly treated, and they weren't about to let a finicky American pass through without enjoying it to the fullest, breakfast included. Now, I'm the type who'd always avoided breakfast, and after the feast of the night before, food was the last thing I wanted to see. I begged off the first morning and slept in. P. reported that the table was littered with dead fish and square eggs. I was happy to have missed it, but when I came downstairs to begin our day's excursions, I was accosted. "Missy-san, you not eat," the hostess bowed. "No," I bowed. "Sick," I bowed. There was much gesturing and picking out words from English and Japanese, and as we left the lobby, P. told me that somehow I'd promised to be downstairs for breakfast, bright and early the next morning. I turned and smiled, hoping I conveyed that I was merely masking my pain.

But the next day, I did try dragging myself down to the morning room. Dinner was served in our room, but breakfast was a social affair. I think it was just a way to keep tabs on errant guests who hated food before ten o'clock, especially dead fish. I loved fish for dinner. But little tiny fish, salted almost beyond recognition and served eyes up at six in the morning was enough to make me wish for my mother's cholesterol breakfast of bacon and eggs, grits and sausage, and plenty of black coffee. These fish came with tea, but from the looks on their faces, they were beyond caring one way or another. Poor things, I thought. They'd fared no better than the eggs. It still seemed like a lot of work to make round eggs square. I settled for tea, bits of potato-like things, and some fruit. This only convinced the hostess that I was either sick or pregnant. I tried to assure her that one was not the case and the other was impossible, but every morning after that, I ran the gauntlet, smiling, always smiling, as I refused to punish one more little fish.

It seemed that P. and I had no sooner abandoned the couple from California than the sun abandoned Tokyo. Everyone said we should be happy. "It's the season of plum rain," Tetsuzo said. "The most beautiful season that brings flowers," P.'s publisher said. "Forty days and forty nights," the translator from the publishing company said. I tried to explain that I had left Seattle, the heart of the Pacific Northwest rain forest. "We get seven or eight months of the stuff," I said.

"Tsuyu, plum rain," they reminded me. "Sweet for summer." I watched it rain and waited for summer. It was a soft, whispery rain that inevitably had me thinking about Shakespeare. *It droppeth like a gentle rain from heaven.* By the fourth day, I felt my Northwest webfeet breaking through. It sprinkled, drizzled, dripped, sprayed, and poured. Sometimes a mist that was more fog than rain. Or a falling rain that fluttered down straight, like a transparent curtain. I stayed wet. Japanese poets wrote lovingly about rain, praising the season that brought blue-green irises and pale gardenias. I wrote in my journal that it was a misty drizzle—my clothes were damp and the walls of cheap hotels were attacked by water bugs and green mildew. (Like home, only wetter.) I'd walk outside into heaven's shower, then run for cover. But Japanese women sauntered through the door as if they'd just come from the powder room. Water seemed to fall away from them. "How do they walk like that?" I asked. "I think they walk between the raindrops," P. said. And you know, I believed him.

The women hurried through the rain without seeming to hurry at all—their clothes dry, their hair immaculate. Some afternoons when we had time for tea—more of a British influence reserved for Westerners than the Japanese ritual of tea—P. and I would watch the women go about the business of the day. (Or night, as the case might be with the girls working the hotel lobbies. The uptown call girls were smooth and casual, always proper in their behavior. In the space of several hours, I watched one make contact five or six times, and not once did she look directly at her prospective client before she led him into the elevators.) On the street, I passed older women wearing kimonos and carrying wax paper umbrellas. They seemed to know how to avoid the puddles without even looking. But the younger ones, in business suits and high fashion dresses with short short skirts, carried the automatic parachute umbrellas that clicked open and closed with precision. Still, they walked as if they had just removed their kimonos. They were a part of the high-rise canyons of downtown Tokyo, but a part of the world of kimonos too, putting a kind of distance between themselves and everyone else, neither encouraging nor avoiding contact. "Think they're looking cute," my mother would have said. But when they passed me with little enigmatic smiles, I'd think: there's one thing that makes us equal—toilets. No matter how graceful those women were, they had to contend with squat toilets. And outside of the Westernized hotels and big buildings in the Ginza and Shinjuku, most of the public restrooms in Japan were squatters.

Let me pause to say a word or two about toilets (loos, johns, w.c.s, potties, benjos): they should be reliable, sensible, and comfortable. I'm talking somewhere way right of the outhouse, and left of those automatic things that have enough power to flush you into hyperspace. Let me put it this way: I've never seen a squat toilet that I liked. Mud or tiles, if it's a hole in the floor, it's a squatter. I'd almost rather go into the bushes. ("Practice with a Coca-Cola bottle," my Aunt Jennie told me. Except I always forget about practicing until I'm outside the states. Then I try imagining the action with a Coke bottle, but virtual Coca-Cola just doesn't quite work. Until I get the knack of it again, I'm lucky if I miss my shoes.) In Turkey, I had to use a squatter in a restaurant near the Istanbul's Blue Mosque. A beautiful restaurant, except for the squatters. And this one was co-ed, almost. There was a half wall partition separating the men from the women. When the men saw me enter, on the women's side, of course, they hugged that wall trying to catch a peek. The women clucked their tongues and spread their black galabiyyas like bats' wings, shielding me from the men until I finished. Sometimes sisterhood extends into the bathroom. At least that one had footrests. In Madagascar, I had to balance on two turtle shells. That certainly won my vote for toilet-of-the-century.

Actually, those damn squatters keep me ladylike. Because of them, I always wear a skirt. Pants only make it more difficult. And those porcelian T-shaped bowls designed by men don't help for squat, literally speaking. Give me the conventional seat, even like the one I once had in Bellingham, Washington, a thing that didn't need a septic tank—it incinerated the stuff. (Great subject for party talk, except my son conducted unspeakable experiments in his efforts to invent new ways to torture his sister.) The rocket seat is as far away from modern convention as I want to get, although I love bidets, but that's another subject altogether. In Japan, expensive hotels featured bidets—my kind of place—and the very wealthy Japanese even have toilets that can run a diagnostic test on bodily functions. (No sh . . . kidding.) But in the rural areas, and in the deep environs of the elegant Kabuki theatre, you get squatters. Rumor has it that the government plans to make the benjos in the whole country go to conventional seats, but don't tell the ladies at the Kabuki, just yet.

Two weeks in Japan, and the rain became our companion. When we took the Shinkasen to Uwajima, the rain was waiting for us when we got off the train. It stayed with us all the while we were in the city. In a way, the rain added to Uwajima's shady fame: the erotic museum. I had wanted to go to that city because Seattle is home to Uwajimaya, one of the largest stores in the International District, but that was just an excuse to visit Taga Jinja, the erotic museum. For that, I figured we needed a map and a taxi. (In Japan, you never hailed a taxi without a map for your destination.) But this time, the map was unnecessary. All I had to do was say the words: Taga Jinja, and the driver nodded. He turned his head so quickly, I couldn't tell if he'd smiled, but I suspected he did. "Everybody knows where the erotic museum is," Tetsuzo said. "You can even make a contribution." Some good sense had told me not to ask him what he meant, and after I'd visited Taga Jinja, I was glad I hadn't.

My first glimpse of the museum was of a patio with stunted red oak and flame trees. On the path to the doorway was a table holding what looked from a distance like the trunk of a fallen tree. Up close, there was no mistaking the object as a phallus. BUDDHA'S PENIS, the sign read. Five to six feet long (and circumcised). Now I understand why he was celibate, I thought. If that was the preamble, I was ready to see what the inside would offer. Every exhibit was slanted toward sex. It was a PBS special made with the censors on vacation. Nothing was exempt. Bugs, birds, and beggars. Everything copulating in all positions imaginable. Tiny geisha riding a giant penis downhill. Lions trying it in tree tops. And upstairs, the greatest show of all: an extensive collection of female pubic hair. (Surely, Tetsuzo was joking!) Each sample, taped to a rice board, was catalogued by the donor's name, age, birthplace, occupation, and status of sexual experience (or inexperience). Nineteen year olds, sixty year olds, mothers, nuns, acrobats, grannies. "One Buddhist collecting for fifty years," the guide said. "How did he do that?" I asked. I tried imagining his interview technique: "Hello. My name is Kâto-san and I need your pubic hair." No, too direct, I thought. Remember tatemae and honne. I'll bet Kâto-san's cheeks hurt from all that smiling, I thought.

P. and I arrived early and had the luxury of being escorted through the museum before the crowds descended. By the time we left, we passed young couples holding hands—newlyweds, by the look of their outfits, school girls giggling into their uniforms, young men who wanted to see if they could outshock the visitors—fat chance, with Kâto-san's collection on the second floor—and a bus load of middle-aged women, the kind the guidebook said would likely be present. They gave me knowing smiles but spent more time inspecting P. than looking in my direction. "Why are they staring at me?" P. asked. I smiled, and it was strictly tatemae.

Taga Jinja wasn't the only place in Uwajima that had gained its fame from "mad, mad monks." Though we doubted if anyone else could beat Kâto-san for his boldness, the guide at Taga Jinja told us that we had to visit Dai Raku Ji. "Very interesting, this Dai Raku Ji. He makes many inventions." So the next day, it was a taxi and a map and plunk—we were in Disneyworld, Buddhist style. Dai Raku Ji boasts fifteen generations of priests from the Asano family. After all those years, you would not expect a neat collection of artifacts, and you won't find one, either. The museum was like a flea market, a mena-

gerie, and an arboretum, all combined, from the mundane and ob-
scure to the imaginative and ingenious. Clocks, bows, swords, old
passports, bric-a-brac, and junk. I saw kitchen items and beauty
helpers from the forties and fifties that I hadn't seen since I was a
child and lived with my grandmother. A washboard and a spindle in
one room. A wooden shoe shine box and a flat iron in another. No
item was too large or too small. I even saw a Captain Midnight glow-
in-the-dark ring. "From all the world over," Asano-san said. I gave my
share—one of my pink hair curlers, a single kinky hair still attached.
Asano-san was delighted. He placed it among the combs and tooth-
brushes in the collection. But now I had his attention. Instead of letting us wander through on our own, he would be our guide.

He showed us a water-powered stereo, a flush toilet made from
plastic garbage cans (one step up from squatters, at least), and a dou-
ble-necked guitar (didn't Mick Jagger have one of those?). We wandered down a wooded path, and modern Japan seemed far behind
us. Bamboo and eucalyptus draped the moss-covered stepping
stones, the shadows leaving dappled patches of light. The air was
heavy with the scent of rain, but in the protection of the trees, there
was merely a fine mist. Asano-san showed us how he grew new
shoots from dead bamboo and how he brought water out of bare
rock—an impossibility, scientists had told him. But his prize was the
creation of a sea world in fresh water. "I make the sea," he said in halt-
ing English. I stuck my finger in the water and tasted it. "Salty," I said.
He grinned. The pond held oysters and seaweed, but the sea was
miles away. "My secret," he said. The garden was full of his secrets.
Under the scent of plum rain, I smelled gardenias, lilies, and roses.
Everything grew in abundance, and so close, it seemed as if one plant
were in danger of choking out the next. But somehow, they thrived.
"First garden," he said. Under the rustle of leaves, I heard the
strangest animal noises that I'd ever heard. Tweets that became
growls, and growls that turned into hisses. A shadow of some kind of
animal flickered through the trees. "Musasabi. Very friendly," Asano-
san said. Perhaps first garden is the right name, I thought. By the

time we left, I was convinced that Asano-san was the closest I'd come to seeing a wizard.

Because I had insisted on visiting the silkworm ranch on the island of Miyajima, P. made me promise to see the bulls in Uwajima. "A Japanese bullfight," P. said. "I've got to see it." I had seen bullfights in Spain and Mexico—bloody messes where the bull didn't stand a chance. But in Japan, it was bull against bull, and the champion was a bull from Uwajima named Kongoriki, weighing in at 2,100 pounds. The silkworms were beautiful, when I could forget that they were worms and that weavers had to play with their mucus, but I was hardly going to forget a two ton glossy black bull. Kongoriki stood like a sumo wrestler, a rope harness thick as my wrist threaded through his nostrils. He would fight by the end of the week, they told us, not a fight of man against bull, but one where two men, in the middle of the arena, held the horns of opposing bulls, and then with the right timing let them lunge into each other. It was called tsukiai, or the thrusting contest, and the bull who could not stand his ground was the loser. Kongoriki had fought for nine years and had about nine fights a year. His next fight, scheduled for the end of the week, was to be his ninth fight of the year. We were told that his opponent, weighing in at 2,200 pounds, was no threat. The rumor was that the opponent bellowed too much, and the Japanese believed that the strong bull seldom bellowed. (That sounded like the proverb of the empty wagon making noise.) But there was one hitch—P. and I had return tickets on the Shinkasen the day before the championship tsukiai. That was how we came to visit Kono-san, the artist who carved images of Uwajima's famous bull.

We made the appointment for early evening. "Kono-san doesn't see anyone before noon," we were told. "Then he works through the evening until dawn." I didn't need to be told that he had a wife, someone to take care of the mundane details of living. (Every artist should have a room of her own and a wife to keep the household in order.) The taxi drove us through a quagmire of streets into the hills above Uwajima. Then the driver parked and waited. "Kono-san?" P. asked. The driver nodded and motioned for us to stay put. It was dark and raining. "Maybe he didn't understand you," I said to P. We peered into the shadows. The only visible movement was the rain beating against the broad leaves of trees hanging over the road. Five minutes more, and even P. began to worry. Then we saw a woman holding a wax paper umbrella. She came up to the door of the taxi, nodded, and without a word, turned away. The driver motioned us to follow her. The woman hurried back to the wet overhang of trees edging the hill in front of us. "I hope that's Kono-san's wife," I said as P. and I bowed into the rain and followed her. She never looked behind her. This venture was beginning to have all the ingredients for a mystery. It was raining; it was dark, and we were following a woman who never spoke. Just before I stepped onto the path, I turned to look back at the taxi. The driver had turned off the head-lights and had snuggled into his seat. My last contact with the outside world. McElroy, I said to myself, your mama's right: one day they're gonna find you dead where nobody else has been. Then I took a deep breath and plunged into the wet, slippery darkness where P. and the woman were barely visible in the dim light of her torch.

Walking up the hillside was like walking onto a scroll, where each level unrolled into the brush painting of another scene. The path was barely discernible, but Kono-san's wife never paused. I, on the other hand, felt as if each step might be my last. I heard frogs and crickets and rain falling onto the bushes on either side of the path, but foot-steps were muffled against the wooden blocks that defined the path. Smells were mingled in the dark: moss and lichen, ginger and euca-lyptus, orchids and roses, the sharp scent of clinging vines. And, of course, the rain. When I'd moved to the Pacific Northwest in the mid-sixties, I began to understand rain as I never had in the Midwest. Midwestern rain was vindictive, that hard stuff that beat at the win-dows, clogged the drains, and flooded the whole town. Its constant companion was wind, and they both came in, full tilt and "crazy as jaybirds," as my mother would say. Then I'd moved to the rain forest and learned to live with different rhythms of rain. In the forest, rain was the sweet smell of young plants or the tender underside of leaves. It was my daughter, laughing in the rain, or my son, jumping in a puddle without his galoshes. It was the three of us walking down the road to the store and surprising a deer at the edge of the woods, those startled eyes blinking in the rain. It was the smell of moss and underbrush. It was what made the Northwest forever green. *Yappari ao kuni da!* "It is green country!" the Japanese say.

As we ascended the narrow, winding path to Kono-san's house, even the shadows were green. At that moment, I could have believed that we were alone in the world—P. and I following a silent woman through the darkness. Then P. took my hand and we were on the veranda, in the entry hall away from the intimacy of the rain and the green hillside. Kono-san was waiting for us. We nodded hello— "Moshi. Moshi"—once, twice, three times in respect for the artist, who was one of Japan's living legends. There was a quick exchange of street shoes for surippa slippers, then into the living room for tea. Nothing was hurried—neither the tea brought in by Kono-san's wife nor his ritual pouring of it. We waited, enjoying the sound of plum rain and the scent of green tea.

Kono-san did not speak English, and P. and I relied on an almost functional speak-sign language and what few Japanese words we had. I could read the Japanese characters for exit, ladies' room, and erotic museum (some things stay with you), but I was frustrated to be so unfamiliar with a language in either its spoken or written forms. P.'s translator had given us copies of our names in Japanese characters, but we could never remember exactly how to pronounce them. We showed them to Kono-san, who smiled, and after that, language differences didn't seem to matter. As soon as P. spotted Kono-san's Wurlitzer piano, the men found the currency of a conversation, and for the next three hours, I smiled and kept to my place in the order of things. I sipped tea and examined the artifacts decorating Kono-san's home. They talked music and discussed the piano and saxophone, trying out their skills with old sheet music that Kono-san had collected over the years. I admired the grain and sheen of wood samples in Kono-san's workshop, some pieces nearly finished, others barely begun. They discussed the tools of the artisan and the charts showing growth patterns of various trees. I admired photos of Kono-san's family in one of his many albums. They examined the prizes and awards he'd received. And when P. seemed very excited about a carving of the great bull Kongoriki that Kono-san had not yet sold, I asked the price, and Kono-san's wife supplied me with the answer. It was the way of Japanese culture. While the men speculated and invented, the women kept their world in order. I was very happy to see our taxi waiting for us when Kono-san's wife escorted us back to the bottom of the hill.

It is said that for Westerners to truly discover Japan, nothing must be taken for granted. Facets reflect both the light and shadow of the culture, the shape of the thing itself. I left the country with images assembling and reassembling in my head. I know that I have not done justice to all that I saw in Japan, but I will end this memoir by stepping out of my Western notions and like the Japanese brush painter, offer you *yohaku,* the space deliberately left bare. Smile.

Take Me Where the Road Turns

I have a theory: first, man invented the wheel, then the taxi. Wheels
evolved. Taxis have remained pretty much the same, except
for changes in name: car-for-hire, limo, hack, jitney,
gypsy cab, pousse-pousse, Hansom, rickshaw . . . You
whistle for them, wave, point, thumb, and yell
But with all that evolution and name change,
the drivers are cut from the same cloth.

No cab ride is simple. It's an engagement between you and the person who at that moment is driving a cab. Most cab drivers think of
themselves as having been on the road to somewhere else when they
took the turn that placed them behind the wheel of a taxi. Ask them.
The nicest cabbie I met in Italy had earned his degree in dentistry but
never had enough money to open a practice. In Chicago, the driver
had been, according to him, FBI—an operative, he called it. I wasn't
about to argue with hair cut that short and nails that blunt. He took
every curve on the Expressway like the Indy 500. I checked my airline ticket and wished I was already airborne, defying gravity at
thirty thousand feet instead at ground level. "Twenty years in service

with the Bureau," he said. "I can rev this baby up to 1 2 0 mph and keep all four wheels on the road." To prove it, he put the petal to metal and floorboarded the cab, shifting lanes and double-clutching. I heard my luggage bounce in the trunk and thunk back toward the middle. We passed an El as if it were standing still. He gave me tips on how to conceal weapons in suitcase frames or slip road blocks. "You learn a lot out there when you hit the road," he said. I nodded, holding tight to my vision of a safer road. "I follow government specs," he said. I shut my eyes and gripped the armrest as we careened toward O'Hare.

That is the proper etiquette: never ever pay attention to how the cabbie drives. Looking too long is liable to earn you a heart attack or, in the long haul, severe facial tics. When the cabbie in Cairo yelled, "Wen-Nabi! Wen-Nabi!" and slipped between a horse-drawn wagon full of melons and an overcrowded bus that was already doing touch-and-go with a truck, I too prayed that the Prophet would guide us.

And then there was the cabbie in San Francisco. I was visiting the city with my translator from Madagascar, and it was to be her first u.s. taxi ride. What a grand initiation! The cabbie took the hills of San Francisco like a roller coaster, all the while yelling directions to everyone in his path. "Don't look at it! You look at it and you never turn the corner." He had no problem with corners, most of them in the whiplash of two wheels. "Adios," he'd shout. "I know I'm good-looking but I got to keep going." José Jiminez, he called himself. "Francisco is my name," he said when I wouldn't accept Jose. "Francisco, I love you," I told him. "You are a cabbie extraordinaire." "Adios, sweet amigas," he called when he dropped us off at Fisherman's Wharf. "Adios," I waved as my Malagasy friend struggled to catch her breath. I've never been on such a ride," she said. "Yeah," I grinned. "Some cabbies don't have the knack."

No matter what they say, I firmly believe that taxi drivers evolved
into a separate species, complete with cultural icons, a
language system, rituals for determining lengths to
which they will go to carry passengers on meta-
physical journeys. They must read the same
book, these men and women who prowl
streets at all hours of day and night.

Consider the taxi driver in Yugoslavia, the one who told me that
curves in the road were not there for drivers. "So many big accidents
on curve," he said. "I drive straight." The road was dark. In the head-
lights, a tree would appear, hog the windshield, and as the cabbie
straightened out the bend in the road, would dance to the side, seemingly of its own accord. I looked out the window. Lake Ohrid was oys-
ter-gray in picture postcard moonlight, ripples lapping quietly at the
banks. Along the curve of shoreline, I could see the town of Ohrid,
dim lights blinking on the horizon. But directly across the lake, all was
dark. "Albania," the driver said, his voice filled with gloom. Then he
pulled onto the apron of the road. "Tell me again why you are in my
country," he said. The road seemed suddenly more deserted than
ever. Moonlight crinkled the water until it dropped into shadows and
fell into that blackness he'd called Albania. "We cannot guarantee
your safety in Albania," they'd said at the Fulbright office in Belgrade.
"Maybe you go also to another place," the cabbie said. He gestured
across the lake. "A short drive, yes?" He pointed to the road behind us
that was pitch black. I said to myself: Think fast, McElroy. When in
doubt, go Island Girl. "In my leetle village . . ." I began, talking fast so
he wouldn't notice how my accent slipped from the Caribbean to
Louisiana to Malaysia and back. "My hoosband, he has very much
importance," I told him. "I must call to the Embahsee and tell heem I
am here or he will have tew much worry."

I still believe that the word *embassy* started the car again. Whatever
the case, the cabbie muttered all the way to Ohrid, his voice like the
loose cylinders on that Yugo coupe.

Remember: an engine that starts doesn't mean the car runs smoothly.
Good cabbies know how to talk to pistons and carbs
better than to a lover. They tell you, "I treat this
baby like a lady or my mother." They dress their
cars in self-defining finery, rearview mirrors
blessed with religious medals, which you
should never confuse with their fears
for your life, because always, it's
the car that matters.

The taxi in Ecuador had two Madonnas glued to the dash. They were sounder than the engine. We jiggety-hicked a couple of miles up the mountain, then stopped. Llamas and vicuñas came to the edge of the fields to watch, chewing their cud as if to say, "We've seen it all. Inca to Spaniard and now the newest crop." At one stall-out on a wild stretch of rocky terrain without a house in sight, a young shepherd appeared—Ecuadorian, no more than sixteen years old, I guessed. He spoke no English except for songs he'd heard on the radio he carried, an Americanized station playing the top ten u.s. hits. They consulted, shepherd and cabbie, on the gringa tourist and the sorry state of the engine while Barry White moaned over the R & B waves. I guess the engine heard him, because it sputtered to life and we groaned to the top of the mountain, Madonnas grinning on the dash.

I've been in cabs put together by wire and glue and the good-times-had-by-all. I'm talking cabs with no gas tanks and floors that are two-by-fours. Cabs that keep picking up passengers even after all the seats are filled. Cabs with no windshields, and cabs with windshields framed in animal skins, the seats more sofas for the living room than comfort for the road. But a cab is a cab is a cab, isn't it? The cab I took in Belize was a cross between a carnival float and a Mexican tribute to the Day of the Dead. The car was a special order that the driver had driven from Houston to Belize himself. Crosses and statues of saints winked in both front windows and back, the windows framed in tassels and red and green lights. It was a queen's barge, a floating bed, a royal coach. Three gold crown air fresheners graced the dash, and everything was cushioned in fake fur and velvet—a true Carib cab, all carnival and flash, especially for tourists.

In Japan, taxis were as clean as brush paintings. Cabbies wore white gloves and car seats were covered with embroidered doilies—white, of course. On a cab's pristine seat, my leather valise, its sides scarred from airline baggage racks, looked not unlike a bad stain on a bedspread. We were changing hotels, P. and I, and only with the promise of a huge tip did the cabbies allow us one car per two pieces of luggage. Even at that, we had to take separate cabs, because by that time, I had three pieces plus my carry-on. (At least airlines post the dimensions of overheads.) I fast-talked the driver into letting me put my suitcase up front. In Japan, if you don't fit, you don't ride. But fit or not, you'd better have a map.

Drivers carry maps by the book: one for street numbers, another for street names, a third for districts. If you don't know where you're going or how to get there, all three books can fail. Once, when P. and I wanted to go across town, three translators drew three different maps. The cabbie dismissed them all. Too confusing, he let us know with gestures. Typical cabbie, I thought, the type who trained in New York or Paris, where cabbies always ask: What route would you like me to take? The most direct, I always think. But in Japan, there are no direct routes. An address may not be simply a slot on a street but the history of a place: one number for the Shogunate, another for the number of times the house was rebuilt, and still another for each owner, all of it altered by wars. Then add language barriers. Result: it's gonna cost you. Unless you're lucky. P. and I were once, if luck is what you want to call it. We had planned to go to shopping in Tokyo's Roppongi district for blue-and-white Japanese fabrics, designs that were famous the world over. The store was called Blue and White. Simple, right? Except we had no map. We cruised Roppongi for half an hour before the driver, unable to find

the shop in any of his books, evicted us on a street corner. We ate his
exhaust as he roared away.

Whatever your trip, there are certain things you should not say. For
example: Follow that car! It only works in the movies anyway.
And speed is a cabbie's middle name, so don't encourage them.
Some get their training in cities where they learn to slip
large cars into spots fit only for bikes or slide between
the breath space of two trucks in order to run a red
light. For a fee, they'll take you down roads fit
only for deer crossings and charge you extra
for assisting with luggage and packages.
And you must never let them know you
are new in town and lost.

In Belgrade, my roommate insisted that she should talk to the driver
because back in the States, she'd once hosted a writer from Yugoslavia. I knew her forté was not Serbian. Even to my atonal ear, her
Serbian sounded like an Ozark drawl stuck in an elevator in Canada.
That didn't stop her. "Take me to the National Radio Office," she told
the driver. At least *national* and *radio* were clear. The driver shrugged
but didn't move. She talked louder—the mark of a foreigner whose
language had failed. I tried interrupting, but she waved me away and
tried again. Finally, the cabbie sighed, turned on the meter, and
pulled into traffic. "See," she said, "it takes patience." We turned the
corner, right at a statue of some Yugoslav patriot. We turned right,
and right and right again, until I noticed we were left of the same
statue. The driver turned off the meter and pointed to a building
across from the statue—our destination. "Pay the man," I said, and
pointed to the building behind us—our apartment. We'd circled the
block, the fare putting a bigger dent in my roommate's pride than in
her purse.

But experience told me how she felt. A few years earlier when I
was in Japan, I had played a similar language game. Thinking myself

clever, I once hailed a cab and demanded to be taken to the Kokusai Hotel. "Immediately," I said. The cabbie shook his head. "Kokusai," P. repeated. The cabbie smiled and took us across town to a love hotel with red brick walls and a red velvet lobby. It's hard to describe how out of place we looked, P. and I in that plush red love nest. But they let us call for another taxi. *Kokusai*, we were told, was Japanese for international, and that hotel, red velvet and all, was one of a thousand called international. At least that cabbie abandoned us near a phone.

Words you rarely want to hear from a cabbie: *So what brings you to town: girlie, little lady, Fraülein, honey?* I automatically start counting my pocket change, thinking my answer will double the fare. But sometimes I'm wrong. There are cabbies who have not put their hearts on a metered clock. They can talk and drive at the same time, getting you there directly and safely. I'd trust those rare finds to take me on an overland trek through mosquito country in Alaska.

I have found good cabbies and bad cabbies. Once, a driver in Pittsburgh saw me running in the rain. I was still wearing high, high heels in those, the foolish days of my youth. I tripped, and she backed up her hack in order to pick me up, then gave me a free ride home—a real samaritan. The next time I needed a cab, I called for hers and gave her a tip bigger than the fare. (Cabbies love tips, the bigger the better.) But it wasn't always the tip that made cabbies generous with their time. What was that song the Mills Brothers used to croon: *Cab driver, once more 'round the block*. With luck, that extra turn around the block could keep me on course. I had just that kind of luck in Venice, where the roads were canals and the taxis were gondolas. When I got off the train, I had expected to walk through the depot and onto a curb where I could hail a taxi. I walked out of the depot and found instead a flight of stairs, about a hundred, it seemed, leading to a pier. And there, the water taxis waited. Some were large, minibus-sized for a dozen or so passengers. Others were sedan-sized with curved prows, the famous gondolas of Venice. But like any taxi station, the rush was on, and no one was willing to wait for the next cab. Folks scrambled down the stairs toward the loading dock in an unruly mass. So, carry-on slung over my shoulder, I clumped down the steps along with them, dragging my luggage behind me, ignoring the fact that my suitcase threatened to abandon its wheels and go careening into the Grand Canal. There was no time to talk practical-ity to a Samsonite Rollabout, so I did the unthinkable and tossed that old bag down the last few steps and onto the deck of the nearest water bus. Then I took advantage of the space I'd cleared and jumped in behind it. Sweating and wheezing, I shouted out the name of my hotel. A couple of Italians repeated my message until the driver nod-ded. And so began my first trip down the Grand Canal.

We passed under the Scalzi Bridge, the Rialto Bridge, and Ponti Accademia, passed docking spaces for great palazzi and churches, Peggy Guggenheim's palazzo, and dozens of Italian Renaissance houses with rococo facades, all of their casements marked by cen-turies of flooding and receding water levels. When we reached the Piazzetta di San Marco, the driver called out the name of my hotel and pointed. Someone unloaded my suitcase on the dock, and the driver waved me off. I was standing there, watching the water bus pull away, when I noticed a commotion on the next set of stairs at the San Marco quay. A woman, a tourist from the looks of the camera slung around her neck, had walked down the boat loading stairs— "to put her feet in the waters of Venice," someone told me later. Stupid, I thought at the time, even without knowing her reasons. Venice may have been beautiful, but the canals were giant sewers with an effluvium that threatened to choke you if you were in the city during the hottest weather of summer. (Those canals had been polluted for centuries. Katherine Hepburn needed several years to recover from an eye infection she contracted while filming a scene where she fell into the canal.) The woman at the San Marco dock had slipped on the slime-covered steps and landed in the water. Within seconds, the gondoliers had snagged her dress with boat hooks and fished her out of the water like a wet rat, sludge still clinging to her hair. That was one time I was greatful to be instinctively aquaphobic. I turned toward the piazza, the Doge's Palace and the Basilica, and on the other side of the plaza, a hotel with an Italian marble bath waiting just for me. I took a long hot bath, then decided on an early dinner and a ride on the Grand Canal. At the quay, I hailed a water taxi.

I was exhausted that first evening in Venice. I had spent the night in a sleeping car with a man from Denmark who snored and a girl from Connecticut who was determined to make every moment of her trip memorable by talking incessantly on the train ride from Rome to Venice. The gondolier could not have helped but notice my fatigue. I fell asleep almost as soon as I'd settled into the gondola and slept through the trip down Grand Canal and into the smaller canals where resident Venetians traveled. I woke up just as we returned to the Grand Canal. He watched me yawn into the last finger of sunlight that kissed the lagoon as the lights from piazzas blinked on one by one. I quickly sat upright, holding my breath at the sight. It was indeed breathtaking, like waking from a dream into a dream, outlines of cathedrals and palazzos turned into purple shadows against a rosy sky. I don't know what I said, or if I said anything, but the gondolier pushed off from the quay and started another excursion down the canal. "No denaro," I told him, indicating zero with a circle of my fingers. He waved off my protest, and we glided past Piazza San Marco while he began singing, "O Solo Mio." (Oh, what a softy I am for an aria and a sweet cab driver.)

The cabbie in London couldn't sing, but I am convinced that he saved my life. It was Sunday, my second day in town, and a holiday for England. Half the city was closed down, so I decided to take the early morning city tour. The double-decker would take me past the London sights—Hyde Park, Parliament, the Tower, the usual London gloss. I'd been on the tour before, but the museums were closed, so I decided to have another go at it. I was one of three passengers, and the driver was giving out a bit extra. We'd no sooner swung into traffic when Victoria's Revenge gripped my G.I. tract. I doubled over, breathed deep, rode the wave of nausea, and came up for air in time to catch the last of the spiel on Whitehall. It didn't crest again until the Old Bailey. I gulped air as we crossed Blackfriar's Bridge. To tell the truth, I don't remember much after that—Waterloo, Westminster, St. James. What I saw was trapped on the floor of the bus, rubber treads almost worn smooth by years of tourists. When we finally returned to the starting point at Trafalger Square, I limped off with a whispery, "Thank you" and made for the nearest taxi. It was a London hack, with a backseat as wide as a tomb, which I was convinced I needed in my state of near death. "What's the matter, luv?" the driver asked. I could only clutch my stomach and groan, spitting out the name of my hotel between moans. I'll give him credit, he tried, that cabbie named Harry, but it was clear, I'd never make my hotel.

"I know what to do for you, luv. Just hold on," Harry said. He took me down a side street, made two turns, and sped down roads that offered no clues to our location. He stopped. Now, I was both sick and lost. He opened the taxi door. "Com'on, luv," he said. I crawled out. I hesitated for a second. The toss-up was the certainty of the rebellion in my stomach or the possibility of a cabbie with a murderous streak. I was beyond caring. What I got was his mum. She rushed me into the loo, clucking at the recklessness of tourists. I was weak when I came out. The cabbie handed me a cup of tea and said, "Mum will tend you, luv. I'll be back in an hour." His mother shushed him out the door and clucked over me like a brood hen. It was exactly what I needed: a cabbie who didn't have to be given directions, and a mother who was every inch an angel.

Brief Moments When I Thought of Something Called Love

A playwright friend who is fond of remembering her love affair in Paris likes to organize a party game where she asks the guests to recall their most romantic moment. Over the years, I've watched her make this happen at various gatherings. In true dramatic style, she demands that everyone participate in her idea of heart-stopping love and sunset romance, regardless of age and present state of relationship. The whole point is to give herself the chance to recall her moment of love and how, because it was Paris, it was all the more exciting. Who can resist? Indeed, what can be more romantic than that fleeting moment in some distant place when love, in all of its splendor, enters your life? The only thing missing is background music, violins, if you please. And although my friend bears no resemblance to Audrey Hepburn, Dianne Carroll, or any of the other Hollywood ingénues who have acted out silver screen images of romantic interludes in Paris, it is a story that never grows old, no matter how many times she tells it.

My playwright friend asks for romance, but what she talks about is passion—sweaty sheets and midnight walks in the rain. I take into account that it happened when she was in school, a young black woman alone in Paris, caught up in the tide of international students wanting to taste the freedom of being abroad. I remember those years, mine mis-spent in Munich, but as I get older, I recall them with a lot less passion than I care to admit. Oh, there were those love-at-first-sight moments during my student days, but they haven't stayed with me as long as I had expected. I have learned over the years that adventuresome love, love caught on the run while I was traveling from one place to someplace called home, hardly ever greeted me directly: it sidled in, stumbled in, tripped me up, and left me confused and happy. Most often it was not even passionate love, but as my playwright friend would have it, romance: the feeling of being in love or being attracted by love. (Are they perhaps one and the same?) But basically I'm a cynic, so it was sometimes hard for me to recognize romance for what it was until after it had passed. Sometimes the feeling was crowded out by the voice in my head saying: Been there, done that! I needed a jolt—or a swift kick in the butt, as some of my friends have put it—to convince me that I, too, could succumb to hearts-and-flowers. So when my friend brings this up at a party, I sort through my memories and give it my best shot.

McElroy, what's your most romantic moment? I ask myself. Well, there was that hint of romance when I was in Yugoslavia, near the start of my Fulbright residency. I remember that I'd had the *been-away-from-home-too-long-in-this-strange-country* blues. As down in the dumps as I felt, I didn't need much, not the kind of heavy Paris nights love where I would give my heart away. After a string of gloomy days, a mere glance would have made me reconsider the possibility of being in love. And that's what I got—an encounter so brief, so fragile that if I'd blinked, it would have vanished into the sweet spring air. It was the stuff of poetry: a handsome young man, a slight touch of innocent flirtation, and a rose.

I had been in Dubrovnik for nearly twelve days and was intent on making my way south to Ulcinj, which was easier said than done. So when I learned that Larry Levis and Phil Dacey, two Fulbright writ-ers, had arrived in town, I put my plans on hold. There were five writ-ers on Fulbrights in Yugoslavia at the time, but Larry and I had become close friends. Each day, after meetings with Slavic poets or touring a local publishing house, we agreed to have dinner in the Starigrad, the old walled city of Dubrovnik. The Starigrad, built in the twelfth century, was a castle city, complete with turrets, palaces, cobblestoned streets, and a moat with a drawbridge. It was almost fairy tale perfect, and in weather that was springtime lovely, the days seemed designed for love, or for the hope of it. The square, in the heart of the old city, was occupied by young people strolling in groups or couples, looking each other over as if they were at the senior prom. "This gives them a place to meet," our Yugoslav host told us. On the main plaza of the Starigrad, the town seemed to be in cahoots with the idea of couples meeting, the square spruced up as if it were ready to receive royalty. Streetlights were festooned with flowers, and music leaked out of the bistros along the side streets.

Only I wasn't impressed. After three months of too many racial incidents, too much red tape, and too many restrictions on buses or trains that never ran on schedule if they left at all, I'd just about had it with Yugoslavia. Dubrovnik might have looked like it was ready for party time, but that was the exception, not the rule. More often than not, I was caught up in the sullenness of cities like Belgrade. More often than not, I could smell the ethnic war that was brewing and within two years would fill that country's gardens with bomb craters. But back in 1988, that trouble was merely simmering.

The first time I visited Ljubljana with my roommate Mary, an American embassy official met us at the train station with the short terse order to "get back on the train. Go to the seashore. Go back to Belgrade. Go any place but here. This town is under curfew." And in Pristina, my host nearly locked me in my room after giving me instructions that I was never to leave the hotel without him and the driver. When I did venture out, I ran the gauntlet of unemployed men from the town staring at the privilege I had of being an outsider. "It's the Albanians," the host in Pristina said. "They have made it impossible for us." The phrase sounded vaguely familiar, then I remembered I'd heard it in Belgrade, except the reference was to gypsies. "The gypsies have made it impossible to live in Belgrade," I was told. But it wasn't gypsies who'd followed me, laughing and pointing when I walked down the street in Belgrade.

"You must get sick of all this," Larry had said. "It wears on you," I'd told him. So by the time I reached Dubrovnik, I had begun to expect the same treatment.

Instead, it was spring and Dubrovnik was heavy with the scent of flowers. The boys, dressed in T-shirts and black market jeans, did what boys do everywhere—they cruised the square, eyeing the young girls who stood demurely to the side, giggling at their ambitious suitors. The boys swaggered past, grinning. So did the Dons—seabirds, we called them—handsome young men in throaty shirts who sold their bodies to foreign tourists. In Dubrovnik, there were just as many women caught up in the world's oldest profession, but the men seemed to be trying to live up to the old street slogan: "Yugoslavia, where the men are pretty and the women are strong." At night, I could hear them through the hotel's thin walls, shouting out their conquests in the appropriate language.

Larry and I decided that the young Slav we'd seen escorting women to the hotel for the past several nights was practicing his English. His voice echoed through the courtyard. "Tell me of what yourself you are doing for business," he'd say. "You coming from where? You going to where?" We could hear the woman's muffled answers, rising in irritation as the young man's clumsily worded questions continued. Judging from the kind of woman I saw him chatting up in the square, I guessed her to be Nordic—Swedish, I assumed, because although more than forty years had passed since World War II, money was often not enough to overcome the average Yugoslav's animosity toward Germans. But money was the weapon in this instance, and since it was in the woman's pocket, it was in her power to hush the questions. After a lull, the moans would begin until finally, triumphantly, the Slav would yell, "It is to come! It is to come!" The next morning, when I met Larry and Phil for breakfast, they threatened to give the Slav an English grammar lesson, "free of charge," Phil said. "Hey, we're supposed to represent the best of American literature for these people," Larry said. "It's our duty to make sure his syntax is in order no matter what the circumstances."

"Maybe," I said. "But I don't think our Fulbright covers these circumstances."

Still, when we saw the young man in the square near Onofrio's Fountain, where all the action was, we'd wave to him and he'd wave back as if we were old friends. I think we were a little jealous of the young Slav's liaisons, but for different reasons. Phil's girlfriend was due to arrive from the States in less than a week. I was recovering from the loss of a ten-year love affair, and Larry was pining for his love back home. We made a perfect team—the cynic who saw disaster in every hint of love and the optimists who saw love in every hint of spring. Larry would say, "Com'on Colleen . . . 'Tis better to have loved and lost than not to have loved at all." And I'd say, "Can it, Larry. I've heard all that crap before." But secretly, I was happy to have his romantic nature on my side.

We had sort of a routine, the three of us. After dinner, we strolled in the Starigrad. That's where we were when love came stumbling by—a fleeting, flirtatious kind of love that would not have been significant at all if I hadn't been in Yugoslavia in the spring of 1988 walking beside a tall, handsome poet who quoted me lines from old poems, and another who could hardly wait to greet his lover from home. But there I was, and in front of me, the courtship of Yugoslav youths was in bloom.

I saw them walking toward me almost as soon as we entered the square—four teenage boys who would have been heading for fraternity row if they'd lived in the States. As it was, they were heading for an insane war that had begun several centuries ago when the Muslim Turks from the Ottoman Empire ruled that part of the world. (That may have been the distant past, but as far as I could tell, the Yugoslavs were like elephants: They never forgot anything.) That day, the young boy and his friends were intent on impressing females.

As Phil, Larry, and I moved closer, I could see that one of the boys was holding a single rose. He looked like a thinner version of Robert Redford, at least Redford during his Sundance Kid days. He was taking up the middle of the road, which is where I was walking. I don't know if I was looking at him in particular, but just as Larry said, "Reminds me of the kids back home on the mall," I knew that boy was heading for me. I pulled myself up tall, all of my street smarts coming to mind as I remembered the rude exchanges I'd had with kids in Belgrade. The boy's friends were giggling and poking him in the ribs, egging him on—that I'd almost expected, but I never expected what came next. He stopped right in front of me, that kid, and in a voice sliding between the adult he would become and the child he still was, said, "Please, for you, madame." Then he thrust the rose in my hand, his face almost as red as its petals. I heard his friends draw in their breath. I smelled the rose. "Sladak," I said. "Sweet. Sweet." I don't know if the sigh was mine or the boy's. He rushed away, his friends laughingly trailing after.

Larry took my hand and kissed it. "Love is where you find it," he said. "Or where it finds you," I told him. I peered into the crowd. I saw a group of young boys near the kiosk but did not recognize the boy who had given me the rose. Then Phil spotted him in the crowd under the arch of the castle gates. The boy looked back, only for a second, then he and his friends crossed the bridge that connected the old city to modern Dubrovnik's main street.

Sometimes love is only just that—a mere flirtation, a chance meeting that makes you feel desirable. "I felt so beautiful," my playwright friend always says. And I always agree. I tell her about a time after I left Yugoslavia. I was on a train in Italy, a commuter between Pompeii and Naples. That in itself is one of the oddities of travel— an express train between the silent past and the bustling present.

Of course, any excursion to Pompeii was a journey into the past. Although I had a sense of foreboding, walking through the ancient city was like walking across a star bridge into a different spatial reference. Sally, my host in Italy, had warned me that the visit would be exceptional. "Pompeii has its own magic," she'd said. Still, I don't know what I'd expected—perhaps charred rubble, like what you'd find after a fire—but the eruption of Vesuvius had left the skeletal remains of Pompeii in all of its architectural glory.

In Naples, you can buy guidebooks that reconstruct several ancient Italian cities, but I had no problems tracing the connection of streets when I walked through Pompeii: the marble hallways and expansive courtyards of upper-class houses, the stingy rooms of servant and slave quarters, the shrines and temples and bathhouses. Where there were no rooftops, the walls remained. Where there were no statues, the pedestals stood ready. I walked past a lone statue in the temple of Apollo, past the brick colonnades of the Basilica, the columns themselves a forest of lonesome stumps that reminded me of hillsides stripped of trees by loggers. I walked through the Forum and the House of the Tragic Poet with its vivid paintings of gods and goddesses, and down side streets where I found houses with no roofs but with rooms so narrow I felt the walls closing in on me. In a house off Via dell' Abbondanza, I swear I felt a presence so strong I could imagine someone breathing.

When Sally found me, I was struggling for my own breath. My good sense said it was my asthma, but my heart's eye told me that something else whispered in the shallow breeze that blew in through the doorway. "This was slaves' quarters," Sally said when she consulted the guidebook. I felt no surprise, just a bit "weirded out," as my daughter would say. What thread was tying me to this place? Perhaps there was some truth in what philosophers call cultural memory. Europeans had been pillaging the African continent for centuries before they took my ancestors into American slavery, but history has it that the slaves in Pompeii were sometimes given more freedom than those brutalized by the American system. Still, I couldn't shake the feeling of disquiet until I went back into the sunlight where wildflowers grew in the ruins of temples, and butterflies, grateful for the absence of rooftops, danced down the Street of

Tombs and into the House of the Fawn. I took with me the beauty of Pompeii and tried to leave behind the uneasiness I'd felt there.

Pompeii was a place filled with unfinished business. What had not been eroded by time, waited as if ready to be reclaimed by the owners. And all the while, the sky held true to its promise of summer. It's no wonder that when Sally and I boarded the train for Naples, I was still caught up in the sense of timelessness. The conductor had already signaled that the train was ready to leave the station when I heard someone banging on the door. The car I was riding in was crowded, so Sally and I were standing, hanging onto the overhead straps. Because I was in full view of the door, I could see a man trying to get the conductor's attention. But when the doors wheezed open, instead of boarding the train, the man fell to his knees and began speaking to me. He was Mediterranean handsome, a little bit too much street but classy in the way of all eternal flirts. "Amore," he said. "Amore." The very act itself caused everyone to stop, the whole scene caught in a freeze-frame. At first he spoke only in Italian, and for all that I understood, he could have been a ghost from Pompeii. Half of my senses were still back among the ruins anyway. "Amore! Amore!" he called to me.

I looked around, thinking he meant someone else, although I was the only one facing the doorway. But the other passengers had turned to look at me. Several women grinned. One, a hefty gray-haired woman in a flowered dress, repeated "Amore," and winked. "Who's he talking to?" I asked Sally. She shrugged. "Maybe he's crazy," she said.

Crazy or not, he'd heard me speaking English. "Amore," he pleaded. "Come with me. I will make you chief dancer in my harem."

I laughed. He was on his knees, his arms spread out as if he were auditioning for a role in an Italian opera. I said the first thing that came to mind. "Fool. You don't have a harem," I said.

"For you," he said, "I will get harem."

And then the doors closed. The woman in the flowered dress said, "Bellisimo." Everyone applauded. Sally said, "He must be crazy." I was laughing. "Maybe not," I said, and felt myself flush with more than just the rays of the Italian sun. "Bella. Bella," the Italian woman said. And I said, "Yes," not caring whether she meant me or my erstwhile suitor, still kneeling on the platform as the train sped toward the harsh reality of modern Naples.

> Given the chance, I would have loved you:
> *more than aureliano buendia loved macondo*
> *more than hector lavoe loved himself*
> Given the chance I would have loved you:
> *more than the flamingoes shoo-do-n-doo-wah love*
> *bein pretty . . .*

"Once I was serenaded by the Italian army," I say. "To be serenaded under the moon, that's romantic." Then I tell them about the moon rising over Lake Como like a great pearl in a sea of stars. Bellagio could have been a backdrop for an Italian opera, but for the forty or so residents there, scholars and writers from all over the world, it was a fellowship from heaven. The studios were what magazines would call "elegantly appointed," with antique furniture, marble bathrooms, and bevelled windows that looked out over gardens terraced like those in Versailles or Rome. In my studio, I'd write to the music of Leontyne Price performing at the Met or La Scala. White linen curtains billowed at the terrace windows and I felt like royalty, a writer of substance. Everything was perfect, except it was 1991 and the Middle East was in flames. "That's why the Italian government had soldiers stationed at Bellagio," I say. By the third night of my stay, the soldiers had figured out which rooms were mine.

Each night after I returned to my studio following dinner, I'd read in bed, the windows open. In the distance, on the other side of the lake, I could see the very tips of the Italian Alps. More Leontyne Price, something from Puccini, as I remember. Then, that third night, a male voice. I thought: Leontyne, your voice is going bad, honey. A second male voice. I turned down the volume on the tape player. A third male voice. "Addio, Fiorito Asil," they sang. Three, no four, voices in chorus. The scent of flowers wafted through the windows. The moon winked between the flutters of curtains. My troubadours switched to "O Solo Mio," and "Gente Mia," their voices somewhere between drunken and homesick. I giggled as they tried "Maria" from *West Side Story*. For four more nights, they sang beneath my window and until I complained that they seriously interrupted my sleep, they may have gone on singing in the moonlight for my entire stay at the palacio by the lake.

"The moon," my playwright friend says, "The moon lets you know you are in love." And I think: Maybe the poet, Al Young, was right. The moon hanging in a distant sky can make you believe in love. When I was leaving for Yugoslavia, Al shared his poems on the moon and love inspired by his stay as a creative writing Fulbright Fellow there in 1985. So in 1988, I had entered the country expecting a clear sky, the moon hanging low and heavy the way I'd seen it in Fiji, or the moon over that beautiful villa in Majorca where George Sand riotously rendezvoused with her lover Chopin. (On the island of Krk, a mad monk serenades visitors with gothic melodies on a pipe organ. The music seems straight out of *Phantom of the Opera*. On the shores of the island, where American oil companies have built acres of refineries that glow like ghostly space stations, an American hotel, reportedly built by Hugh Hefner, stands unoccupied—an ornate love nest. At least the Yugoslavs don't sell miniature pipe organs playing Krk melodies the way Chopin's piano is hawked on Marjorca.) Perhaps along with Chopin's pianos, I could have found Al Young's moon in Majorca, but Belgrade was anything but romantic.

To describe Belgrade is to be repetitive: gray smoke, gray buildings, gray people, rudeness, and paranoia about war. There was no sense of friendliness on the street, and nothing was simple. Everything operated on the principle of time consumption, and everywhere someone was building something. Hammering bricks into walls, away from walls. Laying cobblestones for streets, removing streets. Women had babies—and more babies. Men smoked and quarreled. All day and all night, they walked. Public squares were full of idle men and strolling women. Children out of school joined the walking brigade. I never figured out where they were going, or if indeed they were going anywhere.

From winter, when I arrived, into early summer, when I left, the sky was shaded in smoke from coal burning furnaces. The air was Mexico City and Bogotá, the smog so bad I could wear only one contact lens. A gray pallor hung over the city, partly from the smoke, partly from an economy that was as impractical as the aging furnaces. Everyone, of every age, was a smoker. (Even the pigeons pecked at butts in the gutters.) Boys that seemed no older than seven or eight leaned against buildings, smoking cigarettes like their fathers. (They were just tall enough to watch the previews of porno flicks on the peep screens outside of movie houses.) The air of every bistro and restaurant was thick with cigarette smoke. Social gatherings were cloaked in a blue haze. A reformed smoker, I recoiled at every puff. So it was with some relief that I accepted an invitation to a party at Ivana Milankhova's house. She had befriended Al Young, and since Al was a nonsmoker, I figured I had a fifty-fifty chance of finding oxygen along with my slivovitz.

In Yugoslavia, I'd learned to drink slivovitz chasers with my breakfast coffee. Less than a week after we'd arrived, Mary and I were sent to visit the University of Maribor in the foothills below the Austrian Alps. 8:30 A.M., a breakfast meeting, the English language faculty. As soon as we were seated, the secretary entered the office with a tray of slivovitz to welcome us. Mary looked at me. "Maybe some coffee," she said. "To drink with the slivovitz," I quickly added, easing our host's frowns. "They start so early in the morning," Mary had said later. But we learned that slivovitz was not confined to a special hour of the day; sometimes it was easier to get than a handshake. So when I was invited to Ivana's, I knew slivovitz would flow like the Danube.

"I'm not drinking a lot tonight," Larry said. "Me neither," I said, and sipped my first drink. The good thing about slivovitz was that it slid down easy as water even though it smelled like gin in a dirty toilet. (Perhaps that's because I prefered vodka, which was expensive for the average Belgrade budget.)

The party turned out to be a bit more intimate than I had expected. There were only Ivana; Vladislav, a Russian writer and his girl (whose name was never given); Ratko, a Belgrade fiction writer; Larry; and me—and, of course, slivovitz. "You have a vunderful husband at home?" Ivana asked me. "No husband," I said. "Do you know the beau-tiful Al Joung? Is he your lover?" "Just friends," I said. "Like me and Larry," I said. Ivana's eyebrows disappeared into her hairline. Predatory was the only way I could describe her smile. "So Larry he is not your lover?" she said. "And he too has no marriage?" Except when she said it, it sounded like mirage. "No marriage," I said, looking at Larry. "Let's sit," he said to me.

We parked ourselves on the sofa, Larry and I, the two us of sharing one cushion while the Russian writer and his girlfriend shared the other cushion. And I'm here to tell you, we were packed in tight. That sofa could really only hold three—two, if you figured on accommodating Larry and an average-sized Russian, and Vladislav was hardly the economy package. Both he and Larry were over six feet tall, and almost immediately the sofa began to feel very crowded. With Ivana fluttering about to the tune of Serbian popular music on the phonograph, the smell of raw Yugoslav tobacco, and slivovitz brandy, I began to feel as if I were in the drawing room of some bad Russian novel. Twenty minutes later, I was on my second drink.

Vladislav was trying to talk to me, but I had exhausted my Russian vocabulary after zdrastvujte, dosvidanye, and Kak stranno! Vladislav had resorted to pumping his right leg up and down, the movement doing nothing more than polishing my left thigh. His girlfriend was mute, answering no questions in Serbian, Russian, French, or German. (Did that child understand any earthly language?) Ivana was gaily recalling her encounters with Al Young, "the beau-tiful Al Joung," as she'd say. And Ratko had pulled his chair in front of the sofa in hopes of getting my attention. What got my attention was the peppermill he had between his legs. I'd watched him pick it up from the dining room table but thought he was trying to fix it after Ivana said it hadn't worked since "the beau-tiful Al Joung was here in this house."

"Maybe he wants to immortalize the peppermill in Al Young's memory," Larry said. He winked and asked for another drink.

I thought he was about to get up. "Larry Levis, you leave my side and you die," I told him. Larry handed his glass to Ivana, who filled it to the brim. The Russian polished and polished, murmuring something that I could not and did not wish to understand. Ratko provided the comedy relief.

Rumor had it that Ratko was a successful writer, a hotshot in the Belgrade Writers Union, and friends with Slobodan Miloševíc, who would become infamous as Serbia's president when the union of Slavic states dissolved into war. (Ironically, slobodan means freedom in Serbian.) I couldn't attest to Ratko's skills as a writer, but his conversation left much to be desired. (None of it was helped by Ratko's bad teeth, a condition he shared with many Yugoslavs in a country of appalling dentistry. Even a Serbian dentist I'd met had had brown teeth.) But Ratko wasn't the type to let appearances slow him down.

"You are beautiful woman. Black woman. I know you are wanting to rush across the room and throw your arms around me," he said, grinding the peppermill as if his crotch had a storehouse of spices.

"Not on this planet," I said, and shoved my glass toward Ivana.

"You must tell the beau-tiful Al Joung how I miss him," she said, taking my glass.

"I can't wait," I said.

"I know you are wanting to take off all your clothes and make mad passionate love with me," Ratko said, the peppermill groaning like a gear shift.

I was having less trouble with the slivovitz than I'd ever had. As bitter tasting as it was, already my glass was half empty. And my social decorum was vanishing almost as fast as the brandy. "I'll bet you can't even write about passionate love, much less recognize it," I said nastily. Then I stared at Vladislav, who grinned and worked his leg against my thigh like a masseur on a mission. "Vladislav, do you have a muscle disorder?" I asked. "Da," he answered. His girlfriend never stopped trying to look at something stuck on the bridge of her nose. I decided she was rather attractive with crossed eyes.

"I know you are wanting to take me in your arms," Ratko said.

"I am wanting to go to the bathroom," Larry said.

"And I am wanting to tell you, Larry Levis, that we are joined at the hip," I said. "Wherever you go, I go. Just don't leave me alone in this room."

"OK, you go first. I'll stand outside the door," Larry said.

We rose as one, or at least we tried to rise as one. The slivovitz thought we should remain seated.

Ivana offered to help Larry to his feet. "I think American poets they are so sexy," she said. "But you are so beau-tiful. Like Al Joung," she said.

"Don't leave my side," Larry said to me. I nodded. "We're joined at the hip," I reminded him.

The moon was full that night, an industrial moon that clung to the sky like a shiny manhole cover. Below us, Belgrade rose in a gray skyline of government houses and high-rises. Behind us, Ivana and Vladislav crooned Slavic love songs, and Ratko called me to join them. "My beautiful poet," he said, "I know you are wanting to come back to me." Larry and I laughed and toasted his efforts with one more glass of slivovitz. Before the night was over, Larry and I stood on the balcony of Ivana Milankhova's apartment and serenaded that moon with slivovitz renditions of Jeannette Macdonald and Nelson Eddy tunes. In keeping with Ratko's raunchy intrusions, we changed the words to suit the mood. It wasn't love, but who needed love in the company of crazy Bohemians? By the time the moon gave way to a thin hard sunrise, we yelled a final GOOD MORNING, BELGRADE, and told our hosts good-bye. It took us two days to recover from what Larry called the worst hangover in the Western world.

I tell my playwright friend how theater saved me from utter despair in Belgrade. "In the theater," I say, "you could see the hope of the next generation of Yugoslavs." I tell her how I immersed myself in the theater. Pursued it, sometimes at the expense of attending a writers' conference. I tell her about the grand sets and costumes, about theater-in-the-round, and the theater of protest. "Suddenly we spoke the same language, those theater people and me. In Belgrade, Maribor, Sarajevo, Novi Sad . . . all over Yugoslavia, it was wonderful." I begin with how, in Belgrade, the audience was not seated until the play began. "Then we found ourselves to be part of the play. Audience and players acting out our roles in the theater of protest." I describe how only the costumes made the difference: the audience in street clothes, the actors in elevated shoes, their height raised another foot or so from the floor by those shoes. "The audience entered the theater under the grand parade of those actors striding like creatures from another planet in their elevated shoes. It was elegant, like something by Molière." And I tell her. I spent four days in Novi Sad, how there, I met the actor, Voja Soldatovic, and Clive Barnes, an English dramatist. "I could have been at Kennedy Center for the Performing Arts," I tell her. I spent four days in novi Sad watching theater groups from all over eastern Europe. They came from Russia, Hungary, Poland, Czechoslovakia, Albania, and the Ukraine. I saw *King Lear,* a five hour version adapted Kabuki style by Albanian gypsies. It seemed endless. I loved it, but Clive kept saying, "Wake me when they do it." For me, theater made even the dreariest productions worthwhile. But I suppose I already had a good feeling about Novi Sad anyway. I had been there before, a month earlier, with all of the Fulbrighters. We had visited the local writers' union, the usual round of poets and novelists, the usual discussions of approaches to writing and publishing. Yet the most memorable event had not been the meeting with writers, but the late supper we'd had on our last night in town. We were all tired and a little out of sorts. "That happens when you've been escorted from one office to the next all day long," I say to my playwright friend. "You wait for the time to relax, to really see the place you're visiting." We hadn't had any time during the day, so that night in the hotel lounge, we were ready for bed more than anything else. The waiter was having a difficult time keeping track of our order—so many Americans, so many bad Slavic accents. We had cocktails—maybe slivovitz, maybe vodka—it didn't matter as tired as we were. There was entertainment, a singer, a thin man with a pencil-line mustache and incredibly arched eyebrows. He was trying his best, troubadour style with old-fashioned ballads from the big band era. The only way to recognize some of them was by the efforts of the band, the oldest lounge band I'd ever seen. "That singer looks like he's stepped out of a 1940s movie," Larry said. "They all do," the rest of us agreed. The singer had been seated at the table with an older man, gray-haired and so buttoned-down, he looked as if his face would crack if he showed any emotion. But he never took his eyes off the singer. It was a look of pure devotion, except the singer seemed to be ignoring him. He was flirting with a woman, overdressed, overweight, and wearing incredibly red lipstick. The old man looked fit to burst. The looks passing between the three of them could have been knives. Every gaze and blink of eyelash was full of hope and danger. "Think about it," I say. "The eternal triangle. That smoky room. Those ancient musicians quaking out love songs. That was drama," I say to my playwright friend. Like Larry said: Real life drama of loves sweet song."

I never recount the party at Ivana's when my playwright friend asks for a romantic memory. Slivovitz aside, that was friendship—a camaraderie of poets who were, for want of a better description, "strangers in a strange land." If the talk about romance begins to include the moon, I offer my mother, dancing at the USO club with my father during World War II, some group like the Ink Spots crooning June/moon/spoon songs. Mama was a beauty, and in a picture I have of her sitting in a club, you can tell she was a hit. It's a nice segue into my own story of dancing the night away in Budapest with Anton Pesevkôs under a cornsilk moon. "All that glamour runs in the family," I say. And to make the story all the more romantic, I recount how I'd been introduced to Anton by some gypsies I'd met on the train at the Yugoslavia/Hungary border. "That gypsy business is another story," I say. "But Anton, my wonderful Magyar, he had the manners of a Hungarian count."

"How would you know anything about the manners of a Hungarian count?" my playwright friend snarls.

I lean back on the strength of my years—Paris or no, I've got her beat by at least thirty birthdays. "A woman knows such things," I tell her.

I tell her about my gypsy friends, who'd arranged this one date for me on my first night in Budapest. "To make you welcome," they'd said. And how Anton had called me that afternoon to set up the time for our rendezvous. "What will be the color of your gown?" he'd asked. I'd hesitated. I couldn't think of any Fulbrighter who'd packed evening wear along with her books, so I'd just picked a color. "Kind of light blue," I'd said. Then I spent the rest of that afternoon foraging among the chi-chi shops near Vigadó Square. It only took a few stops to realize that they looked at me and doubled the price. *Tourist,* my face said. I stopped for tea at Gerbeaud's Tea House, where I expected to see dowager duchesses, and where, they said, the Crown Prince of Austria used to meet his paramour. I hoped he'd like Gerbeaud's chocolates as much as I did. Then my luck changed on Régiposta Street in a shop called Lörincz. A "gypsy" frock, the color pale green, but just the right price. What could have been more fitting, since I would not have met Anton if not for the gypsies?

"One of Budapest's greatest opera singers," the gypsies had told me. "He is always a gentleman," they'd said.

Anton showed up at my hotel with a rose. Had the boy from Dubrovnik been reincarnated as an opera singer in Budapest? The settings were similiar: castles connecting modern cities, except in this instance, the old town of Buda was on one side of the Danube and the castle outpost of Pest on the other side. But this suitor was Sydney Greenstreet in an ice cream suit and silver hair. "I am Magyar. Portly and courtly," he said. "I will take you to the city. First the river, then the bistros, where we will dance." I took his arm and we floated out of the lobby and into the Budapest night.

204

"The moon was full," I say when I talk about that night. "A blood-burning moon, tangerine orange. A Yellow Moon like the one Aaron Neville sings about. A gypsy moon, mist covered, as if the castles of Budapest had enchanted even the sky."

The playwright looks skeptical. I tell her that for my tastes, there's nothing more romantic than the moon cresting the top of a bridge—probably because that's the view I get from my bedroom window in Seattle. "And to see that moon rising above the Chain Bridge over the Danube was like a dream," I say.

"You sure you weren't dreaming?" she says.

"Budapest is a city of dreams," I say. "The Paris of Eastern Europe. You know what I mean?" She's quiet, listening now.

I tell her how that night, Anton and I crossed the Danube six times between Buda and Pest, each trip almost more romantic than the last. I tell her about supper clubs where chorus girls in nothing more than sequins made Las Vegas look tame. I tell her about a horse and buggy ride down cobblestone streets in Pest and a moonlight cruise on the Danube. And even though the Danube wasn't blue by the end of the twentieth century, I tell her it was easy to see the reason for all those waltzes. The moon, poised over the river, created its own love song. Anton bought me wildflowers from the vendor who stood under the hedgehog sign near Fisherman's Castle. "Lady Bella," he called me. At the casinos, he knew how to "ease the door" so we could get into the inner rooms. We ended that night dancing on the ramparts of a castle near the White Palace. Anton and I dancing under a crepe paper moon hanging low in the Budapest sky.

"Yes, but you never saw Anton again," the playwright says, dismissing the whole story. "That's a fling, not romance."

So finally I tell her about my last weekend in Yugoslavia.

I begin by telling her how all my bad feelings about Yugoslavia went out the window in the sunlight of my last weekend in the country. The weather was so gorgeous, it was as if I'd received a going-away present, a bonus for the push-pull emotions that had jerked me around during my stay in Yugoslavia. I was on the Adriatic coast, a town called Split. I couldn't have picked a better point of departure from Yugoslavia than Split. "I'm gonna split from Split," I told them in Belgrade. They failed to see my linguistic humor. The Adriatic was postcard blue, the town a jewel that made it perfect. Beaches were practically carpeted with nearly naked sunbathers. The stretch of sand outside my hotel might as well have been reserved for nudists. I figured that after a winter of gray skies, half of Yugoslavia headed for a beach, and half as many took the opportunity to take off their clothes.

In May, while I was in Dubrovnik, I'd made an excursion to a nudist beach with Larry and Phil, but Dubrovnik's beaches were more boulders than sand. And the absence of clothes had not made the Yugoslavs any friendlier. The custom was to pick a rock, shed your clothes, and give everybody a look that said: *Come near my space and I'll kill you.* I'd hugged the rock I'd claimed more out of intimidation than out of modesty. I was hugging my seat on the bus into Split when I met Nikki, my skirt spread over the length of the seat so there wouldn't be any question of someone sitting next to me.

"Scusi," he said. A simple word: *Scusi.* Can I say my heart leapt into my throat? If I did, would you believe me? I was still in Yugoslavia, still the same old cynic. The only difference was that suddenly, after four months in that wretched country, I knew I couldn't go another day without this man near me. We were on the hotel bus that made its twice-a-day trip from the beach into town. It was late morning, but already the temperature was climbing toward ninety. As usual, the bus was late, and although all the windows were open, inside was as hot as a convection oven. I didn't see Nikki get on the bus, but just before the driver closed the door, he said, "Scusi" and claimed the seat next to me.

The heat must have created static electricity, because when his arm brushed against mine, I jumped. I had been fanning myself to cool off, so his skin was really hot. When I turned to complain, he smiled. That smile shattered my anger. "When you do fall, you're gonna fall hard," Larry had said to me before I left Belgrade. He was right. I fell hard. Nikki started with a corny line: "I feel as if I know you. That I am here for you." Had I been sane, I would have laughed, but somewhere between *"Scusi"* and claiming his seat, I'd taken leave of my senses. My nose was open, as they say back home. I would have thought that man was wonderful if he'd said the sky is green and elephants bark like dogs. By the time the bus cleared the ugly concrete high-rises of modern Split and reached the old city, we were friends.

"I thought you were Ethiopian," he said. "There are many in Italy, and they come here for holiday. Split is the most beautiful place on earth," he said, gesturing to the Adriatic, which seemed even bluer beneath the red tile rooftops of the old city.

I had walked through the old city the day before, but that day, under Nikki's gaze, it was indeed beautiful. "Yes," I said, staring at him. "Yes, I can see."

He was from Bosnia, a Moslem. "Turkish ancestors, you know." I looked at him. Turkish? Yes, handsome. I'd believe it. "Yes, I can see," I told him.

I was beginning to sound retarded. Think, McElroy. Think, I told myself. "I was going to the museum," I said. "In the Diocletian's Palace. You know, in the castle. Castles seem so strange, like you could get lost," I said. (Hint, hint.)

He took the bait. "I will show you the museum," he said. "And we will have lunch at the Palace."

Fortunately, I did have an errand at Diocletian, a gift to pick up at a little shop run by a Magyar expatriate from Budapest, one of Anton's friends. (Lila and I corresponded for several years after I left, but finally she was caught up in the war and I lost track of her.) Nikki and I lunched in one of the outdoor cafés in the peristyle of the Diocletian. Having trapped myself in the cloak of "innocent traveler," I couldn't tell Nikki that the courtyard reminded me of castles in Italy and Hungary. I only knew I wanted that lunch to last forever, and already we were running out of polite conversation. But sometimes, at the very moment when language fails you, it also saves you.

"How is your food?" I asked.

"It is good, but the fish has too much sex," he said.

Sex? Did somebody say: *sex?* I gulped, but I think it took us both a couple of seconds to realize the faux pas. "Salt," he sputtered. "Too much salt. How can I say *sex?* I have studied English for years. I have made business in the States. Salt, not sex. You think me stupid now, I know."

But now I was laughing. In that slip of tongue, he had let down his guard. Now he was just Nikki, traveling from Sweden to Bosnia to visit his sister. And I was going in the opposite direction, to Italy to visit my friend Sally. We had three days and a city that became more beautiful each moment we spent together.

That night, we walked the whole length of the resort beachfront. All along the beach, tourists slept in makeshift tents, some in nothing more than sleeping bags. The tide, moving in and out, seemed to whisper of love, or was it all those Germans and Italians camping out on the beach under the stars? I remembered my first week in Alaska in the late seventies, in a house at the foot of the Mendenhall Glacier. After the first several nights, I'd complained to my husband that the couple next door made love all night, their moans so loud, I couldn't sleep. He'd laughed. "That's the glacier," he'd said. "The ice rubbing against the earth." Mother Earth, I'd thought. No wonder it sounds like a woman. After that, the moans lulled me to sleep. In Yugoslavia, some people slept so close to the water's edge, I wondered why they weren't swept out to sea. Above them, the moon, bright as an opal, spilled a ribbon of light upon the ocean. For a minute, I let myself drift into a fiction, where the real world disappeared because I was in love.

"It looks like a road," I said. "If I had a car, I could drive straight from here to Italy."

"I wish I could go with you," he said.

"Yes, but we'd never get there," I told him. "We'd have to stop and neck." He frowned. "You know. Kiss and hug. Like when you were a teenager and you took your girl for a drive so you could find someplace to park and kiss in the moonlight."

He shook his head. "I had no car when I was in school. The first car I ever saw during the war belonged to the Gestapo. They came to search for my father and my sister. Guerrillas, the Germans said. I saw my sister only at night, when she would tap on the window and talk to me for a few minutes before going back into hiding. I was a child, maybe six, maybe seven. I remember the German officer. His boots were shiny. After the war, we had no cars for many years. Sometimes it is better, but the war . . . it is still here," he said.

There was nothing for me to say. I could only hold his hand and promise myself that I would keep my vision in full focus—not hampered by the moon, not by my American expectations, not by the stereotypes of bigotry, but by the possibilities, the small moments that too often break like glass. All I could do was stop and stare at the sky. As I looked at the pattern of stars, I realized that all day, I had been walking along the edge of a cliff, holding onto my balance, teetering between the sense of what I knew to be real and what was still unknown. Then Nikki said, "Hold still . . ." and brushed his fingers against my hair. "I thought there was something," he said, "a little speck, like lint. But it is only the moonlight trapped in your hair." And my heart lost its balance, and I felt myself fall.

Three days later, I caught the ferry for Italy. Nikki came to see me off. He brought flowers. "Uveka sa vama. Especially for you." As the boat left, he threw petals in its wake. The Italian ladies on the deck beside me, said, "Bellisimo. Bella. Bella." And I cried as I watched Yugoslavia fade from view.

Oh yes, we had a love affair. One that spanned two continents and as many years. An affair that carried us to beaches in Finland, Hawaii, and the Northwest, places that lie great distances from Split. And when Nikki went back into the insane war that rages in what was once called Yugoslavia, he left with me the memory of moonlight over the Adriatic. For me, love on the run remains an interlude where the heart outweighs reality. And as sentimental as it might be, Larry was right: Love is where you find it.

This memoir is dedicated to Larry Levis—1946–1996. Those of us who knew him as a friend will miss him greatly.

Mississippi Montage

I was born on the Mississippi across the river from where there was once a city known as Cahokia. By the time Columbus arrived in the fifteenth century, the Cahokians had been overrun by other tribal groups, leaving rich farmlands and some one hundred-twenty mounds, some taller than the pyramids, where they'd worshipped the sun and studied the stars. By the time the Europeans invaded the middle of what is now called America, those mounds were the only trace of Cahokia, and the people called Missouri—a Sioux name meaning "people with dugout canoes"—had cultivated the fields of Cahokia and set up a great trading center on the river. By the time the Europeans arrived, many of the Missouri were dead of European diseases that had spread by traders coming from the East Coast to the Mississippi. All that was left of their trade center were the corn fields and fruit trees. The Europeans cultivated the fields and set up a great trading center on the river. They called their city St. Louis. By the time I was born, all that remained of Cahokia were the mounds, tourists attractions that most folks who lived near the river did not even visit. Instead, they went to the city on the other side of the river, into what is now called Missouri, to the city called St. Louis. Now when the sun rises, it leaves the mounds of Cahokia and blesses the arch that stands on the St. Louis side of the river. And that river just keeps rolling along.

Double-dutch was my favorite jump rope game. Two ropes, clicking clockwise and counterclockwise, your feet moving fast as the ropes swished over your head and under your toes: *Hot Peppers, double-time, double-time,* M-I-S-S-I-S-S-I-P-P-I-*in your eye.*

When I was eight, my mother would shop every Saturday in the market down by the river. A huge place, at least when I was eight. And all enclosed under one roof: fresh vegetables in from the farms that morning, fresh bread from the bakeries, flowers from gardens outside of the city, and of course, the fish. Mississippi trout that folks along the river called Jack Salmon. River fish called buffalo, a bottom fish bigger than salmon, and, Papa said, "meaner than a guard dog." Buffalo, with sweet meat that my grandma fried in cornmeal batter, all the time warning me to watch out for the bones. A thousand bones. A million bones, but oh, the taste was wondrous.

Early evening and fireflies blinking like pen lights. A whole neighborhood full of girls jumping jumping I-S-S-I-P-P-I . . .

When Mama gave me my allowance—sometimes as much as a quarter—I'd go to the fish counter at the market and buy twenty-five cents worth of something like lox or smelt. They must have thought me strange, a skinny legged black girl wanting to buy fish instead of sweets. But I remember there was one man who'd save me a treat, some bit of smoked something that I could eat on the bus going home. My cousins wouldn't sit near me, so fish was the one thing I never worried about having to share with them.

Drifting down the Chao Phraya River to the Floating Market in Bangkok, I was a child again. The day after my lecture at Thammasat University, I rented a sampan for eight hundred baht. A father and son, they spoke no English; I spoke no Thai. They cautioned me to keep my balance getting on the boat, settled me in and warned me about the sun, all in gestures and smiles. I was going on an adventure, and they would make sure I would come to no harm. That morning on CNN International, the weather report said it was snowing in

Seattle, a rare storm from the north that would last for days. It had been snowing in the Midwest for most of December, the Mississippi iced over in places. But on the Phraya, even though it was Christmas, the sun beat down without shelter. The young man, Bä, pulled close to a hat seller's sampan. Within seconds, two other sampans full of hats appeared. The vendors were women. Most of the vendors in the Floating Village were women. The old man Bä made the final choice for my hat. When the boatmen told me their full names that morning, the sounds were jumbled to my farang ear, so they'd offered the tourist version—*Bä*. Old Bä and young Bä. I was simply *Miss*. Before the day was over, they would teach me small words, like the Thai words for snake or melon, simple numbers, directions, or the words for hot with the sun *(ron)* or hot spicy food *(phet)*.

For my time on the river, they became father and brother to me, letting me drift down the klongs (canals), stopping when I wanted to examine yet another sampan offering spices or fruit, weavings or pottery, acting as my go-between when I bargained for beads or ordered my lunch. They held my hand as I walked across the boats rafted together in front of the floating restaurant. Old Bä had more opinions, but this river had been his life, so I listened closely when he pointed out some sight that I shouldn't miss. River traffic surged around us as we glided past small villages, the houses on stilts. Women hung out the wash. Babies cried. Children clamored for space on the walkways connecting thatched-roof houses. I watched snake handlers display their favorites, and when we glided past temples, saw monks in saffron robes walking in exquisitely sculpted gardens. The view changed with each klong, but always there there was the scent of frangipani, melons, coconut, curry, ginger, orchids, and fish. And the river itself, caught up in its own life. When we reentered the harbor at dusk, I was sad to see them go, but within minutes, they were lost in the traffic of long-tailed boats noisily motoring down the great river.

The banks of the Mississippi are crowded. Towns are scattered along the shore from New Orleans to St. Paul and beyond. Every inch of space turned into occupied territory: cultivated, industrialized, and landscaped to death, except every spring when the Mississippi rebels and floods its banks, reclaiming its own.

As a child, I didn't think about the Mississippi one way or another, except to hear the stories my grandfather told of black folks coming up the river after the Civil War, everything they owned on a flatbed boat. "Many black folks died on that river," he said. "Working the boats all day till their backs nearly broke." Tote that barge, lift that bale. And sometimes history books showed black men walking along the riverbank, stripped to the waist with a rope across their shoulders, towing a big paddleboat upriver. The picture read: *The Mighty Mississippi at Work*. Except the Mississippi wasn't doing any work.

In the museum on the island of Antiqua, there is a book of drawings from the early days of European colonialism. One picture shows a barefoot black man harnessed to a carriage holding two white people dressed in their Sunday best. The drawing is titled: *The Horse's Day Off*.

In her diary, Harriet Tubman wrote about how the Mississippi flowed red with blood. Bodies of soldiers and slaves drifted in the current like logs. And at one plantation, when the Union Army boat landed to pick up any black folks who wanted passage out, she wrote that she had never seen so many twins in her life. "That plantation was a breeding farm," she wrote. "A place where black folks were bred like cattle to fill the slave coffles." Tubman said they came running down the hill to the boat landing—twins, double images, two by two, rushing toward the river as if they were heading for Noah's Ark. "That's our legacy," Tubman wrote. The legacy of the Mississippi.

I want to tell you now, I hated Huckleberry Finn. He was a nasty little white boy who needed Jim to keep his sorry butt from dying. I didn't much like Jim, either. Nigger Jim, Twain called him. My problem was that Jim was always helping that fool boy. Let the river take him, I'd think. Come spring, it probably will anyway.

And then there was Liza, in *Uncle Tom's Cabin,* crossing the river on an ice floe, her braids blowing in the wind while the dogs, all drool and teeth, kept the paddy rollers on her trail. Well, at least, Sweet Jesus, she was trying to escape.

Mama told me that Paul Robeson was the only one who could really sing "Old Man River." I was glad she told me that because all through high school, any black kid who could carry a tune in bass or tenor got to sing that damn song. Sometimes they threw in "Summertime" for good measure. It didn't matter to me. It all sounded like Jim singing and grinning while he poled Huck Finn's raft down the mighty river.

Fish cakes deep fried southern style. There was one place that made them so sweet. We walked six blocks from Sumner High just for a sandwich and near black root beer to drown it all. Jack Salmon turned buttery under a tide of Louisiana Hot Sauce. Mrs. Crutcher marked us truant, but the lines snaked around the block. Then came talk of integration and anyone loitering off the school grounds got expelled because of all the fights with white kids. I heard the Fish Shack closed down. Never tasted anything like it since.

The Columbia River is a spawning ground for salmon. In the spring, you can watch them begin their journey at the mouth of the fresh-water channels in the Ballard Locks. They travel into the locks from the ocean to begin their journey up the fish ladders to the lakes and on to the Columbia and the spawning streams. They jump—the silvers, chinooks, and cohos—leaping from the water as if joy is the chance to go upstream, lay their eggs, and die. Sometimes one executes five or six leaps, like a rock skimming the surface of the water. They arch and flip like Olympic divers. They throw themselves forward and up, going against the current in that beautiful deadly dance. When I take visitors to the locks, I tell them they can ooh and aah all they want, but the first one who dares to sing *Fish are jumping and the cotton is high,* gets to walk home.

I was sitting in a café called Three Hats or Three Pigs, or something like that. In Belgrade, restaurants that weren't named after Vuk Karadzic usually took on names of convenience. This place was right around the corner from one called Two Fishermen. They were both in Skardarlija, the nicest part of Belgrade except for the bistros along the Danube. Skardarlija was all cobblestones and quaint cafés—almost hippie, if Belgrade had allowed any hippies. My roommate and I had chosen Skardarlija that evening because it was a weekend, and anything along the Danube would be crowded with families dragging behind them half a dozen kids and the grandparents. Skardarlija was a younger crowd, artists and musicians a lot less concerned with how many Turks had invaded the country several centuries ago and more concerned with where they were going next week.

It was late May, and Belgrade was struggling into spring. Café tables were decorated with flowers, and outdoor seating at the edge of the cobblestone street was available if you didn't mind the slightly uric smell from the gutters. But if I blinked, I was back in New York's Village or London's Soho. Mary and I tried the schnitzel and something meatless with eggplant. (They roasted the meat in the vegetarian restaurant near Café Vuk. They insisted, therefore, that the menu was vegetarian.) Then we smothered everything in baklava and Turkish coffee. After dinner, the breeze was still warm enough to let us sit outside until early evening. Three musicians were strolling among the tables. (They were not wearing hats.) They were playing accordion, bass, and guitar. The guy with the bass fiddle was as thick and bulky as his bass. When they came to our table, I was slightly embarrassed as always when roving musicians drift in my direction. They smiled; I smiled. The bass player plucked his strings; the accordion player limbered up his fingers. And then the bass began belting out "Stari Reka . . ." as if Paul Robeson had taught him the Serbian version of "Old Man River." Everyone in the café looked at me and grinned. I applauded, of course. Like it or not, I carry the burden of that damn river with me.

The most recognized poem by a Black American poet is Langston Hughes's "The Negro Speaks of Rivers." Some students at Thammasat University in Thailand knew that poem by heart, but none of them could sing "Old Man River." That was fine; I'd been serenaded with that song in more languages than I cared to remember.

Her name was Mrs. Ishikawa. She was a poet, one of Japan's Living Treasures, one of the artists so admired by the people that government support allowed them to continue their work without the distraction of having to earn room and board. She had received Japan's equivalent of the Pulitzer for her last collection of poems. Our meeting had been set for dinner in a restaurant in one of Tokyo's posh highrises. Below us, the city spread out in exacting patterns like a landing field for UFOs, a river of lights twinkling along broad streets leading to the center of the city. Patterns of triangles, squares, circles, and swirls were geometrically repeated in the scene below us. The same artistry appeared in every dish. Delicately fried fish seemed to be swimming on a white porcelain lake, their tails arched as if they were about to leap above the bits of parsley decorating the plate like algae. Radishes were lotus pods, the artistry all in the symmetry of color and form. I put my fast-food habits aside and ate slowly. (In Tokyo, only the traffic moved at breakneck speed.) We drank cups of lightly scented green tea. At first, our talk was hesitant, slow and as deliberate as the dishes arranged by the waitress. We began by discussing poetry in our respective countries, and moved on to how poems are important, how music lends itself to poetry, pausing to allow enough time for the translator.

Mrs. Ishikawa began to talk about how hard it was for poets to escape the world's horrors. "She speaks of children and war," the translator said. "So much loss. So much is lost." Then, in bits and pieces, she described Hiroshima and the bomb, how the city burned with a fire so intense, the river was in flames. "She says that people threw themselves in the water," the translator explained. "They thought they could quench the fire, but instead of water, they found flames." I found myself turning over the image, trying to grasp it. Our gestures became more eloquent and our intonations more emphatic, until suddenly I noticed we were speaking directly to each other without pause. We turned to the translator. She had sat back in her chair and was smiling. "I don't think you and Mrs. Ishikawa need me," she said. "What you speak is closer to the heart than anything I can translate." I nodded yes, but I knew I could not translate into my own experiences the image of a river consuming everything in its flames.

In Belgrade, my translator Nada Obradovic served me tea in delicate porcelain cups. "From Hungary," she said. "My trip to Budapest." I remembered the tea shops I'd visited in Budapest, the bone china tea service in Gerbeaud's Tea House, each set enameled in a design pattern taken from the royal houses of the Hapsburgs and Romanovs. Nada's flat carried that same Old World flavor, her furniture all damask and brocade, the upholstery elaborately flowered. Paintings covered the walls from ceiling to eye level. "Some are originals," Nada said. "Yugoslav painters. From my late husband's family." She served me Belgian sweet cakes—"Imported," she said—and told me her family had died during World War II. "First there were the troops. Then the Gestapo. We were afraid." She told me how the men had hidden from the Germans and how the Germans would round up the women and children in retaliation. "They made us gather in Terazije Square, then marched us to the river." Nada stopped and passed the tray of sweet cakes again. She began to talk about the Danube, but this time it was the Danube of her youth, before the Germans came. This was a Danube of ladies having tea under parasols and men in proper suits escorting them. Along the shores of this Danube, children played innocent games, and sailboats drifted with the summer wind. The more she talked, the bluer the Danube became. Then her tone changed, and I began to understand why she needed to recall the river as it had been before the war. "The Germans marched us to the river," she said. "They told us to go in. Then they began shooting. Everyone. Women and children. My mother fell upon me, pushed me underwater. There was an air bubble in the billows of her dress. I stayed there, and when the shooting stopped, my mother and all the others were dead." Nada said that the Danube had run red for days after.

By the time all the engineers and architects got through with the river, by the time all the painters and poets and writers got through with the river, the Mississippi had no place to go but over its banks and into everybody's house, messing with their business whether they liked it or not.

I could not have gone to Egypt without sailing down the Nile. It was a river of myth, and I felt enchanted as I sailed on its waters. It carried me through a country of contrasts: from Cairo in Lower Egypt to the more southern reaches of Luxor and Aswan in Upper Egypt. And always the feluccas, their lateen-rigged sails like white palm leaves blown into the wind. At Cairo, an urban landscape full of luxury hotels and the domes of mosques dominated the skyline. Where the city faded into desert, camels replaced cars. A few miles away downriver, oxen plodded in a circle around the sakyeh (waterwheel), pulling water from underground pools. Young boys spent their days keeping the oxen moving. They waved as the boat glided by. Men in white galabiyyas strolled to their places of business, and women clad from head to toe in black carried water jugs on their heads. Their garments billowed behind them like sails. Amidst it all, the pyramids, palaces, and the great Sahara. But no matter where I was on the Nile, the river commanded the geography. Each year for centuries the Nile had flooded its banks, shifting the landscape into and away from the encroaching Sahara. What was rich land one year could become desert the next. For centuries, the Egyptians, both Upper and Lower, fought to harness the Nile. Their latest effort was the Aswan Dam.

Near Aswan, I was mistaken for Nubian. I let them know that despite my Sudanese ancestry, I was not Nubian. "American," I told them. "This is Black Egypt," they reminded me, as if they suspected that, like most foreigners, I would be unaware of the differences between the lower and upper regions of the country. The felucca boatman who had taken us to shore at the White Palace across from Luxor, arranged a visit to a fellahin house. It was a typical country house: a courtyard surrounded by rooms and nothing closed in by a roof. (It rarely rains there, and when it does in the flood season, it is a momentary downpour.) We were ushered into a middle room, one for visitors. The family rooms, always off limits, fanned out on either side. As I watched the boatman talking to several women, I realized he was a member of that family. That explained the ease of arranging our visit. "Nubian," the boatman said, pointing to me. "Nubian," he said, pointing to himself. I was tempted to correct him, but on second glance, one of the women wearing a pale blue galabiyya, her face uncovered because she was at home, looked somewhat like my cousin, Loveta—the same complexion and high cheekbones, the same pout of lower lip. I thought, if I could be mistaken for Ethiopian in Italy, Tuareg in Morocco, and Garifuna in Belize, I could certainly be Nubian in Egypt. Besides, I was being treated one step above the average tourist. But nothing is free.

After cups of hibiscus tea—the favorite of Cleopatra, I heard—and a chance to buy beadwork made by one of the boatman's relatives, the time for baksheesh arrived. We tipped the woman who made jewelry. We tipped the woman who made tea. We tipped the boatman. We tipped the cousins. But when they said, "Baksheesh the baby," I drew the line. "Understand, the Aswan has taken away the land of the Nubians," a rug merchant told me. "Everyone is very poor." He was showing me rugs woven in villages near the Aswan. "The water has covered hundreds of pyramids. Much of history has been lost with the Aswan. It has flooded land that had been in families for centuries." I pulled out a rug that showed a woman cloaked in black, a water jug on her head, walking up a dusty road that led to nowhere, the Nile rising on either side of her. "That is from the painting of a famous Nubian artist. It is called *The Sorrow of Nubia*," the rug merchant said. "Everything has changed now that the government controls the flooding of the river."

There are days when I stop along the banks of the Ship Canal in Seattle and watch the bridges open to let the factory ships from Alaska glide into dry dock. The bridges and the canal dominate my neighborhood. It is said that when engineers dredged the canal, a dozen or so salmon spawning streams were consumed. You can still find the tail ends of those streams running through neighborhoods on Queen Anne Hill, surfacing in odd places as if the water has leapt up out of the ground to find its old course. Dozens of small bridges connect one side street to another, but it is the Canal that finally commands the traffic. At night I hear the bridge tender's horn signalling the passing of another ship under the drawbridge, some vessel with a mast that is taller than the bridge. Day or night, that is when all traffic stops. Mornings when I drive to work, fishermen in yellow slickers and deck boots walk the edge of the road from the convenience store to the docking area like ducks in a row. On land they have no shape, but onboard they flow with the constant movement of deck and water. Sometimes as I wait in the north- or southbound traffic lanes at the open mouth of the bridge, I see them walking east on the deck as their boat moves west, and the Canal, that artificial river, oblivious to us all.

Some say that one hundred slaves from the Roman Empire pulled Cleopatra's barge upriver in Turkey from Kusadasi to Ephesus just so that she could catch a glimpse of Mark Antony in action. When I saw the Büyükmenderes River, skinny as a Missouri stream, I thought: After knowing the glory of the Nile, ol' Cleo must have felt truly grand sitting under her peacock fans while her slaves from Turkey and Greece towed her along that shallow river in Asia Minor. And those slaves, pulling Cleopatra upriver like they were coming home for a holiday.

Once in Yugoslavia I went down the Danube with an Englishman, a drama critic named Clive who had an obsession with pig farms. The trip was a relief since the day before we had sat through five hours of

King Lear done by Albanian gypsies, Kabuki style. (You had to be there.) The Danube lulled me to sleep, and when Clive nudged me awake, we were at a farm that looked as if it had been pulled off of some medieval landscape, something old world and muddy from Sir Lancelot or the Crusades. The farmer was quiet, somewhat puzzled that we had come all that way to see his pigs. Those pigs were as big as small ponies, only fatter. They were clean, arrogant pigs—huge, white, shiny things with a sort of "I live here and you don't" look. The look that house cats sometimes have. I kept trying to figure out how they'd gotten so big, except those pigs had the best view of the Danube than I'd seen in all of Yugoslava.

It was my second night in Brisbane. I'd spent most of the day in the museum, and my feet hurt. I knew I didn't want any of the hotel food, that kind of sturdy stuff that would having me saying "G'day" and "Throw one on the barbie" if I wasn't careful. I checked my dining guide. A thousand and one Chinese cafés, an East Indian place or two, the usual English fare, then something called Caffé Opera at Caffé Barnardi. I wouldn't have stopped there except that one of the singers listed in the ad, Sani Muliaumaseali'i, was Aboriginal, and there wasn't any other mention of Australia's first people in the rest of the ads. There wasn't any comment on the kind of food either, but with a name like Barnardi, I was hoping for Italian. Whatever the food, I hoped the singing would be worth the trip.

The place was all heavy dark wood and sensible tables, like an English pub. The Australian influence, I assumed. So was the wine— a delicious rosé that didn't assault my sinuses with poisonous hista- mines. And the ad was right about the ambience: a little conversation and a lot of service. I was feeling comfortably fed when the singing began. The soprano, Melanie Duncan, simply set down a tray of sal- ads and launched into an aria from *Così fan Tutte*. Nobody seemed to mind. Diners stopped chattering and listened attentively, applauding when she finished on a lingering high C. Some of them were appar- ently regulars, putting in requests as soon as the singers seemed ready for action. Sani had a beautiful voice, a sweet tenor who carried his notes from the chest, none of that warbly stuff that makes all the notes sound strained. They cruised the room, answering requests, timing their songs to fit the dinner service. By the time they reached my table, I was already suspicious. What were they saving for me? Melanie offered "Summertime" (so what else was new?), but it was a little too thin, a bit high for her range. I couldn't take it seriously. Then Sani waltzed in. Yes, "Old Man River," a tender version, more movie musical than lyrical opera, but nevertheless, he got my attention. I smiled, of course, and applauded. He apologized for not being as comfortable with the song as he'd like to be. "I am a tenor," he said. "My brother Eddie does this better. He's a bass." I told him, "That's OK. I've heard that song in three languages. You get as close to the Mississippi as any of them." On the way back to the hotel, I walked along the Brisbane River. It wasn't spectacular, just a respectable sort of river, with arched stone bridges and parks littered with statues. But it was silent, floating along without song.

No Stops Until Darwin

In 1994 I took a motorcycle trip across the Australian desert. Fifty-eight years old and on the back of a Harley, a handsome Australian driver guiding me through Aboriginal Land. It was great. At least I thought it was. Something to talk about with the folks back home.

My son said: Are you crazy? You could've been killed out there. I reminded him of the accident I'd had less than ten city blocks from my house. The sweet sports car I'd owned for eighteen years, folded around me like a handkerchief.

My lover said: You never get up at 4:30 in the morning for me. I said: You're not a big red rock in the middle of the Australian desert.

My daughter said: *Mo*-ther! the word stressed with reminders of my responsibilities to her. I said: Hey, you're going to Russia for two years! "That's different," she said. I didn't bother to tell her that the difference was a matter of who was traveling.

And I didn't bother to say anything to my own mother. They've become bookends in my life—my daughter, the Missionary, and my impatient mother—they alternate between scolding me and making sure I've packed everything I'll need.

"You need to stay home," my mother said. "I don't know what you're looking for out there." "Me neither," I said. "But I'll tell you when I find it."

And each time, I have told her what I found. This time, how long it took to get my body stirring at four o'clock in the morning, even with the anticipation of watching the sunrise paint Ayers Rock from earth brown to fuschia. Four A.M., and I crawled out of bed to watch the sun do what it does so well every day without me. "This had better be good," I told the driver. "I only get up this early for babies and air-planes, and thank goodness I no longer have to get out of bed for a baby." My driver, David, looked as if he'd heard it all before. I blinked sleep from my eyes and tried to concentrate on the thermos of sweet-ened tea I'd brought with me. But even the sugar refused to take hold. It was winter in Australia and cold in the desert at that time of morn-ing. Everyone in our caravan was stomping around, trying to bring enough blood to their hands and feet so they could set up camera equipment. I was huddled on the back of the Harley with my trusty point-and-shoot set for automatic consecutive photos. "You call that little thing a camera?" David asked in his delectable Australian accent. At four in the morning, I was having trouble thinking of his accent as delectable, so I answered snidely, "I don't care what name you give it as long as it comes when I call it," and went back to my tea. After that, everyone left me alone to mutter to myself.

Even in a group, I can manage to travel alone. In fact, as a black woman, that's easy to do. Most often I'm the lone black female on the trip—sometimes making folks rethink the notion that black women never travel except to Africa and the Caribbean, sometimes an uncomfortable reminder of America's racial history—but always I am aware that my vision of the world will differ from that of my usual travel companions. Not that I need to travel to be reminded that I see the world differently. Sometimes that realization takes no more than discussing a movie. For example, I say I cannot understand how a con-temporary film director can make a movie on the streets of down-town New York without having any black people in the scene. "What happened to the black folks?" I say. "Did they send them all to Reikers? All the cleaning ladies and bankers, the bus drivers and shop clerks, the messengers and cabbies? All the black women shopping Bloomingdale's and Sak's?" But my friends, those who haven't lived in big cities or have never found themselves excluded on the basis of color, give me puzzled looks. They haven't noticed that black people were missing from scenes that were supposed to reflect the general American public. Often I'm given a lecture on the filmmaker's right to be selective about who is included in a film depicting reality. "Selective?" I repeat. "Sounds like some kind of warped Darwinist theory of evolution," I tell them, "but fortunately, life isn't like that. Like my grandma said: Black people are everywhere."

Everywhere I went, in big cities like Sydney, Melbourne, and Brisbane, there were references to Aboriginal culture. But if I hadn't really been looking for them, I could have left the country believing that there were very few Aborigines living in Australia. I don't mean in the Outback. On any given day, I could find a dozen tour guides competing for the chance to take me to Aboriginal Land. But in the cities, Aborginals were only symbols. Their country had been turned into a world of white faces where they'd become, like Ralph Ellison's Invisible Man, conspicuous by their absence. Yet, every public park was infested with blonds playing the didgeridu, and every shopping mall had an art center of tourist souvenirs—wood carvings and cloth emblazoned with dreamtime images, ethnicity for sale, "genuine made in the Bush," white shopkeepers told me. "Aborigines don't like the city," I was told. But I took a second look. Under the cloak of urbanization, they worked in banks, hospitals, law offices, and schools. Some owned homes in the suburbs. Some were mixed bloods but of Aboriginal descent nonetheless. Book stores stocked special sections with their stories: *Portraits of our Elders, Inside Black Australia, Aboriginal Folktales.* Traditional stories and emerging writers. "Last aisle, third shelf from the bottom," I was told. Just like home, I thought. What was it that Darwin had theorized: The struggle for survival between individuals is based on continuous variations.

We were on the highway heading toward King's Canyon beyond Ayers Rock and the Olgas Mountains when I saw it—a sign that read: No Stops Until Darwin.

"How far to Darwin?" I asked. "Several thousand kilometers," David said.

I grunted. That's a helluva lot bigger than Texas, I thought. "How long would it take to get there?"

"Well, you've got to get off the Gunbarrel Highway and back onto the Lasseter, then take the main road. Ten days, a week, if you're lucky."

"So there's nothing between here and Darwin?" "Depends on how you look at it," he laughed. When I didn't laugh too, he added, "Rest easy, luv. It's just a little Outback humor."

I never found out whether he meant his laughter or the sign, because just then he swerved to avoid a frilled lizard sunning itself in the red dust of the road. It raised its head, ignoring us as it paid homage to the sun, the frill flared about its neck like a monarch's ruff. "I hear tell, they used to eat those things back in the Bush," David said. Then we roared off, the Harley spewing dust, King's Canyon in front of us, the lizard on the road behind us looking down its nose at the passing world.

Ayers Rock: Uluru, sacred place for the Anangu, the Aboriginal people. Even from a distance, it is clear that Uluru is no ordinary mesa. It rises in majestic splendor out of the dust of the desert, a landscape of brick red sand and spinifex scrub brush, the horizon occasionally broken by a lone tree—and, of course, by Uluru, the rock itself, thrust abruptly some 1,200 feet above the desert like a giant rust-colored beast come to slumber under an endless sky. No one fails to find it magnificent, its sheer size and steepness massed on the plate of the desert. I think of it as rising up like a mountain, but the Anangu believe it fell from the heavens. They regard the rock as a sacred place, each crevasse, cave, and indentation blessed with spiritual pow-

ers. They take a dim view of tourists who climb it, but that doesn't stop the tourists. Throughout the day, they crawl, mostly on all fours, up the perpendicular sides to the top of the rock. From a distance, they look like a line of ants crawling up a giant sugar cube. In fact, that's what the Aborigines call them: minga, the Anangu word for ants—all those white folks, the Germans and French, the Americans and Italians, the Aussies and Kiwis, crawling up the side of the sacred rock. "Have you climbed Ayers Rock?" I was asked later. I answered, "No, but I didn't climb Notre Dame, either." What's one sacred place, more or less? I thought. My answer was met with a puzzled look. "How could you pass up such an opportunity?"

Uluru became my whole reason for visiting Australia. I wanted to partake of the Uluru Experience, as it is called, and so, motorcycle parked, I hiked around Ayers Rock, an outsider's walkabout approved of by the Aborigines. In predawn light, the rock was muddy brown and looked anything but spiritual, probably because I was out of bed at an ungodly hour and the only spiritual experience I was really interested in was sleep. But I trudged ahead, moving quickly in the cold windy air of early morning. The cold surprised me, since I still insisted on holding to the illusion that the word *desert* meant heat. But an icy wind whistled against the sides of the Uluru. As dawn approached, the ranger, a young woman from Melbourne who led the hike around the rock, took us to a sheltered recess. We ate breakfast as the sun rose against the eastern face of Uluru, colors spreading in layers on Uluru's surface: from the deep brown of night to gray brown to mauve, pink, orange, and finally to bright red as the sun engulfed the sky. It was definitely worth getting up at the crack of dawn, and my point-and-shoot camera was as trustworthy as a Labrador retriever. Uluru seemed to beckon photographers, its slopes and valleys sensual as a woman's body. A shift in angles, and the light and shadows offered new surprises. Turn one corner, and suddenly I was staring at a waterfall that came out of nowhere but tumbled down the rock as if it followed stair steps. Turn another corner, and the surface was sandy dry, lizards and insects the only signs of life. I could see cave openings high up on the sheer face of the rock, no visible footpaths leading to them. "That's a ritual cave," the ranger told us. "Only Aborigines can enter." It's no wonder, I thought, looking at the steep climb.

We had been standing near a cave opening at the base of the rock, watching the sunlight spread in our direction. As light erased the shroud of darkness, the cave walls came alive with paintings. Here a warrior. There a woman and child. There a kangaroo, a snake, a ribbon of sunlight, the desert dreaming itself. I remembered the rock paintings I'd seen on cave walls in Spain, where stories also were told in figures that symbolized the real world and the world of the spirits. At Uluru, the ranger elaborated upon legends of the ancient ones, pulling the tales from the drawings, the spirit of the desert, the verbal art of Ayers Rock which was detailed as surely as the Gutenberg tradition might detail a story in alphabet and script. The sun grew stronger and warmed us. For a while, we were silent, then, as the ranger ended a story of Aboriginal dreamtime, a young man from Scotland gestured toward the symbols and figures on the walls. "So," he said, "it is no' a real story, eh? They jus' pull all this from the imagination?"

On the desert, I began to believe nothing was real. At any given moment, I was convinced that even the desert itself lived in a dream of the mythical past. By midday, the heat had forced us into shirt-sleeves and I couldn't remember the chilly air of early morning. By midday, the desert was cloaked in shades of russet and ochre, clumps of pink paper flowers and yellow rattle pods blooming near billabongs that still bore traces of the great sea that once covered Australia. In places, saltwater shield shrimp lay dormant in the dry beds of rock pools where spinifex grass was clumped like Texas sagebrush. The ranger picked up several shrimp. They rested in her hand like badges, their backs flattened into the shield shape that cushions them against accidents. "They wait for the rains," she said, "then they come to life. In the span of one rainy season, some will live and die. Mate, lay eggs, then fall into a half-life when the dry season comes." In her hand, the shrimp were stony as fossils. I asked if they were sleeping. "Not sleep as we know it," she said. "Just waiting. But they scurry like beetles when the rains come." When she tossed them back into the spinifex, they sounded like sand falling to the ground.

A thorny devil darted out of the clump of spinifex and disappeared almost before we caught a glimpse of it. For some strange reason, it was a lizard I'd liked the moment I'd seen one, maybe because it was so homely, like an old scab with doleful eyes or a cactus stalk on legs. "That one's a pet," the ranger said. "Well, as much of a pet as you can expect a lizard to be." "What do you feed it?" I asked. She laughed. "You don't really feed a thorny devil. You just let it have its run. Keep it out of traffic. I saved that one from a tumble with a tour bus. Sometimes they take off in the wrong direction." I remembered the ochre-colored lizards I'd seen on my way to the shower building that morning. Half-hidden in the shadows on the edge of the walkway, they were barely discernable in the light from the cabin door, but something had made me stop. They were waiting as if to let me know that the path had been theirs for centuries and I was nothing more than a newcomer. They gave me a look that said: What's your problem? So I stood there until they decided to let me walk past, making their point with a slight flick of the head before they slipped out of the halo of light and vanished back into the deeper shadows, their passing no more than a faint trail left in the sand.

In a village on the desert west of Yulara, I stand under the shadow of a paperbark shelter and watch an Aboriginal woman decorate bowls with ancient designs: lizards, birds, turtles, and snakes, their trails painted in geometric patterns. Several unfinished bark tapestries are resting against a corner post in back of the hutch. In the next lean-to, a man carves snake and bird tracks into spear heads. I've been standing there for nearly ten minutes before the woman speaks. "You a daughter come home?" she asks. She never looks up. In fact, she hasn't looked up since I arrived. Her voice, in a gravelly overlay of Australian English and her own language, startles me. For a second, I'm not sure I understand her. I cup my hand behind my ear. This time, her question is more distinct. "You from Oz?" she asks. "Oz?" I repeat before I remember that Oz is a shortened way of saying Australia. "No," I say. Several other women enter the lean-to. They inspect me. Will I pass for a daughter come home? I wonder. But my nose is not flat enough, my hair not straight enough, my brow not strong enough.

"You don't look Aboriginal, but you'll get around alright," Sloan Baybury told me. He had become my unofficial guide in Brisbane. We'd spent the afternoon in the museum at the Queensland Cultural Center. Sloan knew one of the curators, and after we left the convention hall, he managed to get me an introduction. He said he was impressed with my speech on oral traditions. He was an archeologist, and I was flattered when he called me an international researcher, but as I walked through the museum, international became a matter of opinion. Every room reminded me of how little I knew of the connection between Aboriginal and Pacific cultures. We went from rooms full of shields and spears to rooms filled with pottery and paperbark patterns. One room held an enormous free-standing exhibition of beautifully decorated didgeridus suspended from the ceiling like slender acrobats—so many that for a moment, I could imagine myself lost inside the music of the instrument. In the ethnography of myths and totems, the museum exhibits spelled out a small portion of the history of Aboriginal cultures. I tried my best to hold up my end of the discussion, asking what I hoped were intelligent questions about differences between the art of Australia's Northern Territory and that of the Southern Territory, and how much cultural exchange there was between the Aborigines and the people white Australians called Kanakas, who had been captured in the Pacific and brought to Australia as slaves. "How do you make the distinction," I asked, "between those who were enslaved and the disenfranchised?" The curator looked slightly embarrassed, most likely because Kanaka, like Negro, was a colonialist term. But Sloan grinned, pleased that I had not accepted the standard spiel. "You know more than the average bloke who comes here to give a talk on

folk culture," Sloan said. I told him I had my reasons, but he brushed his hand against my cheek and said, "That's pretty obvious. But it takes more than color to make a match, luv."

A woman is painting a serving bowl with birds and mythical bunyip. Another woman sits beside her and continues weaving a basket she's brought to the lean-to. Two others stand nearby, watching me. "You a daughter come home?" she asks. "You come from around W.A.?" Her name is Caralee, or something that sounds close to that. My ear has retreated into the sounds of my childhood and refuses to distinguish any words that do not hold a Missouri accent. My hearing is dulled; sounds are snarled. I catch a word here, a word there. I say, "No, not W.A." Caralee goes on with her work without looking up. "Eh, from the Queen," one woman says. I think they mean Queensland. They all grin at me. "No, the U.S.," I say. "America." They give me a look that is both sad and disappointed. Home doesn't stretch that far, they seem to say. "She needs some tucker," Caralee says. This brings a round of giggles, but they gesture to a seat, a log stump smoothed across the top. I have been accepted, up to a point, but more than I had expected to be. The women stir the cooking fire.

I begin to talk about the wooden serving bowl Caralee is painting. It is remarkably beautiful, close to one of the designs I'd seen in the museum in Brisbane: a pattern of concentric circles in pale ochre denoting the movement of birds, and surrounding those, ghostlike bunyip in bright blue—arms, legs, and tails all akimbo under the red ochre limbs of trees folded around the edge of the bowl. The women pull something that looks like a split log closer to the fire. With flat sticks, they begin to rake the bark pulp. I'm thinking about blue bunyip and trees with limbs like arms, so I don't notice that there's something moving under the edge of the flat sticks. Then I see it: a worm, pale and plump on the end of a stick, then plop—into the fire. "Tucker," they say. "Eat." Another hits the fire. Then another. Witchetty grubs, a delicacy, I remember. It takes all my nerve to keep from leaping away, my stomach in my mouth.

I tell myself: Chill out, McElroy. But witchetty grubs are crawly things, and I hate bugs. I remember an awful encounter with bugs in Kansas City before I moved to the Pacific Northwest. I'd been standing by the garbage cans, dreaming of an ocean that seemed light-years away from that prairie town, and because I'd been daydreaming, I was still holding the lid to the can, not paying attention to its resident predators. The cockroaches in Kansas have wings, and they move like guerrilla warriors, fast and heading for cover. One flew in my ear. My neighbor, watching me from her kitchen window, swore I invented a dance that had not been seen on this planet before that day. All I know is that for days after, I flushed my ear with warm water, but still I heard the flutter of wings against the drum. As far as I'm concerned, a worm is nothing more than a bug without wings, and witchetty grubs qualify. I watch the grubs nose blindly from the heart of the wood. I shudder. There's a slight crackle of flames. They could be clams, I tell myself. Or escargot. Or those chocolate covered ants sold in Africa. But I've seen the grubs move, and I've long since come to the conclusion that I'm a carnivore with a delicate stomach. "Eat what you shoot," my father told me. I was ten years old, but had managed to bag one poor chicken hawk that boiled for days and was still tough. That was my last hunting trip. I even walk away from a crab boil. If it's already cooked, I'll eat it. Just don't ask me to watch it die. The women scoop the grubs from the fire and giggle. I rub my stomach and cough. "Not today," I say, praying they'll believe I'm hopelessly ill. We bargain for a shallow serving dish instead. I'm no longer thought of as daughter, just outsider. I take the best offer on a dish painted with the images of witchetty grubs. I leave behind the birds and blue bunyip nesting in the limbs of mythical trees. I tell myself that I've made the best of what was probably a touchy situation.

I talk to myself quite a bit when I'm traveling. It eases the tension and helps me check my expectations. Sometimes it keeps me from being pulled into the madness of someone else's conversation. On a bus between Cairns and Moseman Gorge, Rosie, an Aussie tourist from Perth, described fourteen ways of making meat pies, in detail. There seemed to be no connection with the tour and Rosie's need to let us know her finesse with meat pastry combinations, unless you count the bus driver's penchant for telling dirty jokes in dialect. On that trip, I learned more words in Australian slang for a woman's private anatomy than I ever knew existed. In the end, I had a choice: Rosie or the driver. My only relief was when we left the bus to take a close-up look at a scenic view. But as soon as we took our seats again, Rosie was there to fill in the gaps between the bus driver's bad jokes and announcements of other sights to see. Only those in the back of the bus missed Rosie's endless meat pie advisories. I, unfortunately, had garnered a seat in the front, near Rosie. She had a face not unlike the giant wrasse, a fish I'd seen a couple of days earlier while diving in the Great Barrier Reef. The wrasse appeared in a school of smaller fish and seemed to take charge, examining every diver with an expression full of corporate meanness, as if it were there to determine your next promotion. As my Aunt Claudia would say—and she was the meanest of all my mother's sisters—they looked like they wouldn't lend a crippled man a crutch. I was holding my breath, a lifeline of oxygen stuck in my mouth, my legs steadily cycling for balance. The wrasse didn't back off. Neither did Rosie.

We were sitting under the dome of a double-decker, Queensland rolling by in waves of farms, small towns, mountain streams, and incredibly lush green forests. After a week of red sands and spinifex, this gave me a chance to recover my memory of landscapes that looked like Seattle. Early on, Rosie explained that she was from Perth, "Freemantle, really. We've got all the modern conveniences, eh?" She nodded to her husband, but he'd fallen into some kind of trance, his eyes glazed over. Early on, it was obvious that Rosie was less interested in what she might see on her fortnight away from Perth than in what she could say—or rather, for some inexplicable reason, how she could describe meat pies. So I became my own tour guide. While Rosie lectured on red pies versus brown pies, I made mental note of the several species of evergreens growing side by side with tropical vines. While she allowed that spinach pies were best with four eggs, not two, I examined the mist hanging over the gorge like a bridal veil. Who could possibly want so many variations on meat pies? I thought as I counted the number of brush fires clearing the land so that one more suburb could be built. Only those whose mental illness drives them to describe their obsessions in public, I told myself. Of all the tour buses in all the world, she had to pick mine, I sighed. At the end of the day, as the bus wheezed onto the highway back to Cairn's, Rosie's parting shot was full of onions and carrots and how lean the meat should be. "Never buy from a Koori," she said. "They're cannibals. Eat anything, they will." I closed my eyes just as we passed a field smoldering under a farmer's brush fire. I was back cooking witchetty grubs, except they all looked like Rosie. My serving dish was almost full, but nobody would touch the stuff.

"We couldn't have survived without the Aborigines," Eric says. I'm on another tour, this one into the Daintree Rain Forest. I've traded in Rosie for a smaller group: the guide, Eric, a German family with two teenagers, a lesbian couple from Sweden, and me. It's a manageable size. The adults keep to themselves, except to fend off teenage angst. The boy, fifteen, wants to personally dismantle the Daintree; the girl, seventeen, is repulsed by it all. Has she read the German version of the *Barbie Doll Book of Teenage Etiquette*? Eric leads us quickly along a well-marked trail into dense underbrush. He tells us he's from Perth. I gulp. How could Hermes, god of travelers, cast bad karma my way twice on the same trip? I hope you're not Rosie's neighbor, I think, imagining endless days of meat pies.

Eric explains Australia's origins. "Forty million years ago . . ." he begins. My brain turns off. I haven't yet come to terms with the fact that the paint I saw on Egyptian tombs was done some four thousand years ago, but a million! Eric shows us red gum trees and hoop vines, three different varieties of wattle with spiky orange-and-yellow buds that look like cactus berries, tea trees with sap that heals insect bites, and blunt leaf plants good for cuts and scrapes. "I've seen those before," I say. "In Malaysia." "Right," Eric says. "Same botanical family. Just a

variation." The fifteen year old snarls at me; the seventeen year old yawns. Eric digs around the base of a tree. "The first settlers ate these," he said. Not witchetty grubs again, I think. But it's a seed, brown and shiny as a walnut, and it doesn't move. "The Aborigines showed them how. Kept them from starving to death," Eric says. The fifteen year old is game for something new. He pops one in his mouth and spits it out almost in the same breath. His sister makes ugh-ugh sounds; their parents look apologetic. The lesbians look as relieved as only childless couples can look under the circumstances. Eric watches the teenager spit and spit trying to get rid of the bitter taste. "Take a lesson from that," he says. "You can't go rushing into anything out here in the rain forest." I begin to like Eric and think I can forgive him for his Perth roots. The kid starts whining; his sister takes up the chorus. Eric keeps walking, but after my ordeal with Rosie, I've had enough. I take a fork in the road; one of the Swedish women follows me.

We don't say much, the Swedish woman and I—just a grunt or two to indicate a tree or flower that has taken our fancy. Besides, when we are quiet, we can hear the others plodding along on a trail not far from where we are. Maybe it's our need to be quiet that offers us an extraordinary experience. We have been examining a flowering bush, a thorny sort with stay-a-while leaves that threaten to take pieces of your clothes, or your skin, if you brush against it. Suddenly, there is a thumping sound. We both look up. My life may have been bound to the city, but I'm savvy enough to know that thumping sounds in the woods are bad omens. But I also know not to run until I'm sure of the direction of the sound. You don't want to run toward the bear, my ex-husband had warned me when we were in Alaska. The Swedish woman obviously has not been warned. She takes off like a rabbit. I go torpid and freeze. There's more thumping. Then I realize I can't move. That damn stay-a-while is threatening to keep a piece of my index finger with it. That finger starts to sweat—I think the rest of me is too scared to do anything—but the moisture on my skin lets me pull my finger away from the plant, and that act may be what saves me. The next thing

I know, a big bird breaks through the bush. I mean a big big bird—at least my height with a bright blue head and a big fat brown behind. I look at it; it looks at me; we both squawk and do a runner in opposite directions. I don't know how fast the bird's going, but I reach the group only seconds after the woman from Sweden. "Blue bird! Big blue bird!" I announce in what little voice I have left. Eric turns calmly. "Was it blue all over?" he asks. "Just the head," I pant. "Just the head." The Swedish woman nods in agreement. "A cassowary," Eric says. "First cousin to the ostrich. They are on the endangered list. Did you get a photo?" Maybe he doesn't understand the word *Big,* I think. "It's sort of hard to take a photo when you're running," I say. The teenagers giggle. "Pity," Eric says. "I think you missed a great opportunity." I look behind me. The leaves rustle a bit, then still to their usual gentle sway. "Just call me Missed Opportunity," I say. The seventeen year-old breaks her composure and laughs out loud.

If you think you missed the sixties and the hippies, go to Cairns. Outside of San Francisco's Haight and the Village in New York, you probably won't find so many flower children in one place. Old ones and new ones, dyed-in-the-wool and corporate escapees, all there and all using hair as a signal of their break with middle-class tradition. The difference is that this generation decorates itself in Rastafarian natty dreads, or the Dreaded Dreads, as my father calls them. Of course, Rasta hair doesn't have much to do with traditional Rastafarian religious beliefs. Now it's all surface: music and the latest mind-altering drugs, the haute couture of whatever marks the wearer's rebellion. Rebellion was the keyword in Cairns, where everyone seemed to be rebelling against something, if nothing more than being in Cairns. I saw more dirty blond dreadlocks in Cairns than I had in the States, except at some folklife festivals where everybody goes ethnic, meaning non-Anglo-Saxon mainstream. In Cairns, the hippies offered the usual market items: tie-dyed T-shirts, homemade candles, leather vests and bead necklaces, and of course, their version of Aboriginal art. I resisted. After all, I owned a dish full of witchetty grubs.

Cairns was a stopping off place, a divided town, crosshatched, really, where one group sometimes fell all over the other to gain right-of-way: tourists and Aussies, hippies and reef divers, Aborigines and shopkeepers, deep sea fishermen and opal miners. Visitors "go native" along the esplanade or head for one of the offshore resorts on Green or Fitzroy islands at the edge of the Great Barrier Reef, where room rates per night averaged more than the annual income of Aboriginals in the outback. Those places are done up like any time, resort time, any beach in the world. Still, if you could afford it, the reef was worth it. I resorted to day trips from Cairns.

I'd promised myself before I left for Australia that I'd see Ayers Rock, dive the Great Barrier Reef, and put my toes in the Tasman Sea. By the time I arrived in Brisbane, I'd added to my must-see list Botany Bay, the Daintree Rain Forest and River, the Kuranda Railroad, and all places leading to Darwin. I made it as far as the Tasman Sea, even stuck my feet in the water, although the wind was wickedly cold that day and the waves were full of raging froth. ("The deep breathing sea of Tasman," Seine Finay had called it in her journal entry.) My attraction to the Tasman Sea probably started when I was a child watching Saturday matinees where the image of Tasmanian devils had been abducted by Disney for cartoons. But the only Tasmanian devils I saw were in the zoo in Sydney, mean looking motor scooters, certainly closer to the mythical spirit chasers of folk stories than they were to the cute little cartoon creatures in Disney's world. So after Ayers Rock, all I had left on my original wish list was the Great Barrier Reef.

I dropped my swag at the luggage lockup in my hotel and headed for the reef. Ten minutes out, and I was beginning to think the barrier wasn't so much the reef as it was all those folks who'd come to see it: the swimmers and boaters and surfers and divers, and on the edge of the horizon and beyond, commercial fishing boats hauling in great nets of fish. The Great Barrier Reef might have been bountiful, but it was never quiet. There was as much activity on the surface of the water as there was below it. I booked a regular tour on one of the eight or so dive ships out of Cairns that gathered each morning at designated spots along the reef, each ship carrying more than one hundred passengers. Not all of them would dive, but most went into the water—some, like me, only once. I went down with a group of Japanese divers, powerful swimmers who seemed more graceful in the water than they had been on deck.

"You did what?" my doctor asked me when I returned home. "You're asthmatic. You're aquaphobic. You've got no business diving."

"I couldn't pass up the opportunity," I told him. "And it was only for twenty minutes." "Too long," he said. "Make that your last dive," he said.

"OK," I said. "But if you could only see what these eyes have seen," I said, paraphrasing a line from *Do Androids Dream of Electric Sheep?*

My doctor wasn't impressed. You had to be there, I thought, under-water where the world turns upside down and you are foreign to your own planet. The reef was alive, a living, amorphous form that stretched for miles, blue water covering it like a veil. Above the coral, I'd seen fish that looked like tigers, like leopards, like zebras, twisting among rows of pink lace fan coral. Beautiful jellyfish, delicate as veils, undulating with their poisonous invitations. When I turned to get my bearings, I was surrounded by rainbows of fish: red stripes, cornflower blues, and yellow chevrons. I could not remember ever seeing so many fish in one place: butterfly and goat fish, eel fish and fish with bug eyes or those with seemingly no eyes. The water was clotted with divers, but the fish swam by as if they were simply avoid-ing traffic jams. I even saw fish that looked like hippies, their colors patterned like a tie-dyed shirt. Somewhere in that mob scene, I'd spotted a giant wrasse, or rather, it had spotted me. It came up slow-ly, its look intense, its face almost too human, one of those "smart-ass" kind of looks, rude and unbending. No wonder I later thought of the wrasse when I met Rosie from Perth. But while I could endure the bus trip, being captive underwater was another matter altogether, at least for an aquaphobic. It was sort of strange to be stared down by a fish, but that's what happened. I followed the bubbles of my own breath to the surface and quit his kingdom, making my ascent through the gaudily dressed crowd of parrot fish, angel fish, and coral trout. Below me, the wrasse flicked its tail and disappeared into the darkness of deep coral waters where it had been spawned.

As splendid as my visit was, I felt my trip to Australia had been cut short because I never reached Darwin. Too many places; too little time. The lack of time is a frequent complaint for most travelers. "I don't have time to go there," they'll say. "I'm running out of time," they'll say. But in Australia, I constantly had the feeling that as I moved forward toward some beginning, my sense of time had fallen into a holding pattern. I'm sure that was partly caused by the land-scape. When I was on the desert, time seemed to have slipped into some sort of primordial pattern. From shield shrimp that looked like fossils to the way in which the sun cast the desert in primary colors, I felt as if time had shifted to the dawn of the land itself, the past rear-ing its head like a frilled lizard basking in an eternal sun. Scraggly opal miners from Coober Pedy and Bush Aboriginals both seemed to have stepped out of the same time warp. The sense of timelessness was trapped on the desert. In an Aboriginal arts and crafts shop, I saw a T-shirt that read: *Three thousand years of dreamtime / Three hundred years of colonialism / Thirty years of T-shirts!* Time, alas, that final mea-sure. But it was not just on the desert that time seemed to warp back upon itself. In the mangrove forests along the Daintree River, croco-diles with faces full of that "spooky, dreadful-ancient-knowledge look," as Elizabeth Gilbert termed it, floated like logs. In the trees, kookaburras laughed at my amazement.

It doesn't take much to amaze me; my vision is steeped in American sensibilities. Even the sight of kangaroos grazing like cattle in pastures near the Cook Highway made me think I'd found a place where time stood still. Hadn't those kangaroos been there long before the intrusion of the highway? This didn't happen in the city. The mystery of time seemed to fade in the tangle of cars, buses, and high-rises. In places like Sydney, Brisbane, and Melborne, everything was in present tense and urgent. Urban landscapes seemed to be outside of the notion that time was fluid. (Anyway, I've always held to the idea that office buildings are intolerant of history.) But outside of the city, I felt as if I could see where I'd been while I was moving away from that place. Like traveling on the train between Cairns and Kuranda: when I leaned out of the window to take a picture, the end of the train, still snaking across the three-mile trestle, was curving away from me while the front section where I was seated plunged into a tunnel. For one dizzying moment, it was as if I had turned away from myself, as if I had glimpsed a place of spirituality that I couldn't give a name to—as if I was moving forward while parts of me still lived in the past. That was as near as I came to understanding anything about dreamtime, the sense of coming out of myself to understand what moved me forward. Of course, it was my own naive view of dreamtime, and perhaps as close as I would get, being outside of Aboriginal culture. "Do you think these blokes really have visions?" a man seated next to me asked at the end of a Tjapukai Dance Theatre performance depicting dreamtime stories. "I mean, what do they know that we don't know?" he asked. "I don't have enough time to explain it," I told him.

I've done a lot of traveling alone. Sometimes on purpose, sometimes inadvertently. For a black woman, traveling alone can be an awakening, a way of defining myself that is not dependent on the American system of color coding. I know the traps are out there, the biases set for race, religion, and gender, but skin color is no longer an absolute measure on that thin line between black and white. There are shades of difference dependent on history, ancestry, and boundaries of land. Perhaps I am the traveler G. K. Chesterton referred to when he wrote: "The more I see of the world . . . the more I come back with increased conviction to those places where I was born . . . narrowing my circles like a bird going back to a nest." In Australia on the Red Desert, I started to believe that was what I was looking for—the daughter come home, the evolution of me. These memoirs are filled with the detours, the half steps and circuitous routes I've taken, where strangers became neighbors, where towns blended into maps of ruins, and fellow travelers remained surly in every language. A world of enchanted shores that beckoned me with its forests full of primal wonder, its seas connecting continents from the South Pole to the equator, its languages singing of vowels, its songs filled with the warnings of a hundred ancestors.

On my flight home from Egypt two years before my trip to Australia, I received the usual customs declaration slip asking me to list my purchases. I made my check-and-balance listing and was ready to complete the declaration when I noticed the directive above the signature line. *Sing on the reverse side after you read warning.* I rang for the cabin attendant. "What song shall I try?" I asked, pointing to the customs form. She frowned. "There must be some mistake," she said, and handed me another one. There was no mistake. They both held the same command: *Sing,* they ordered. *Sing.* "Perhaps it is a new trend," I told her, and kept the extra slip. Why not sing on your way home, I thought. That's what the folks from Fiji had done, and the ones from Yugoslavia. As the planes neared home, they indeed began to sing. Home was the heart, the place of birth, the starting point. Home, where I learn how to survive. Where I dream of trips I've yet to take and identify outgoing airplanes by the insignias on their tailfins. I return home to replenish my friendships, to touch base with my family and snuggle down in my own bed, but the sound of jets streaking overhead fills me with longing. There's something out there beckoning me—I don't know what; I don't know where. But I can hardly wait for my ticket to get there. And I don't plan to stop until I find it.